BETWEEN HEAVEN AND EARTH

This book is dedicated to my mother, Margaret,
whose life had just begun.

BETWEEN HEAVEN AND EARTH

THE LIFE OF A MOUNTAINEER, FREDA DU FAUR 1882-1935

Sally Irwin

WHITE CRANE PRESS

White Crane Press

Copyright © Sally Irwin 2000

First published 2000 by White Crane Press
PO Box 525, Hawthorn, Victoria 3122, Australia

1 3 5 7 9 10 8 6 4 2

National Library of Australia
Cataloguing-in-Publication entry:

Irwin, Sally.
Between heaven and earth: the life of a mountaineer, Freda Du Faur 1882-1935.

Bibliography.
Includes index.
ISBN 0 9578183 0 0.
1. Faur, Freda du, d. 1935. 2. Mountaineers - Australia - Biography. I. Title.

796.522092

Cover design by Michael Guz
Edited by Neil Thomas
Text designed and typeset in 11/15 Berkeley Book by Scooter Design
Printed and bound by Australian Print Group

This project has been assisted by the Commonwealth Government
through the Australia Council, its arts funding and advisory body.

*'I lost contact with the rocks and hung...
between heaven and earth.'*

MALCOLM ROSS
From a speech to the English Alpine Club, 1914.

Contents

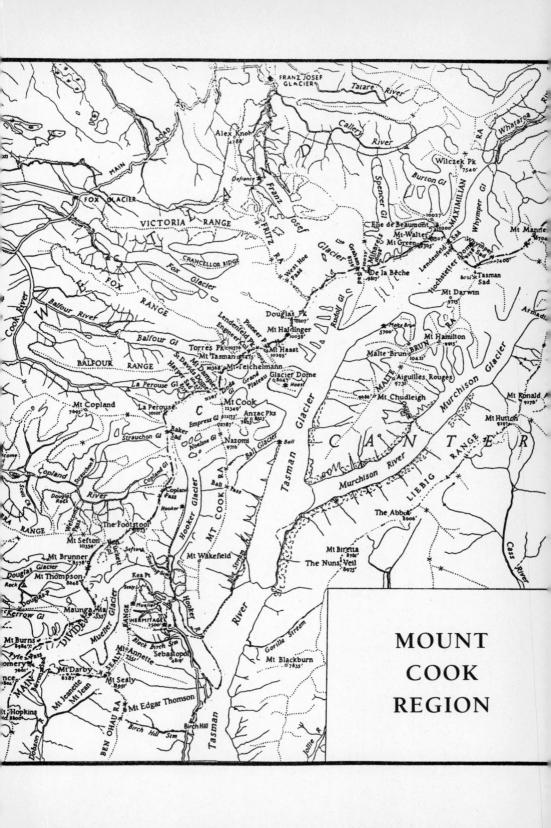

MOUNT

COOK

REGION

I

TOWARDS HEAVEN

'To a restless imaginative nature the fascination
of the unknown is very great; from my childhood
I never saw a distant range without longing
to know what lay on the other side.'

Freda Du Faur

1 DREAM WEAVERS

'I grew up with an ambition and determination without which I would have been a good deal happier. I thought a lot and developed the faraway look of a dreamer, for it was always the distant heights which fascinated me and drew me to them in spirit. I was not sure what could be accomplished by means of tenacity and little else, but the target was set high and each rebuff only saw me more determined to see at least one major dream to its fulfilment.'

Earl Denman
ALONE TO EVEREST

In the Southern Alps of New Zealand, early summer is the time for those who dream of finding a true heaven on earth through their own endeavours, when mountaineers attempt to grasp a fleeting vision of perfection. During those days the heavy snows that reach far down into the valleys and fill the great aquamarine chasms of the glaciers begin to melt, and the layers and layers of high white peaks lie sharp against clear blue skies with summits firm enough for those dreamers to stand on and look to what lies beyond. It was then, in 1906, that Freda Du Faur first reached these mountains and fell passionately in love with them. 'The great peaks towering into the sky before me touched a chord that all the wonders of my own land had never set vibrating, and filled a blank of whose very existence I had been unconscious',[1] she wrote; and, from that moment, she was determined to climb, reach those peaks, and be the first woman ever to do so.

Peace should come to anyone whose romantic desires and endeavours are fulfilled as Freda's would be, yet the photo taken after Freda climbed the highest of them all, Mount Cook, does not portray fulfilment. True, it shows her standing proudly, and with justification. One hand rests on the rock, the other grasps the blade of her ice axe. Her body is strong beneath a severe knee-length skirt and a prim, high-necked, white Edwardian blouse, pinned by a cameo against her throat. Sturdy leather boots and puttees encase her legs. Her hair is drawn loosely back, exposing her face, the determined mouth. But her eyes, although bold, are still searching, for climbing a mountain can only provide the illusion of achieving peace. However, fleeting visions of perfect breath-taking beauty and the exhilaration of conquering danger are also capable of creating a deep dissatisfaction with ordinary life so nothing below is ever enough again.

On 3 December 1910, the night before her ascent of Mount Cook, Freda had the experience to believe she had the skills to reach the top, but knew also the doubts that come from previous failure; the possibility of some unexpected crevasse, rotten rock, an extraordinary storm, black ice. It was already freezing. Although the sky was clear, there was no moonlight. She and her guides, the brothers Peter and Alex Graham, had bivouacked on a tiny plateau under the harsh sweeps of Mount Cook and attempted to sleep inside a tent created from a piece of canvas slung over posts made from ice picks, and in sleeping bags, sewn together from woollen blankets. It was too cold to consider doing the morally proper thing – for the men to sleep apart from their female client.

At 1.00 a.m. the men requested Miss Du Faur to wake for breakfast. She at least had the luxury of the warmth from a meths stove and breakfast, then, at 2.45, with lanterns lit and roped together, they set off into the bone-aching darkness, Peter leading, Freda next, followed by Alex.

Peter Graham had been Freda's guide on lower climbs and on an earlier attempt on Mount Cook, but she had never climbed with his younger brother before. With the two best guides possible, it had to be her climb. If she failed this time – with perfect weather, perfect mountain conditions and with these companions – some other woman, and they were beginning to arrive, would take the next opportunity.

But that morning, it was the reality of the snow, ice, rock and weather, not the possibilities of being first, of filling that 'blank ' in her soul, that kept them moving as they concentrated on the dimly lit steps cut by the men the previous day. There was little more than that as their boots crunched up hard snow that blurred away into darkness and unfathomable depths. Above, stars spiked an inky sky. Breath came hard in air, so cold, that it razored their throats and hurt their chests, bit through layers of inadequate clothing, stung unprotected eyes and skin, even through the layers of grease Freda had smothered over her face and lips. Warmth from movement, flexibility, strength, that was what was needed as they left the snow slopes and reached the first demanding section of the climb, the schrund, a deep cutting at the junction of snow and rock, that had stopped them on Freda's first attempt the previous year.

Back then, she and Peter had been on their own, and had faced much trickier conditions. This time, despite the darkness, they climbed through the schrund without incident and into a steep couloir above it. After tough climbing, halfway up there was enough light for them to extinguish their lanterns and by 4.00 a.m., as harsh cords of sun shimmered yellow across the mountain tops, they reached the blue ice and numbingly-cold rocks under the western buttress of Mount Cook. Ahead was a good rock climb, something Freda always loved. Peter was still leading so she concentrated on the rhythm of his boots as he moved above her; she knew him well enough to judge, by those deft movements, his state of mind, his strength and confidence, as he could trust her to keep up with him, even dare, she considered, rely on her. Alex was more protective; she was their client after all, but had to give up when she 'disdained' his help and his brother teased him that 'he'd catch it hot' if he kept checking on her.[2]

At 5.30 a.m., the three climbers stopped for food and tea and to take the time to discuss how to deal with what lay between them and the summit. The climb was going perfectly to plan but the men, always cautious, scanned the westerly peaks and the deep valleys, looking for a turn of light, a darkening aspect of the clouds, any shadow that might hint at a sudden storm. They climbed on, out of solid rock on to rotten brown shale held only by ice. One climber moved at a time, fearful of dislodging rocks onto the climber below, and then only when every hold had been tested. It was slow but they had still made better time than any other climbers had before them so, when they reached solid rock, they had every reason to feel optimistic.

Then, at 6.00 a.m., about 1,000 feet off the summit, when Freda was tempting herself with the exhilarating thought that she was certain to be the first woman to get to the top, they struck a stretch of rock covered in the thinnest film of treacherous green ice. Footholds and handholds were impossible. This was not a time of razor-fine, steel crampons and pitons that cut through ice and into the rock beneath, nor were there Antarctic-tested synthetic fabrics, plastic helmets, computer-designed equipment and back-up teams. Freda and the Graham brothers had little to protect them; the men wore woollen jackets, ties and shirts, always immaculate, always formal and hacked steps out of the ice with wooden handled picks; Freda wore boots and puttees and a suit, designed by herself, consisting of a short tweed jacket and a short skirt, cut to knee length. On this ice their gloves and skin, axes and ropes stuck to anything they touched.

Freda, wearying, deeply regretted her premature exhilaration. Her mouth was dry, her muscles strained from stress as well as exertion, but she forced herself to concentrate on nothing but the dense white form against a vivid blue sky, the summit, so tantalising above them. They traversed a seemingly unending icy face of another couloir until they finally reached the ice-cap. Here they encountered crisp wavelets which snagged their precious rope and threatened to fray it. But they pushed on. The risk was worth it, the momentum was there, and they knew they would make it, as Peter cut the last 200 feet of steps onto the summit snow.

The two men stood aside. It was a first climb for Alex but, as their client, it was officially Freda's climb. She did not expect the honour and was grateful when they sent her 'on alone the length of the rope' and there, on the summit, she waited for them 'feeling very little, very lonely and much inclined to cry'.[3] But the men were only moments behind her. Just as excited, they shook hands and congratulated each other, especially as it was only 8.40 a.m.; they did have a record. Freda wrote 'and I a mere woman', a comment that was at once humble and not as tongue-in-cheek as she liked to pretend. But, on that summit politics and attitudes towards women were the last thing on her mind. It was enough that she had arrived, that everything she had dreamed of for years had been achieved. She could even consider the previous year's failure as a fortunate event.

For two hours there was New Zealand, all of it, beneath them. Freda took off her wide-brimmed hat and placed it on the ground, out of the way, in order to use her camera, so regretting she did not have the skills to match the view, especially as no one had yet managed to take good photos from the summit. She savoured the colours and shapes, the movement of the wind and the sun, storing the memories to be drawn on and lived with over the years ahead. 'Never was such a glorious day', she wrote later, but she was too restless, too imaginative for her ambitions to be permanently satisfied. On the summit of the cloud piercer she might have been enamoured of the perfect moment but she was already looking for more, beyond to the other possible climbs she and the Graham brothers had discussed.

South of the summit there was a good view down the ridge leading to the two lower peaks of Mount Cook; it was named the Grand Traverse, but it was so 'razor sharp' that they concluded the only possible way to tackle it was up it, south to north, from the lower peaks to this, the highest. Freda, growing in confidence with her mountaineering, vowed silently that she would be the first ever, man or woman, to traverse those three peaks. As well – naturally there was an 'as well' – she wanted to add the other great peaks of the Southern Alps: Mount Tasman, the second highest mountain in New Zealand; and the third highest, Mount Dampier, and whatever else she might see from this vantage point. That way sheer volume would surely provide fulfilment.

But cooler heads than hers were dealing with the present. They had greedily squandered time and energy, the sun was high and already melting the ice, solid rock was becoming unstable, the rotten face disintegrating.[4] Two years later she would recall: 'Even now ... the thought of the four hours we spent upon them makes me feel sick and shaky.'[5] They began to move again, one at a time, ready to brace a fall. A dislodged rock hit Freda on the back; as well as unsettling her, she was in pain for the rest of the climb. Her legs trembled and, when she thought they were through the worst, an overhanging rock she was traversing, collapsed. Peter managed to hold her on the rope but it was her own quick instincts that saved her as she leapt back and stood pressed against the cliff, with only a foot between her and the stones showering the glacier below. She 'crawled' round to join Alex who was leading and Peter followed.

At about five foot two inches and eight stone, Freda must have appeared alarmingly small to her well-built guides. Tired themselves, they were increasingly concerned that they had pushed her too hard and their numerous critics had been right: women did not have the strength for such an adventure. Freda was well aware of their fears but she could cope with anything that was direct and physical and it was not in her nature to have men she admired anxiously overseeing her. Angrily she pushed through her pain, achieving through passion what rationality couldn't, and continued her descent, within herself again.

At 5.30 p.m. they reached the bivouac. They had been out for fourteen and a half hours – six hours up, two hours on the summit and six and a half hours down – and had the record that Peter assured her 'would take some beating, little lady'. Freda loved that. Then, too tired to eat properly, they drank tea and ate frozen tinned peaches that softened in their mouths and oozed down their dry throats as steam rose, opaque and grey against the snow. A couple of hours later, rested, Freda got up to a feast being prepared on the cooker: tomato soup, cold meat, tinned fruit, bread and butter and copious amounts of freshly brewed tea.

The next day, the sun was well up and warm but they lacked the necessary energy to go off climbing elsewhere, so instead lay and 'lingered lovingly' over the details of their latest achievement. Freda wrote of that time with great clarity and nostalgia:

We know again the pride of the steady head, the long reach, and the sure foot, muscle and brain pitting themselves against the mightiest forces of nature as when life flows wild and free in the beginning of the world. All the primitive emotions are ours – hunger, thirst, heat and cold, triumph and fear – as yard by yard we win our way to stand as conquerors and survey our realm. And then the primitive sinks back into obscurity and all those unplumbed depths within stir at the call. Spirit, imagination, name it what you will, it steals into the heart on the lonely silent summits and will not be denied.[6]

It was poetic, free, even Biblical; she likened it to the testing of Christ going into the mountains; it could, almost, be called contentment. Sitting there, by the fire, with Peter and Alex Graham, she was a companion, disconnected from what she saw as oppressive civilisation. She could have so easily remained, as did most of her friends, in the narrow society of upper middle-class Sydney, which clung to Victorian ideas that were already outmoded in liberal Edwardian England. Queen Victoria feared that 'the mad wicked folly' of women's rights would turn a woman into some disgusting horror and all kinds of illnesses were wished upon women who tried to 'unsex' themselves by developing their potential roles in life. All these accusations and dire warnings would be levelled at Freda: that she would suffer loss of child-bearing ability and interest, egotism, anaemia, hysteria, selfishness, even somehow be responsible for the destruction of society. Freda knew she was looked at with some sympathy by her married friends, aware that many regarded her as that unfortunate 'type', a spinster, 'dying for a man and worthless without one'.[7] A woman was only valued as a wife and preferably a mother, a condition that certainly threatened her freedom, her property and even her health.

On her own, climbing, freed of such notions of civilised behaviour, Freda felt she could forge a life, as the Graham brothers already had, in a world she coped with better than that of the 'whaleboned and corseted'[8] women now slowly stirring in the Hermitage below. She had always hoped such a place existed but feared it was just in her imagination, just a notion, fed from child-hood, by the works of the Romantic poets – Browning, Tennyson and Arnold – who had imbued nature with a sense of God and of magic and of some other waiting-to be-discovered world. Now she knew it was all true. Mountaineers were just like these true poets, created at birth and with luck, instinct and tenacity, both had found a way of melding all they felt with what they experienced in the natural world.

It was the ultimate endeavour as she was attempting to live in the world of the ideal, a heroine as daring as any she had read of in poetry, or discovered in history.

The irony of Freda's desire to achieve more than what was regarded as appropriate for a young, upper class woman is that it had its gen-esis in her family, through her acquaintance with a series of verses used to school young ladies in moral charm in the French court of Marie Antoinette. Dressed in flowing skirts and tight corsets, their noses covered to protect them from sunburn, they walked the gar-dens with a little book, *The Quatrains*, from which they had to learn several pages each day. The 126 verses were written by the famous poet Gui du Faur, Seigneur de Pibrac (1528– 84), Chief Justice of Toulouse and, under Charles 1X, Attorney-General of the Parliament of Paris. He was also a member of the du Faurs de Pibrac, a family which traces its lineage to the mid - fourteenth cen-tury, to the du Faur d'Ecuns, headed by Jean du Faur, Seneschal of Armagnac. Their small land holdings expanded in the sixteenth century and the name Pibrac was added to du Faur when the Gausine Douce, Dame de Pibrac, married Comte Pierre du Faur. She brought to the marriage the Chateau de Pibrac, in the Haute Garonne area near Toulouse, which is still the family seat. By the eighteenth century Duc D'Orleans was added to the family titles.

Freda well knew these verses from an early age. One, the Thirtieth Quatrain, was particularly appropriate:

'Tis no small thing illustrious birth to claim,
And from our forebears to have gained renown:
But better to leave sons a self-earned crown,
Than from our sires alone to have won a name.

Quatrains de Pibrac XXX

Her family had 'won a name' and her father, Eccleston Du Faur, would go to great lengths to prove it and push, both himself and his children, to win a 'self-earned crown' as was appropriate for all true Du Faurs, those hybrids of practical dreamer, of politician and legal intellectual, of artist, occasional adventurer and poet.

But Freda's great-great-grandfather, Jean du Faur, born in Pau, Gascony in 1733 to the eldest of the du Faur line, actually left the title, estate and France behind when he emigrated to England, apparently part of the Huguenot exodus after the Revocation of the Edict of Nantes.[9] He left, not out of fear for his life, although later pogroms proved that would have been justifiable, nor just for religious freedom, but in search of a place where the intellectual life was valued. This he found in London.

Naturalised by a special act of the English Parliament in 1768, he married an Englishwoman, Sarah Stubbs, daughter of the Proctor and Registrar of Rochester. As the French were not the most popular nationality in England, in order to marry, Jean had to change his name to John and change 'du' to 'Du' in Du Faur, drop the Pibrac coronet and use his wife's crest and shield. But there was little change in his ideas, character or even personal appearance and he never completely lost his foreign accent. Among the French émigré society he was always addressed as de Pibrac or Comte de Pibrac.

John Du Faur, the new 'Englishman', and Sarah had three sons.

The first two died without male children but the third, Cyprian, made up for such failings by not only siring Freda's grandfather but also reviving the adventurous life, dormant in his own father, that would eventually be embraced by both Eccleston and Freda Du Faur. Cyprian's romantic and foolhardy escapades from the age of fifteen would be used as a deterrent to later generations of fearful Du Faurs who detected similar aberrant adventurous spirits in their offspring, but Freda fortunately was not limited by such a parental attitude. At the age of nine, the version of Cyprian's activities she received from her father, Eccleston, contained no cautions.

He described with admiration and envy how, in 1790, at the age of sixteen, Freda's great-great-grandfather joined an African expedition lead by a family friend, Major Haughton, in search of Timbuctoo, only known at that time to exist from accounts of Arab traders. The expedition departed from the mouth of the Gambia River but, soon after, Cyprian became ill and was left behind with friendly natives, an event that saved his life as the rest of the party were murdered. After struggling home, and encouraged by his parents, Cyprian tempered his activities until, at the age of nineteen, he decided on a quick trip to Paris to visit relatives. It was 1794. With the confidence of youth and his English birth, he believed the Reign of Terror would not touch him. He was wrong. His name was enough to put him in the Luxembourg Prison, condemned to place his pale young neck under the guillotine. Three days before the event that would have extinguished the chance of Freda ever being born, Robespierre fell and the prison doors were opened. Cyprian hurriedly left, with a portrait of himself, painted by a young student. Freda's father brought the painting and a very similar one of Cyprian's wife, Sarah, two long, pale-faced, pale-haired images, to Australia.

Cyprian never left England again. He would say, and the saying was passed down the Du Faur family, that 'a cat may have nine

lives but a man has only three. I have had my two chances – in
Africa and the Terror. I will stay in quiet England to await the
third.'[10] Cyprian may not have moved out of England but his
repressed adventurous spirit moved just about everywhere in it. His
son Frederick, Eccleston's father, was born on 19 January 1800 at
56 Sloane Square, London but the family frequently moved house
around the country: to Worcester, back to London, to Vicarage Hill
and Stroud in Gloucestershire, back to London, to the New Forest,
Hampshire, then to Twickenham, Middlesex. Such restlessness produced in Freda's paternal grandfather a man who loved ideas but
loved stability more. He became a solicitor at South Square, Gray's
Inn London, dynamic only in his choice of wife when, in 1826, he
married Mary Elizabeth Harsant, the daughter of Thomas and Mary
of Wickham Market, Suffolk. Mary was an artist, a pupil of Samuel
Prout and a member of a social clique based on the studio of the
English master painter Turner. She would introduce her children,
and especially her only son, to the joys of the artistic life of that
period. It was a love affair of both art, adventure and nature that
would drive the activities of Freda's father and dominate his life and
that of his own children.

Eccleston was born on 14 September 1832, the second child
and only son – there were three daughters, Frederica, Mary and
Ellen. The family lived at Flowton, 23 Queen Anne Street,
Cavendish Square, London, a large, formal, two-storey brick home
with a shingle roof, curving lawns and gravel paths. Adding to his
social and artistic connections, Freda's father had a good enough
education to pass him onto Harrow in 1846, with the intention of
going up to Cambridge but Eccleston was determined to get as near
to squandering as many of his lives as possible before he was placed
in the family grave in King's Road. When illness interrupted his proposed university career, he escaped to his 'west Africa' and, with two
close friends, sailed for Australia, to Victoria, to the gold rushes.

In 1853, the three well-brought up, young men in their early twenties arrived in what Eccleston regarded as an 'inferno', the city of Melbourne, then travelled on to the inland goldfields of Bendigo and Ballarat. Once again Eccleston became seriously ill, this time with 'Colonial fever', which he later believed to be typhoid. For five months he struggled to recover and would suffer poor health for the rest of his long life. Despite this, he managed to spend several more years travelling around an inhospitable country until he arrived in Sydney, to a raw, exciting 'inferno' of the kind he had learned to thrive on. It was there that Freda's father found a single life among the sprawling, disorganised conglomeration of warehouses where traders established their shops and soldiers and ex-convicts lived side by side, neither one more corrupt than the other. Transportation of convicts had ceased only fifteen years earlier, public hangings near the Quay even more recently. Tradesmen and merchants, whether free men or freed, were racking up fortunes from land, wool and gold while wide boys and entrepreneurs ran fast and loose with the connivance of the law. Sailors, with money earned from whaling and sealing, patronised hotels and grog shops with names like 'Rose of Australia' or 'World Turned Upside Down'. Pubs, pig pens, stalls and terrace slums pressed against gardens where peacocks shook their tails and vied for admiration with the flower-bedecked mansions, domed ballrooms and silverware, initialed with fake crests. Within a generation origins would not, and could not be questioned.

During his first trip back to England in 1858, Eccleston's father died. Although now head of the family, the young man had changed too much and knew the life he wanted so, in 1863, he returned to Sydney. A merchant in burgeoning Sydney was the usual way to make a fortune but Eccleston was not interested in that. He had a great 'blank' as well that needed filling with events and adventures so he joined other expatriate Englishmen in the Surveyor-General's office, an ideal position from which to explore uncharted lands and be paid to do so.

By 1866, at the age of 34, Eccleston was working as a surveyor out of Port Macquarie, a small coastal town north of Sydney, when he fell in love and married Augusta Crummer, the daughter of a captain in the small local army contingent. Within a year, the new Mrs Du Faur was dead and their new-born son, named after his father, died soon after. Eccleston would never recover from such a setback. Afraid of such losses again, he would not allow emotional commitments to dominate his life. He would never permit his next family to come too close and devastate him in such a way again. He moved from the town of his hoped for family life, back to the distractions of the city and to long sojourns through unsurveyed mountains and plains west of Sydney. He became one of those great avoiders of personal life, a workaholic,[11] but he was also his mother's son. He loved the company of the new poets who used brush and canvas instead of pen and paper, as he was one of the rare immigrants who could see the new world with new eyes.

In 1878, Eccleston was instrumental in setting up the New South Wales Academy of Arts, the forerunner to the National Art Gallery and eventually the Art Gallery of New South Wales. Backing him was a small number of influential men whose families would be part of the Du Faur social connections, including Judge Backhouse, the lawyer Charles Windeyer, the Member of Parliament Joseph Abbott, Sir Charles Nicholson, Provost of Sydney University, and the Reverend Dr John Woolley, Professor of Classics and Principal of the University, whose daughter, Blanche, would become Freda's mother.

Eccleston was a practical man fascinated by creative forces, Freda's grandfather was an intelligent visionary whose passions overwhelmed practicalities. John Woolley's father, George Woolley, was a physician, his mother a Gell, a well-known and wealthy Derbyshire family. John was born in 1816, in Petersfield, Hampshire, the last of four children and the second son, a position that provided him with the attentions of two older sisters and mother, but saved him from the pressures of being the eldest. As the beloved baby, he was allowed to indulge in contemplation and ideas in which he was encouraged by his father who, looking for intellectual stimulation and what he called progress, moved his family to Hyde Park in London where two more sons were born. Neither boy would tilt John from his favoured position.

John's father insisted his clever son attend a new university, University College (the University of London), which did not award degrees and was described by many as godless but which provided young John with an open attitude to intellectual endeavours and the opportunity to obtain one of the few scholarships open to anyone, to Exeter College, Oxford. His emotional inclinations assisted him in choosing a wonderful wife when he married Mary Margaret Turner in 1842 but also worked against his preferred academic career – marriage meant the forfeiture of his fellowship at Oxford – and from then on he had to make a living as a schoolmaster. The Woolleys moved to one of the oldest schools in the country, Hereford, where their first child, Emmeline, was born. Their second daughter, Blanche, was born in 1844. Later in that year the family moved to Rossal, Lancashire, one of the newest schools, a posting that provided a pleasant life and gave Woolley the opportunity to practise as he preached to both pupils and his own children 'that school is society in microcosm with a gentle moral value provided by knowledge'.[12] It was a great theory, and the ability to believe in a theory, regardless of reality, was a trait he passed down through following generations.

The only academic seats where it was possible to fully carry out John Woolley's ideas were not to be found in England. He applied for Corfu and failing that, the University of Calcutta. Going there was his 'oldest day-dream'.[13] but it was totally fanciful, as the society running the university was High Church. Woolley had been ordained in 1841 but as a cleric in the Low Church. Eventually in 1849, and not without considerable push from the influential Bishop Stanley of Norwich, he found a posting as headmaster of Norwich Free Grammar School in Norfolk. The family were content there, for a while. Freedom could be found in the Fens, romance in the ships setting off for wondrous lands across the sea, and inspiration from the beautiful daily services and choir in the Norwich Cathedral. The music and singing encouraged the young Emmeline to become a musician and composer and Blanche, then five years old, to become a pianist.

But such pleasure and comfort was not enough. John Woolley was offered a slim chance to fulfil his ideals. A university was to be built in Sydney, a rector was needed. It was not a choice posting but Australia had not yet built up the conventions Woolley had been struggling against in England. His references were impeccable: 121 testimonials included one from the Equerry to the King, the poet William Wordsworth and the Lord Bishop of Manchester who, in July 1849, summed up Freda's maternal grandfather as a 'sound elegant scholar, amiable in disposition, irreproachable in character' but noted with some relief, as did others, 'that in Mrs. Woolley he has a valuable aid'.[14]

The Reverend Professor John Woolley needed all the help Mary Margaret could give him. He was a lovable, irritating man, adored by his uncritical children and wife, although she would have been more valuable if she had sometimes questioned her husband's decisions, particularly where money was concerned. Although described in 1851 by the Registrar of Cambridge University as 'a very agreeable fine woman who wears her beautiful hair floating over her shoulders',[15] Mary Margaret Woolley was more than just that. She was the emotional support to her husband and his practical, diplomatic face.

In July 1852, on a mild winter's day, the Woolley family came off the ship, at Circular Quay, Sydney. Six well-behaved children, dark-haired and dark-eyed as Freda would be, stood on solid ground for the first time in weeks. There was the strong, clear-eyed Emmeline, aged nine, devastated at being taken away from the musical world to which she was already devoted. Gentle Blanche followed. A year younger than Emmeline, with a pale face and thick hair, she was dominated by her brilliant older sister and the deformity of a dropped top lip. Following the sisters was the only son, Turner Severin, who hid his nervousness in boldness, then sharp-tongued, witty Constance, Charlotte and Agnes, the baby, barely three. And the devoted parents – would they have come on this adventure if they had even suspected that, within a few months, their youngest child would be dead and the struggle and pain would not stop there?

A cab took the Woolley family quickly away from the quay into the main street, George Street, a wide thoroughfare lined with smart hotels, shops and houses tiered with balconies and lace work of wrought iron, through the markets and into Parramatta Road where the University of Sydney was to be built on a north facing slope. A number of colleges and a home for the Woolleys were planned in the same grounds.

Almost immediately Woolley set out to enhance this 'unformed' society with his Utopian dreams. Appalled by his students who were 'unable to handle their minds', he was nevertheless impressed by their 'quickness' and set up a Grammar school system to train (male) students to a standard acceptable at university. Schools of Arts were established to inculcate the values espoused in the colonies of the Ancient Greeks. Woolley enthused about their 'brilliant' empire: 'colonial merchants laid at her feet the wealth of the world and colonial philosophers lectured in the schools, sometimes even colonial princes rewarded and encouraged learning and genius'.[16] Impressive, but Freda's maternal grandfather reached too far, too quickly and, at times, frequently expressed views about the nature and ideals of a fair society that irritated the wealthy, the politicians and bishops who felt he should be beholden to them.

A painting of Dr John Woolley, in the Great Hall at Sydney University, shows a fine-skinned, sad-eyed man, with thick, dark eyebrows, flat dark hair and white mutton chops that disappear under his chin. He appears vulnerable and to lack the pomposity customary in photos of a Victorian gentleman. The Woolley household too was not typically Victorian. It was informal, with 'dear Papa,' and 'darling Mama'. Everyone had a nickname, based on the bear family. In letters, they addressed each other as Bruin. Papa Bear often signed off with a sketch of himself as a plump bear with spectacles.[17] The five girls – another sister, Lily was born, two years after Agnes' death – were as well educated as their brother in languages, music and the classics but, naturally, did not have access to outside study as Severin would.

'All except poetry are in constant danger of degrading the ideal to the real',[18] Dr Woolley wrote, and he ensured that the family shared the fantastic internal life he thrived on. Poetry, classical stories, myths and legends had more reality for the children than the educated society they moved in. It would always be difficult for the Woolley children, and their children, to live in what they considered to be dull reality without gilding it with romantic visions. At the Darling Point Mutual Improvement Society, in December 1860, Dr John Woolley gave a long discourse on a poem by his favourite poet, Tennyson. The Idylls of the King epitomised the world as Woolley wished it to be. He taught his children to see it in this light; as creative dreamers who looked at what might be rather than what really is, and was more successful in this education than he ever dreamed, especially with his second daughter.

John Woolley talked about two kinds of women, but women defined only in terms of their love for two kinds of men. In *The Idylls* there were two women, Queen Guinevere, who loved King Arthur and Enid, her closest friend, who loved the dynamic knight Geraint, and unlike Guinevere, 'remained wholly sweet'. Enid would not compromise such gentleness. Woolley saw his own wife in Enid, as 'not a heroine of Romance. She is a pure woman such as many of us love and know.' His daughters were encouraged to see themselves as young Enids, as 'Loveliness, Holiness and Wisdom, the three angels linked arm and arm in gracious sister hood'. [19] For the impressionable Blanche such notions could not be criticised and underlying hope for her only daughter was that she would view life in the marvellous way Papa Woolley had encouraged Blanche to view hers.

As music was to her admired older sister, the humanising of these illusions became the purpose of Freda's mother's life and it sentenced a generous, talented, intelligent woman to drift in a haze of hope and idealism before and after her marriage to Eccleston Du Faur.

In 1858, Blanche's situation had been made more difficult when Emmeline, then aged fifteen, left for Florence to study pianoforte, theory and composition under the master Kraus and later under a famous teacher, Ducce. She then joined Julius Von Kolb, a favourite pupil of Liszt, in Munich for three more years. All this cost much money and Dr Woolley was unstinting, regardless of the hardships it meant for the rest of the family. In the time Emmeline was away, Blanche learned it was a noble thing to sacrifice herself and to adore anyone with apparently greater gifts. She took over the role of stand-in elder daughter and grew to womanhood in a temporary position and as a semi-permanent, assistant-mother to her younger siblings.

When Emmeline returned in 1863, Blanche immediately lost what status she had in the family to her sophisticated and independent older sister. Emmeline became the keeper of the Woolley flame, especially as Severin would spend most of his adult life out of the country. Blanche bore her secondary role as 'a pure woman' in 'gracious sisterhood' and considered nothing more than that for herself. It was an example Freda would loathe.

Finally, after thirteen years in Sydney, Freda's grandfather cemented for himself a place in the kind of legend he had adored. In January 1865, exhausted by his struggles with what he felt was 'a not very appreciative society', he sailed to England to see his family. Woolley described himself in his papers as 'not a lucky man'. In that he was correct. He returned on what was described in the newspapers as, an auxiliary screw steamship, *The London*, which left Plymouth on 5 March 1866, but he was in the hands of what he regarded as destroyers of civilised ideals, 'odious merchants' who overloaded the ship. After five days of storms, it was wrecked in the Bay of Biscay. Nineteen men out of the two hundred passengers managed to get off, as they apparently had their own small boat. John Woolley did not survive. Sir Alfred Stephens, the Chief Justice of the time, quoting from an English journal, described John Woolley moving among the passengers and ministering to them as the ship went down: 'very nobly our brothers and sisters took the message of their doom and quietly gave their souls to God…There was a great silence, broken only by the waves finishing their work and then crew and passengers mingled together, some prayed…or …patiently held hands with their loved ones.' [20]

Blanche was 23 years old. The protected existence was over. She could only clutch her dear Papa's ideals to her heart and believe that her purpose in life was to pass them on. There was little else. A public meeting in the Prince of Wales Theatre was held in Sydney on 26 March to testify to the 'Public Sympathy with Dr Woolley's family'. Sir Charles Nicholson opened what was essentially an appeal for money: 'my lamented friend has left a widow and six children most inadequately, if not wholly unprovided for, like many intent on the highest objects of life, he was ever ready to give where he had little of worldly goods to bestow.'[21] The latter part of that description could just as easily have been applied to another man in the audience, the family friend, the widower, Eccleston Du Faur.

2 GOD'S WORK

'If God's work ever is to be done on earth it must be by the
union of perfect womanhood with perfect manhood.'

Rev. John Woolley

The money raised at the public meeting to acknowledge John
Woolley's contribution to the colony did not last long and the
Woolley women were soon faced with the problems of maintaining
Severin at school in England, themselves in their role as keepers of
the flame of Dr John Woolley, and at the same time in a morally
sound, middle-class existence. It soon became clear that Emmeline,
as the only member of the family capable of earning money, would
have to modify her aspirations and become a music teacher. To that
purpose she rented a house for the family, in part of a group of red
brick terraces collectively called Craigend, at 25 William Street, the
main thoroughfare east from the city. This was a convenient position for her music pupils, who lived in the larger estates and fine
houses of the eastern suburbs of Bellevue Hill and Vaucluse.

It was also a convenient street for Eccleston Du Faur, who
came to live just up the hill in Rialto Terrace, at 45 Upper South
William Street. Rare for Victorian times, particularly for someone of
his standing, he had not remarried. He saw himself as a bachelor

who devoted himself to the needs of the colony. His house was a place to lock up and leave.

By the mid-1870s, financial worries had eased for the Woolley family as Emmeline had a good business head and, despite her shyness at performing publicly, was described as 'a pianist with a style both scholarly and sparkling'[1] which would later be enhanced by a creative relationship with a young, English-born violinist, Ethel Pedley. As well, the number of dependents had dwindled as Severin had joined the army in India, while Charlotte had married and as Mrs Courteney had also gone to India with her husband. Sadly for Blanche, Constance, the sister closest to her, whose cheek and energy would always enliven her life and whose younger sons would become Freda's close friends, had sailed for Sarawak to stay with a relative. It was an exciting place to be. Ellen Woolley was a missionary, who had in her first few months in the country survived an insurrection of Chinese gold workers attempting to throw off the paternalistic rule and taxes of Britain. While Bau, the town nearest to the mission, burned, Ellen had never doubted they would survive because they were white, British, and had God, Right and the British Navy on their side. Afterwards Ellen married another English missionary and, grateful to God for both her survival and the deliverance of a husband into her life, devoted herself to the needs of native women. Constance was sure that this kind of devotion was a noble path for herself to pursue, but was diverted when she met an exciting soldier, the handsome Captain George Henry Bacchus.

Poor Blanche's narrow life was in complete contrast to that described in her sister's letters. Connie exalted in the brilliance of Sarawak, the excitement of her love, the pink satin she was married in, the uniforms, and parades, the raw square wooden buildings, exotic flowers and even pirate boats. In 1873 a son, Reginald, was born and, despite the wonders of army life in paradise, Constance was content to return when Captain Bacchus was posted back to

Sydney. According to his soon-to-be written obituary, the captain was 'an enlightened and humane officer, excelling in manliness of spirit'.[2] While he dedicated himself to men and duty, Constance, along with her mother and unmarried sister, dedicated themselves to the already indulged Reggie.

Spending so much time with her adored Connie only emphasised the probability that Blanche would, unwillingly, become that unfortunate of unfortunates, a spinster companion, first to her mother, then to some wealthy older woman. Or worse, she could become a housekeeper or a governess, all which meant living in other people's houses, on other people's terms. Instead, on 23 January 1878, Blanche married Eccleston Du Faur and opted to live in his house on his terms, all which were civil and not unkindly, intelligent but formal. They exchanged vows at St Mark's Church, Darling Point, a small charming church of neatly cut sandstone, popular then and now for society weddings. Captain Bacchus and Mrs Woolley were witnesses. Constance was pregnant again.

Eccleston looked older than his 45 years. Photographs of him out in the bush or on art camps, casually dressed in white flannels and navy blazer, show him unrelaxed, his mouth hidden behind a fine, clipped white beard. His features were small, his eyes cautious and impassive, his ears large and long lobed. He had that dry skin that Australian winds were not kind to, skin that wrinkled easily and freckled. His 'indifferent' health never seemed to prevent him from any activity that interested him but would be useful as a means of withdrawal from anything less than a higher purpose.

It would be too idealistic to imagine that Eccleston, knowing Blanche as a child, saw her finally as a woman coming and going from their homes in William Street and fell in love. Or met her as an old family friend, at the soirées for the university or at garden parties, to which the Woolley women were always welcome. Evening dress would have shown Blanche off at her best. She was a graceful woman, with intense dark eyes, a smooth neck, pale skin and well-rounded shoulders enhanced by dark hair tied back and knotted at the nape. Photographs as an adult never served her well for she had been a pretty child. Taken at an awkward angle, designed to disguise her mouth, they overemphasised a high forehead from which dropped a straight nose and a tiny chin inherited from her mother.

Their marriage would have been regarded as a suitable pairing. Blanche was demure and formal, restrained, not too young, and a good housekeeper, all attributes that would ease Eccleston's life and not cause emotional upheavals. They were both intelligent, well educated and interested in the arts. In the intervening years Eccleston had become a man of the establishment, renowned for his work as Chief Draughtsman in the Department of Occupation of Lands but, as he grew older and his need for long and adventurous surveying trips waned, he realised that, for all his achievements, a good name and praise were not enough.

Blanche would not have taken any man who made an offer for her. Loving a darling husband had not saved her own mother from near penury and she had no desire to be dragged from one South-East Asian post to another like Charlotte, or have a husband more attached to his men like Constance. She believed, above all, in the perfect man and she may have believed she had found him. The premature death of John Woolley ensured the eternal perfection of his views on womanhood. All her life she would strive to be 'Enid' with an 'evenly balanced mind, whose strength only trial reveals'. Such a belief would leave Blanche always hoping for consideration and never expecting anything for herself: the very fact she was not entirely happy might even be verification that she was doing the right thing by her husband. Eccleston appeared to Blanche as Gerwain: 'an explorer, a doer, a creative yet practical man'.[3] She ignored his reserve, preferring to view it as part of his nobility rather than intractability. Eccleston, on the other hand, was not required to adapt to a wife; it was how most marriages were but most women did not have Blanche's idealism. It would only have become clear, after many years of marriage, that Eccleston was more like Tennyson's King, about whom Blanche's father had written 'his idealism had too far drawn him from the communion of those whom he loved and sought to bless'.

Even in tragedy Constance's life continued to be dramatic. On 28 July 1878, at the age of 35, Captain Bacchus died of unspecified causes and was buried with full military honours. The cortege travelled from the Barracks at Paddington, through the main streets of Sydney to the cemetery. So admired was he that a description of the man and the event took up a half column in the *Herald*. Three weeks later identical twin boys, Ralph Lancelot and John Harold, arrived prematurely.

Three months later in the quiet Du Faur household, a son, Guy Cyprian, was born, with a dropped lip inherited from his mother. He was a gentle, timid baby and always Blanche's favourite. Two years after that another son, John Bertram (known as Bertie), was born and two years after that, on 16 September 1882, two days after her father's birthday, a daughter Emmeline Freda. She was tiny with sharp, determined eyes, dark hair and large ears like her father. In 1885, when Blanche was 42, another son would be born to whom Eccleston Frederic Du Faur dared give his name but, as with that first son eighteen years earlier, baby Frederic did not live long past his birth.

Even a rather unfanciful man as Eccleston may have felt jinxed by this although, in that era, he could have counted himself fortunate that three out of his five children had survived and he'd lost only one wife in childbirth. Did Blanche feel uneasy when the name of her older sister, Emmeline, was dropped and her three-year-old daughter, the only child named for the Woolley side, was renamed after the Du Faurs? Emmeline Freda became simply Freda.

Freda's first home was a terrace house, Marfa, in Grosvenor Street, Croydon. The suburb had been divided only two decades earlier, when it was described as being the most valuable, suburban property ever offered for auction in the colony. Selling for £44 an acre it could be afforded only by the wealthy, primarily merchants who desired large blocks on which to build mansions in an attempt to rival any manor house in Britain. Among the property owners were influential acquaintances of Eccleston Du Faur's: William Hemmings, the New South Wales Commissioner of Stamp Duties; Anthony Hordern, son of the founder of Anthony Hordern department stores; and the Member of Parliament Joseph Abbott. Genial and popular, Abbott was also the manager of the pastoral interests of Morts, one of the biggest companies in the colony. He held large parties, to which the Du Faurs were invited, in the wood-panelled ballroom, billiards room and on the tennis courts at Ivanhoe, Abbott's 25 acre estate. Eccleston bought a smaller block, during the second wave of settlement which occurred in the vicinity of an overly expensive and elaborate railway station provided for the convenience of the wealthy and powerful.

Moving there was proof that he had succeeded in business and had made the transition from lone traveller to a settled family man. Croydon was significant enough to have a Church of England and its own post office from where the postmen, in high-buttoned jackets and white topees, shouldered large leather satchels to deliver the mail. Two drapery establishments in Elizabeth Street provided everything a conscientious wife and mother might need, there was a butcher shop and even a coffee shop selling pastries and cakes, where ladies could ease full skirts into tiny chairs and dip plumed hats over their tea cups.

Apart for an unsettling period between 1881 and 1882, when Eccleston decided to retire from the Land Office and set up the pastoralist company Donkin and Du Faur, (which three years later became Du Faur and Gerard, when Donkin retired) Blanche had no reason to believe that her life was anything but blessed. She had two living sons and a daughter. She had, unlike her mother, her own house and garden to tend to, in which a family could grow in grace and style, and a relevant permanent place in society. Her husband was stable, hard working and public spirited, did not interfere in the running of the household and there were to be no more children, which would have taken pressure off both of them: it would have spared Blanche from the obvious physical dangers and suited her restrained approach to relationships, and allowed Eccleston to follow work and his external pursuits with fewer distractions.

There was one catch in this perfection. Blanche had expected, as the children left babyhood, that her husband would then become a devoted father as hers had been, a Papa who popped home to play with his children and delight in their development and their idiosyncrasies. But Eccleston liked mature people who could exchange heightened ideas with him; he was too set in his own ways. Unfortunately Blanche, continuing in her belief that 'a life more eloquent than words restores our [men's] faith in duty and truth'[4] remained silent in her disappointment and harboured, in that silence, a lonely sadness.

When Freda was six, the family moved again, to Tintern Road, Ashfield, about half a mile away. The new house was a larger, airy establishment and, in keeping with their rising wealth and status, was filled with weighty furniture imported from England. Family portraits, including those of Cyprian and his wife, were placed on walls big enough to take them.

For Freda the greatest pleasure in moving wasn't the house but access to 'out there', beyond the lace curtains and blinds pulled to protect the interiors from the raw Australian sun, out among stands of iron bark trees and beyond again, to the acreages and bush filled with possums and gliders, fair sport for any child with the inclination and a good aim with a sling shot. There was the added lure of Iron Bark Creek, which meandered through the bush out into Iron Cove on Sydney Harbour. Guy and Bertie didn't mind their young sister tagging along on these expeditions, on the proviso she didn't challenge them in any way, but that was impossible. Freda refused to be dominated; she would not miss out. She pestered her parents into buying her a horse, not as swift or as expensive as Guy's and Bertie's. Although she rode side-saddle she was more daring, had precise balance, greater need, and it became impossible for them to outrun her. Tennis was physical, social and competitive and there were ten children to beat in the Abbott family but, during regular tennis matches on the Ivanhoe courts, Freda had only one player in her sights, Guy. Frustratingly, she could never beat him but it irritated him that she constantly tried. She was not a sister but a rival and it became harder for her brothers to like her, harder for them to protect her. They banded together against the nuisance. Even as an adult on Mount Cook, she remembered how they 'always jeered at me for being a girl baby if I dared funk anything'. Her only defence was to seem not to care. Even if her 'mind was in chaos, nerves on edge'[5] she would not show any weakness to what she viewed as an unsympathetic world. She was proud of, and practised this skill.

Freda, through all her battles, did not realise that in her home her gender gave her an advantage over her brothers. Despite his abstracted ways her father was a courtly, respectful man who, through his three sisters, was accustomed to dealing with, or perhaps ignoring, female vagaries. Also, fortunately for Freda, although when young it must have been frustrating, her attempts at equality in a 'male way', to be competitive, articulate and direct,

gave her the essential skills of a mountaineer. There was no simpering with her. She did not ask guides, like Peter Graham and
Conrad Kain, as did other women, 'Do you have a girlfriend, are
you married? Do you have children?[6] – questions that came out of
an awareness of their sexuality. Freda wanted male companionship,
that distant, friendly mateship that allowed for things to get done
and emotional needs to be repressed. She was everything a father of
that time could have wanted – intelligent, articulate, physically
brave – in a son.

Eccleston and Blanche were concerned with their daredevil
daughter's relationship with her brothers, but Freda found her own
diversion, a young British immigrant named Bertha Ealing, who
was hired by her mother as a kind of nanny/maid. Under the older
girl's polite demeanour was an ally in adventure and they soon
developed a mutual dependency – in keeping each other out of
trouble. It was Freda's first real friendship and it was a passionate
attachment. No one thought to explain to her that Bertha was
engaged and when she married would not remain for long, and certainly would not go with Freda's family if they moved elsewhere.
When these events occurred, Freda would perceive the separation
as a betrayal. As her mother did when low, she turned inward, and
felt bitter that her friend, her family, the world was against her.

This dark oppressive mood only lifted when a stray dog,
a black and white bitser with long, soft fur and a patch over his eye,
turned up. He was impossible to resist, especially as it was too late
to train him properly and he was only obedient when it suited him.
Freda called him 'Possum' or 'Possie'. He was as keen as his mis-
tress on the exciting life, although Guy and Bertie had discovered
another 'get Freda' game. They could lure Possie off with them.
Again sibling fights escalated but, by then, Freda was making
friends elsewhere and her brothers' activities were becoming less
important.

Two girls were of particular importance. The first was Ruth Gerard, the daughter of Eccleston's partner and close friend, Francis Gerard. Although the Gerards lived across on the north side of the harbour at Mosman, the families were inevitably thrown together. According to her daughter, Ruth was the epitome of 'Judy' in the classic Australian tale *Seven Little Australians*.

> If she did not dash madly to the place she wished to get to, she would progress by a series of jumps, bounds and odd little skips. She was very thin, as people generally are who have quicksilver instead of blood in their veins. She had a small, eager, freckled face, with very bright dark eyes, a small determined mouth, and a mane of untidy, curly dark hair that was the trial of her life.[7]

Even a few of these qualities were enough to endear Ruth to a girl looking for allies, but she had a serious side that Freda, as a child, never needed to develop. Francis Gerard was infinitely more strict than Eccleston and, as her mother was ill with pernicious anaemia, Ruth, as the eldest, had to take care of the house and the children. She would eventually marry one of the Abbott boys of Ivanhoe.

Despite a queasy stomach even on the calmest day, Freda always found the trip out to the Gerards' home exciting. On the ferry she felt she was finally going 'somewhere', reaching for 'something unknown', almost touchable beyond the Heads where a silver horizon met a silver sky. Anything could happen. And it did, although only when they reached land. While their mothers took tea, Freda and Ruth would marshal the three younger Gerards at the wharf. Originally the site of a whaling station, the area was redolent with the kind of life nice young girls shouldn't know about, although Freda and Ruth incessantly discussed possible scenarios and scared their charges with their stories. Old iron rings bolted into rocks became convict chains rather than rope pulleys and there were pirates over the road at the Badham house, The Nest, where 'a deaf employee who somehow fired the old cannon … kept repeating excitedly "I heard it, I did!".[8] The Badham house had thick, bullet-scarred walls and barred windows designed, so the girls imagined, to keep mad people in or to keep out marauding escapees or the cannibals (the fairly amiable indigenous population) that passed round the bays in search of shellfish.

The Badhams meant little to Freda then. What was it to her that Professor Charles Badham had come out from England to replace her long dead grandfather as Professor of Classics and Principal at Sydney University? Nor would she give a thought to Badham's grown daughter, Edith, who would one day become her headmistress.

It was as well Ruth was not a jealous child, because another girl, from up the hill, began to join them in their games. This was Enid Blanche Dorcas Harnett, who became Freda's best friend, an attachment secured by their naughtiness and cemented forever in life when Enid eventually married Freda's cousin, Ralph Bacchus. Enid was the most spoiled and youngest daughter of an influential, somewhat nouveau riche family. Her father, Richard Hayes Harnett, was an early entrepreneur in real estate and transport, whose confidence only took a denting when he occasionally went bankrupt.

Regarded as the founder of Mosman, he later named another northern suburb, Chatswood after his second wife, Charlotte (Chatty), Enid's mother, who was only seventeen when she married the 51-year-old Harnett. Chatty was never concerned with order in the household of eleven children from Harnett's first marriage and six from this second. The Harnetts had once lived in The Nest, but by the time Enid and Freda met, had outgrown it and were living up the hill in the Buena Vista, called the 'Mirror Castle' by the children as each brick had been dipped in liquid glass. Without a strict

father and an ailing mother to inhibit her, Enid could lure a willing
Freda away from fantasy games to real ones. She would dare Freda
to ride the wagons at the wharf, which was forbidden, climb
through the bush and roam away for the entire day. Once they
climbed on a stationary tram, took off the brake and rode it down
the hill. There were no punishments so after that anything was possible. Freda admitted that her parents were unable to control her
and that her self-reliance caused them 'some alarm'.[9] Blanche, holding hard to her ideals that being sweet and kind and uncritical
would eventually engender a similar response from her recalcitrant
daughter, was helpless. And Eccleston was never quite the heavy
Victorian father. He was not keen on the careless Harnetts but he
loved individuality and his emotional distance meant he was rarely
irritated enough with his headstrong daughter to reprimand her.
She was too like him, with the same spirit that had taken him to
Australia. He knew how dull his life would have been if he'd
stopped home safely in England. He could not crush her. Instead he
exposed her, in the pursuance of his own obsessions, to greater
stimulation.

3 NATURA ARS DEI

> *'O nature, why do I not name thee God,*
> *Art thou not the living garment of God*
> *Is it in every deed*
> *He that ever speaks through thee and lives.'*
>
> inscribed in Alex Graham's copy of
THE CONQUEST OF MOUNT COOK

Eccleston Du Faur, as a lover of art, was his mother's child; although for him the greatest works were those created by nature, and he was determined his opinion should apply in Australia. In this he was given the unstinting support of his wife, artists and influential friends. However, he wished to communicate his enthusiasm to his fellow citizens, primarily British stock who still did not find the dry and seemingly monochromatic local landscape particularly attractive, let alone a place to visit. So, as John Woolley had started the Schools of Arts, Eccleston initiated a re-education program through art and photography camps with the intention of rectifying this backward-looking view. He wanted to create national parks, accessible to the public as they were in America, and regarded it as ridiculous that Sydneysiders went all the way to the soft greenery of New Zealand or Tasmania to escape the enervating summers when they had access to areas like the Blue Mountains, a low, bush-covered range of valleys and sandstone escarpments that divide Sydney from the vast, inner plains.[1]

He was in, what his colleagues, called his 'Blue Mountain craze': such areas provided, he felt, 'a kind of cultural uplift ... in these rather unappreciative colonies'.[2] It was not just idealistic talk. Freda's father organised and paid for camps that might last for weeks, where artists could be supported financially to paint the landscapes and bring back their paintings for the edification of the citizens. Such camps were also a base for exploration into the vast inner tracts of the western districts of New South Wales as Eccleston was always in an exploration 'craze'. Apart from his personal forays, even before Freda was born, he had helped finance and organise major expeditions to the then unknown parts of the New Hebrides and New Britain. The latter expedition was regarded as successful enough to name an island after Du Faur, despite their vessel, *The Star of the East*, foundering on the uncharted reefs in the area. But another expedition Eccleston planned was a complete disaster. Led by the explorer and criminal Andrew Hume, the intention was to search for the remains of the famous explorer Leichhardt, who disappeared while attempting an east–west crossing of Australia in 1848. Nothing was found of Leichhardt and only one of the three explorers of the Hume expedition, Lewis Thomson, survived. Guilt ridden, Eccleston kept him on to become a kind of family retainer and companion in exploration, and the tragedy remained in the household as one of those things that must never be mentioned. But, for a child like Freda, death only added allure to the men and to their papers and maps, their works of art which were often in various states of completion about the house, and the spread of the latest photographic equipment, a feast of gleaming steel, dull black cases, worn leather and smooth black and white prints. Eccleston was formidable in such company and during intense discussions around the dining table. Speaking of the thorny native plant, the bush lawyer, he was to say, its 'sting is more cruel than any advocate's tongue and sharper than his wit',[3] although such dry, unfathomable humour ensured there was always distance between him and his guests as well as his family. All this only made the world of the explorer more desirable and her mother's world, the world of a late Victorian upper class woman, even more bland.

Frustrating as this was, it was even more so when there were exciting journeys Freda could only farewell, which left her with impressions of smell and image that stirred her imagination. A journalist described a train carriage filled with the equipment on its way to one of Eccleston's camps in the Grose Valley:

> On stepping into the saloon our olfactory organs at once advised us that photographic materials formed part of the luggage and we were somewhat surprised at the size of the bath, plates etc especially considering the difficulty of conveying large packages through the bush.[4]

True to Eccleston's beliefs, every summer the Du Faurs migrated to Mount Wilson in the Blue Mountains, a journey requiring a train trip to Weatherboard Station and a buggy ride along the bumpy track of the Five Mile to their destination. It was the nearest to an adventure Freda was going to get at that point in her young life and, at times, it did appear to be the real thing: the landscape looked like the wilderness as water trickled off great sandstone cliffs and thick vines and ferns crowded the edges of the road. It felt as if civilisation, epitomised by Croydon and all the other suburbs the train had passed through, had been left far behind but, in reality, Mount Wilson was rapidly becoming an area of holiday homes for the wealthy who regarded England and English ways as the true standard. The township was built on a rare volcanic extrusion, in what was essentially a sandstone range, where the rich soil nourished lush and beautiful ferns, known as beowangs, and dense bush as well as plants and trees, imported from England. The settlement was enthusiastically described at the turn of the century by a home-sick English journalist as thankfully having 'no vestiges of the usual rugged Blue Mountain scenery: ... the continuous song of birds and a sense of peace and tranquillity is of some gentle corner of England set down in a fertile corner of Australia and retaining that sense of gracious and spacious living that has all but passed from the world.'[5]

Even more disappointing for an eager young girl, as soon as they arrived she was invariably bundled off with her mother to the Backhouses or to Wynstay, the big wooden house belonging to the businessman Richard Wynne, who had been involved with Eccleston in the original subdivision. There she was squashed back into the world of beautiful homes, manners and etiquette, while the boys, her grizzling brothers, were allowed to go with Eccleston to stay in the primitive bush cabin, not unlike the huts in the Southern Alps made of corrugated iron with tiny windows and a single door, that Eccleston owned and used as a base for explo-ration.

As well, she had to watch her brothers ride off, often overnight, with their father and, as the final insult, sometimes traitorous Possie disappeared with them. She was only allowed out into the bush on picnics, which were formal events involving considerable organisa-tion between various families. She had to wear a white frilled pinafore, straw hat and laced boots and sit up on the wagon as the horse plodded on, amidst talk, jostling cautions, the squeak of hampers, the smell of fresh bread, damp undergrowth and horse manure while the plump-faced Backhouse boys and lucky Guy and Bertie ran alongside.

The closest to freedom Freda could get was a walk along the paths and roads as far as Du Faur Rock (named for her father's work in the area) or to Wynn Rock and, from these places, gaze down the valleys into the infinite distances of blue haze and steep cliffs. There she could recall those maps of mystery, the power of exploration and her family name that marked such places forever. Her father's stories came back to her: the difficulties of coming to Australia by the ship; his travels through Australia as a young man; the heroism and drowning of her maternal grandfather; the loss of the explorers Leichhardt and Hume; Chateau du Pibrac; Cyprian Du Faur's brushes with death in Africa and during the French Revolution; even the drawings of the spirits in the Aboriginal paintings in local caves held an allure Freda never wanted to resist. At times these events seemed as vivid as if she'd lived through them herself, but her common sense reminded her that this was self-deception. To be a real Du Faur, to live up to all that had gone before, her grandfather's dreams and her father's aspirations, she would have to create her own stories that generations after her would talk about and wish to emulate. Life wouldn't be worth living if she didn't.

The importance of this had been emphasised when, in 1887, Freda's restless father returned to England to visit his family and fit in a trip to Toulouse, to the Chateau Pibrac. Eccleston sent back postcards of the chateau which proved to be nearer in style to a castle, designed as it was to defend the valley of the Garonne River from invaders with walls of thick stone topped by turrets and with windows little more than slits. He was most impressed with it and the on-going renovations which the incumbent Comte de Pibrac, who was based in Paris, cared enough to finance.

Because of the loss of papers during the French Revolution there had been some difficulty in establishing lineage. Eccleston, however, tirelessly searched out the evidence and to his great pleasure, on his return to Sydney, the Comte wrote to acknowledge the visit and the relationship. He stated 'the particulars, thus cited are sufficient to assure you, in my family and in myself personally, the most sympathetic reception should you, as I hope, ever return to our country'.[6]

Despite this, Eccleston's return was miserable for his family. He was impatient with everyone. He was 56 years old and painfully aware that he had not built his 'castle' to attest to the family Du Faur in Australia. After seeing ten years of specialised work in drawing a detailed map of NSW burnt in a fire, he was determined to put his efforts into something less destructible than survey papers. Buildings and estates seemed the obvious choice but that conflict-ed with a growing conservationist conscience and dislike for urban life. Even at a young age Freda recognised how urbanisation oppressed her father with the narrowness of its existence. It was what he regarded, and therefore she regarded, as 'over civilised'. That he could not tolerate and, to be her father's daughter, neither could she. He could not, even if his wife could, live in what he saw as an increasingly bland, upper middle-class existence in Croydon and Ashfield. Parties, balls, billiards, concerts all seemed fleeting, excessive and wasted his time. Other intellectuals and artists were escaping the materialism and the mundane crowds they saw as rampant in the city. The pastoral company of Du Faur and Gerard had already invested in land in the upper North Shore, in an area Eccleston had officially called by the Aboriginal name 'Turramurra', meaning Lofty Place, and the Gerards were renting a house in near-by Warrawee from where Francis was overseeing the building of his new house, Cheddington. So Eccleston bought land up there as well in Eastern Road and chose one of his few close friends, the renowned architect John Horbury Hunt, who had already been commissioned to design the new National Art Gallery, to design a house.

Freda adored the little American, as she would adore a number of much older, eccentric, intelligent men. He seemed like a magi-cian, full of winks and tricks, and she was never sure whether he was teasing or not. In a time of navy suits, pinstripe and black coats, Horbury Hunt wore a long, plum-coloured frock coat, with special pockets to hold pens and instruments, high-waisted striped pants, and a brightly coloured waistcoat (usually blue) with silver, domed buttons. His boots were self-designed with raised heels to compensate for his small stature. The bicycle he rode everywhere had a mobile studio attached to it. Inside his exaggeratedly high top hat, he created a ventilated area with room for paper, 'so he could whip off a new drawing for one of his buildings, literally at the drop of a hat'.[7] Once he even arrived at the site of a nunnery in his pyjamas. However, when Horbury Hunt's radical designs and his personality failed to endear him to the establishment (he eventually lost the Gallery commission), he turned his attention entirely onto the new Du Faur home.

Blanche did not want to move from Croydon, with its easy connections with friends and family, to a place that wouldn't even have a railway line for another five years; but, inevitably, when Freda was eight, the moment her mother dreaded arrived. Everything the family owned was packed up and carried down to the harbour's edge, then barged across and up the Lane Cove River to Fidden's Wharf. From there bullocks dragged drays, full of their belongings, cross-country, up the tracks used to bring building materials, firewood and fruit – apricots, pears, nectarines, orange and apples – down into Sydney. There were few real settlements and what existed were little more than squalid sawyers' huts and pits. It was as rough as Blanche had feared, although as she became more settled, her fears would be mollified by the beauty of her new home, the company of the largely creative and self-motivating Sydneysiders who moved into the northern region; and there was the chance, as the boys were going to school, of getting Freda back on an even keel.

Pibrac, the house the Du Faur family lived in from 1890 to 1895, is a large, two-storeyed home classified by the National Trust that curiously, surrounded by beautiful exotic trees, looks no older than the newer houses nearby. Its simplicity of style and high gabled roof that sweeps low down over the shingle walls and ground floor windows invokes the plain styles of the 1920s rather than the 1880s. The five bedrooms, entertainment areas and billiard room with plastered walls and polished floors are cool and expansive, the extensive gardens, although now subdivided, still require constant maintenance. The house provided the existence Eccleston had believed he was trying to escape from, but it was also a mark he needed to make and it could be justified on the grounds that, as Pibrac was placed among natural surroundings, he was still serving the beauty of the natural world. However, he was also rarely there.

Eccleston and Francis Gerard, with Guy and Bertie, travelled to work by two-in-hand down to Milson's Point where the boys were left at school and from where the men crossed the harbour to their office. Sometimes they stayed overnight at the Metropole Hotel, but it was not Eccleston's absence that Blanche found she missed, it was that of Guy.

While his younger siblings more selfishly pursued their own desires, which did not include quiet times with their mother, Guy kept her company. Blanche had become accustomed to confiding in her elder son although this meant he often found himself caught between her needs and his father's high expectations. Going to school, going on a trip with Eccleston felt like a betrayal of Blanche. Constantly torn, Guy would survive by becoming a quiet adolescent and an even quieter man, eager to please, but even more eager to avoid being seen as preferring one of his parents over the other. He was only safe in his own company. In time, he would refine his behaviour to such a point of calmness and sweetness that he appeared to have no real desires or opinions and therefore did not need consideration. His wife said of him: 'It was love at first sight … and if I had searched the world I could not have married a nicer man.'[8]

Guy's loyalties could be seen in his deeds rather than in his words. In 1899, when Eccleston bought twenty acres near Pibrac for him, Guy removed most of the native bush and turned it into what his father did not value, a showplace of exotic plants with cottage gardens, European trees and, as a centrepiece, a grass tennis court surrounded by climbing roses. It was everything Blanche loved.

Bertie did all the things that worried Guy. Tall for his age, and robust, he often wandered off exploring on his own, to build dams and make what he called 'inventions'. He seemed uninterested in the rest of the family but, underneath his self-sufficiency, was a growing resentment of his place as the second son. There might be two years between him and his older brother but Bertie knew he was the explorer and had the right to be by his father's side. When Bertie did go out on camps, he spent his time trying to outdo his older brother and succeeded only in irritating Eccleston. Bertie could not understand this and, in time, turned away from the family to become a loner who would feel he had been hard done by all his life.

Freda's life did become more structured. In the morning there were lessons from both her governess and her mother. In the afternoons they attended 'at homes' at the nearby Edwards', where there were three daughters, Dorothy, Marjorie and Mona, and at the Sulmans'. Annie, the second wife of the artist and architect, John Sulman, became Blanche's friend although Freda had little in common with the older Sulman daughters, Florence and Edith, despite the latter being the same age as Freda. She preferred going to Cheddington, where she and Ruth Gerard could create dramas along the big verandah, re-enacting Joan of Arc or Boadicea, any heroine at all, as long as Freda was lead. But even that became too sedate and she longed for Enid and her escapades. The Harnetts were, by then, relatively close in Chatswood, but they and the Du Faurs were not on each other's visiting lists and contact was spasmodic. So, frustrated by the lack of excitement, Freda began to creep off and roam though the local orchards. From there she ventured north along the uninhabited parts of Eastern Road or into Cockle Creek, always with a wary eye out for snakes. Gaining confidence in her own ability to get about in the bush, she progressed out into the periphery of a vast and pristine area of sandstone gullies and deep waterways around Cowan Creek, which her father had already begun exploring. There a local Aboriginal tribe, the Kuringals, had left their life stories and history in long strokes of ochre in caves or stretched out over large rocks. There also the native bush protected koalas, ringtail and brushtail possums and echidnas; wild flowers grew in abundance, reflecting on the ground the colours painted in the sky by rosellas and lorikeets, whose raucous voices cracked through the foliage.

After the building of Pibrac, the summer visits to the Blue Mountains came to an end. Apart from the inconvenience of getting the entire family across the city without railway linkage, Eccleston was far too interested in the environment around Cowan Creek to bother going elsewhere. When the weather became humid and unbearable, the family instead began staying in one of the tiny cottages locals had built on the edge of creek, and Freda loved it. There was a wooden boat to row up the inlet and deep cooling water in which to become an expert swimmer, and ensure she was better at it than her brothers. The hardened men of the Southern Alps considered she was mad when she took a dip in an icy pool in the mountains and, when it was raining, the comment would be made by a climbing companion that 'Miss Du Faur was reduced to taking her exercise in bathing dress and waterproof'.[9]

As well there was the cottage, which was primitive enough to feel like the rough old hut she had not been allowed to stay in at Mount Wilson. And there were no rules. Down by Cowan Creek no one nagged her about her dress, and behaving in a lady-like manner. There were no visits to make, no study to do, no needlework. And at night around the campfire it was glorious; there were stories told and secret bush sounds – the cries of frogmouth owls, late flying bats, the sharp crack of dry eucalypt to identify. Then too soon, they'd have to go home. Compared to the creek, home felt even more oppressive. Only out in the natural world did she feel a calm kind of happiness. But it was never enough; the joyous times, once she was back inside, faded too quickly.

By 1892, when Freda was ten, her brothers' attendance at school came to an end. The sheer newness of the colony, the expanding infrastructure of roads and railways, an economy predominantly dependent on millions of sheep, and the appearance of quick money that many had little interest in repaying, had created a buoyancy that was an illusion. Farms were the first to feel the effect of a full depression, pastoral companies weren't far behind and Eccleston had taken his eye off his source of income. He had found another passion in which to invest his time and money. This project would take precedence over everything, including his sons' schooling. He wanted to turn the 35,000 acres around Cowan Creek and up to the Hawkesbury River into a national park.

The depression was laying off men all over the country so the last thing a cash-strapped government was interested in was a land reserve, but lack of finances never deterred Freda's father. He had contacts and he used them. That September, the family and other interested locals went to meet the Governor of New South Wales, The Earl of Jersey, and his son, Lord Villiers, down in Cowan Creek with the intention of showing them what letters and photos had failed to prove. Three boats waited at the head of the waters to pick up the party and take them to the lower reaches to glimpse, what a journalist would later describe as, 'a New Zealand sound minus the tumbling waterfalls … a Norwegian fiord plus an Australian sun. It has not some of the things these others boast, it has beauties distinctly its own.'[10]

For long anxious hours they waited until the Earl, who had lost his way, finally arrived, but by then it was too late to explore the waterways as the tide had gone out, marooning the boats on the ugly mud flats. Freda was perturbed by the event. She had believed her father to be all powerful and yet she had seen him waiting anxiously on the opinion of someone who knew far less than he did. It was the one blot in her father's perfection and she did not like it. Nearly twenty years later, when the English Alpine Club was interested in publishing her articles, she wrote: 'I like making the aristocratic club beg for favours. It is much more sport than giving them unasked.'[11] The Earl must have discovered more than just a way through the bush for, within two years, Ku-ring-gai Chase was gazetted as a reserve.

At the same time Eccleston had increased his involvement in the National Art Gallery and became its president in 1892. For Freda and Blanche it meant rare trips to town to attend art exhibition openings. It meant staying at the Metropole or at Emmeline's, with morning tea at fancy shops and window shopping in expensive arcades. Art connected mother, father and daughter, but it also put Freda on equal footing with her brothers. At openings she ensured that she was tucked close enough to her father to bask in his glory and to ask complex questions that required his full attention.

Over the following years she became expert enough to distinguish between the famous painters, to discuss their techniques and who painted in the way of the 'Old World' and who, truly, was managing to paint with some appreciation of the light and landscapes of the 'New'.

By early 1895, although the economy was on the rise and the Du Faur and Gerard Pastoral Company was doing well, Eccleston decided Pibrac was too expensive to run. They should, he considered, consolidate, and where better than on land he already owned, twenty-five undeveloped acres 'four miles from anywhere' as Freda put it,[12] but right beside Ku-ring-gai Chase at the end of what is now Bobbin Head Road, Turramurra North. But such convenience for Eccleston was terrible for Blanche, who would never adjust to the change and isolation. Freda knew how her mother felt, but much as she loved her and tried to be considerate, she could not get past the feeling that to sympathise too much would draw her into Blanche's world or, to put it unkindly, she feared she could be tainted by, what she perceived, as her mother's weakness.

By the end of 1895, a new, practical house, designed by Horbury Hunt but tiny compared to Pibrac, was built on the slopes above the Chase and Pibrac, beautiful Pibrac, with its gardens and fountains, was gone. The new house, that plain little building, would be named after the large graceful Du Faur family home in England, Flowton Hall.

It was done. Eccleston was finally where he wanted to be. However, whatever light-heartedness he might have once exhibited was gone, and by the time Freda was old enough to really comprehend the dynamics of his personality, her parents had settled into formalised rituals and her father's obsession had made him a stern patriarch, determined to create a minor kingdom in the Chase. His time was spent writing letters, arguing, pleading and working. He organised influential trustees and surveyed the land and even dug some of the Zig Zag Road to Bobbin Head around Cowan Creek himself. He fought constant threats of encroachments: applications to mine the area for kaolin; to build country clubs; and, in 1899, to create a city called 'Pacivica', as the capital of the Commonwealth of Australia. This extraordinary plan included a copy of Windsor Castle and the Tower of London as well as an assortment of lakes, gardens and bridges.

All this suited Freda as it put her outdoors, and even more so when she and her brothers became part of the observer system protecting Ku-ring-gai Chase around Christmas, when the flower sellers from the city came out to steal native flora, especially the brilliant red blooms of the waratah. Such protection was essential as usually when these were 'looted', most of the plants were destroyed and every flower taken meant there were fewer seeds to replenish the natural stock. It was in those silent times, waiting with her brothers in the bush, that Freda began to appreciate what was nature and what was beautiful and what it meant when man destroyed the natural heritage. Naively she concluded that civilisation meant destruction and, in her fanciful youthful musings, she decided that, given a choice, the noble savage's life was preferable, even a condition to aspire to.

But at the same time as Freda, then thirteen, was making these discoveries, other plans were being made for her. She was intelligent enough to pursue academic interests but there was no system to her knowledge and she only applied herself to subjects she was interested in. She showed little interest in home duties and appeared to be losing interest in Ruth Gerard and the Edwards daughters and the other young women heading towards marriage and motherhood. Freda still preferred the wilful ways of Edith Harnett. Her parents did not. They decided something should be done and, as they couldn't do it themselves, she should be sent off to school.

4 IN THE SCHEME OF CREATION

' ... the aim of all education is to fit
the individual to master the environment ...
The ideal is to help that individual to rise to the height of destiny.'

Edith Badham

Advice on a place for Freda came from Aunt Emmeline Woolley, who may well have financed her schooling. Emmeline was formidably successful, financially well off, impatient at times with Blanche's inability to say what she wanted, critical of her niece's inability to apply herself to anything and definitely at odds with Eccleston over his disregard for his wife's needs. Emmeline considered the best place for the daughter of an upper class family was the Church of England Girls' Grammar (later Sydney Church of England Girls' Grammar, SCEGGS). Originally only daughters of clergymen had any real education outside their homes but this school, although established by the church and a bastion of Anglo-Saxon Victorian heritage, lent itself to the education of daughters of professors, politicians and business men as well. Opened on the 17 July 1895 by the archbishop and six bishops, it was run by a board of six men and, radical for the time, six women. On the first day only one pupil arrived, although five had been enrolled; but in less than a year the premises were too small for the numbers.

If the Du Faurs had any doubts about who to entrust with the delicate process of turning their daughter into the flower of the family, instead of scuttling through the bush in search of them, the fact that Miss Edith Badham, the only surviving daughter of the Professor of Classics and Principal of Sydney University, was head-mistress settled their concerns. Early in 1896 Blanche took Freda to E. Way and Company at 213–217 Pitt Street, who supplied 'young Ladies' School Outfits at very reasonable prices'. Her new uniform consisted of a long, grown-up navy skirt to the ankle for winter and a white dress with leg o'mutton sleeves and the ubiquitous straw boater for summer. There were also dresses for formal occasions and dinner, white in summer and navy blue velvet or cashmere in winter. Fees as a boarder were eighteen guineas a quarter, there were laundry costs of one shilling and sixpence for a dozen pieces, and with everything paid, Freda was packed and suddenly a schoolgirl.

It was devastating for her to leave both her home and her beloved Possie but, by the time the cab reached William Street and passed by Craigend and the Rialto Terraces, then turned into Victoria Street, mourning was over. There was too much to see: the cobbled road busy with cabs and buses; wisteria-covered houses with balconies containing cases of singing canaries; hawkers calling out in rhyme and song as they walked the pavements selling muffins, bread or fish. It was lively, it was irresistible.

At 65 Victoria Street, Darlinghurst a maid, dressed in an after-noon uniform of black topped with a white frilled apron and cap, opened the door and ushered them through to the drawing room where Miss Edith Annesley Badham was waiting. Miss Badham was described by a pupil with great admiration as 'tiny and neat in per-son – her pretty light hair, now brownish fair. It was crinkled and vital; so much so that one expected sparks. Her skin was finely

etched, still like a rose petal; her spotless clothes stiffly starched.'[1]
Born in 1852, she had come out from England to Australia at the
age of fourteen. Brilliant, with a gift for languages and extensively
educated by her father, she was, as a woman, unable to be admitted to the university run by him, despite the fact she was to assist
him in his work until his death. Unwilling to be dependent, she
took one of the few jobs available for an intelligent single woman.

The building Freda arrived at was described in the prospectus
as having 'a commodious schoolroom, drawing room, dining room,
two balcony rooms, seven bedrooms, large balconies and splendid
kitchen arrangements'. However, it was actually unprepossessing
and was even without a garden. Before long, due to rising numbers,
the school moved to a more appropriate house, Chatsworth, in
Macleay Street, Potts Point where most of Freda's four years at high
school would be spent. Chatsworth was more to Freda's taste with
pleasant, open, decorative rooms and grounds surrounded by
wrought-iron fences that ran down to the harbour where there was
a swimming pool, boating shed and tennis courts, from where,
through the jacarandas, the imagination could be stirred by the
sight of sailing ships heading off to the Old Country, Asia or New
Zealand.

The school day was strictly divided, a shock to Freda, but such
discipline would ultimately be useful. Lessons from 9.15 to 3.30
were interrupted only by a lunch cooked by 'Huge Henrietta'.
Subjects studied included English, geography, history (ancient and
modern,) the classics (Latin compulsory, Greek when desired)
maths, French, music, art and drawing. Exams were discouraged as
likely to be burdensome on a young mind. As a church school there
were three prayer meetings a day and strong leanings toward missionary work. It was easy to appreciate the purpose of good works,
but such evening activities as knitting socks and samplers of
encouragement for Australian soldiers in the Anglo-Boer War was

not Freda's idea of fun, nor was she good at it. She didn't mind the dancing classes. School dances were frequent and were held in the ballroom lit by glistening light from the candelabras. Below the ceiling of painted mythological figures, Miss Badham's youthful students turned on the polished parquet of native woods, as the huge gilded mirrors reflected and re-reflected the filmy white dresses, the formal dark suits and the serious faces of the students from the equivalent boys' school, 'Shore'.

Freda could play the piano almost as well as her mother but preferred popular tunes. She enjoyed sports, including tennis and swimming. There were reading periods; 'low brow', a reading of light fiction in the library with one of the teachers, or 'high brow', with Miss Badham, who read such classics as Milton's *Paradise Lost*, or the works of Dante, Chaucer and Spenser. Edith Badham was keen on the classics and Freda was keen on Miss Badham. Few fitted Miss Badham's ideal, and those on the outer knew it. An old girl wrote to the school magazine:

> One of her [Miss Badham's] girls – Lucy Peel – was burnt to death saving horses out of a burning stable. Another – Olive Kelso King – took convoys of wounded across the Balkans in winter – the only Englishwoman among the lawless Serbs. Freda Du Faur was the first person to climb Mt Cook ... and wrote a book on it. Lucy, Olive and Freda were Miss Badham's types.[2]

Sometimes the favoured girls rowed across the harbour to the Badhams' 'Nest' where afternoon tea was served in the drawing room. Nibbling on very thin bread and butter and sometimes cake which was kept in a portable safe that the girls called 'the coal scuttle', they perched amongst the rich brocades and tapestries, beaten brass and hand-tooled leather bindings that the Badhams adored. So too did Freda, and she learned to carve, a popular craft of the time. One piece survives, a wooden mirror, carved with gumnuts and eucalyptus leaves entwining the initials F.D.F.

Miss Badham carried the same sense of privilege and exotic taste into the school. There her rooms were decorated with wallpapers in a rich scroll pattern and her bedroom was an unusual gold, dominated by a high four-poster bed, smothered in quilts and pillows gathered in her travels.

The headmistress came at a perfect time for Freda, searching as she was for an example of womanhood to emulate. 'To be wise and sincere and outspoken' – how that side of Edith Badham's teachings rooted itself in Freda's heart and into 'the sensitive delicate mechanism ... of her mind'.[3] The motto for the school, was *'Luceat Lux Vestra'* (Let Your Light Shine'). Miss Badham would stand 'upright before her class vibrating – one might say scintillating – with life – her steel gray eyes humorously alert'.[4] What Freda wanted to do all her life was to keep that light of her individuality shining as honestly as she could. What more could a future mountaineer ask for?

Miss Badham followed Freda's later activities closely. More impressed with Freda being the first person to do something, not just being the first woman, she wrote, in the school magazine in 1912, years after Freda left her school: 'I wonder how many old girls know that one of their number, Freda Du Faur, is a distinguished Alpine Climber. She is the first Alpinist to have climbed to the top of Mt Tasman.'[5]

Freda, although the first woman to reach the top, was not the first Alpinist. She later supplied photographs and an article on the Mount Tasman climb to the school magazine, *Lux*, similar to the account in her own book *The Conquest of Mount Cook*. But she also included a poem chosen to enable schoolgirls to imagine what such a climb was like. Eager to encourage admiration of such individuality, Miss Badham reviewed the article with enthusiasm: 'Miss Du

Faur writes with an arresting simplicity which usually marks the doers of fine things, of toilsome and prolonged climbs in the teeth of bitter winds over the ice fields when not only each step, but even grip holes for fingers must be cut with an axe'.[6] Such a pupil was proof of her success as a headmistress. There is more admiration in this than for any of the young women who gained, as the school had promised, 'beauty of the truly feminine character above the price of rubies'.

But there was one blemish in Freda's idol. Despite providing a contrary example, Miss Badham stated at the first prize-giving: 'We also desire to show that it is possible for a girl to learn Greek and Latin without at all desiring to step out of her proper and subordinate place in the scheme of Creation and we aim rather at teaching her the duties than the rights of woman.'[7]

This opinion wasn't an affectation to please a conservative board, for Edith Badham refused to assert the rights of women, perhaps believing that the full rights were for the rare woman like herself and the light of most women was never destined to burn bright enough to deserve a vote. Freda knew better. At SCEGGS, Florence Nightingale was revered for her nursing skills but at Aunt Emmeline's, where Freda visited on afternoons off, the famous nurse was lauded for her feminist ideals and her rejection of marriage on the basis that 'women must sacrifice all their life if they accepted that ... behind his destiny women must annihilate herself'.[8] Annihilation was an unappealing prospect for a young girl whereas the other choice, of not marrying and living like Emmeline and Ethel (and Edith Badham), seemed quite reasonable.

Freda's aunt and Ethel Pedley did everything together including writing music: Emmeline was the composer, Ethel the lyricist. They founded St Cecilia's Choir, which became the focal point of fundraising activities for charities as diverse as Women's College, the Thirlmere Consumptive Home and the Women's Industries

Exhibition, and performed at balls attended by the elite of the city. Their charm and style were evident in their home as well, where the rooms were decorated with fresh flowers, painted in gilt and pretty colours, and gold ribbons were strewn over paintings and held back swags of curtain. There were always visitors, mainly influential, intelligent women friends and, at times, gatherings included Blanche and her daughter. Blanche was relaxed there; it was like old times, as sisters together in a household of primarily women. She played duets with Emmeline; although never as skilled as her sister, Blanche was as passionate as she was about music; it was both a solace and a joy.

Despite the closeness of the sisters, Freda was, at that time, apprehensive of her Aunt Emmeline, who appeared stern and intimidating, but she adored the slender, dark-haired, lively Ethel. As well as a musician, Ethel Pedley was famous (posthumously) for the Australian classic, *Dot and the Kangaroo*, a story about a small girl lost in the bush who befriends a kangaroo in search of her lost joey. The book raises questions about the dominance of one group of people over a demonstrably weaker group. The kangaroo complains that 'The Black Humans kill and devour us; but they, even, are not so terrible as the Whites who delight in taking our lives and torturing us just as an amusement.' The book questions the damage done by the British colonists and lauds the strength of the female, a not uncommon topic of discussion in the Woolley–Pedley household for they and their friends were at the forefront of feminist thought in New South Wales. Through them Freda would be thoroughly indoctrinated, at a relatively young age, in the push for suffrage and in feminist argument.

There was always a practical side to anything Emmeline did, which enabled her to get to know people quickly and without fuss. Any finer points of friendship were provided by Ethel. Emmeline had maintained connections with Sydney University, specifically to ensure her father's name would continue but, in doing so, became involved in setting up the Women's College in 1892, which was intended to provide a residence and supervision for young women attending university. She quickly befriended the woman appointed to run the new college, Louisa MacDonald, an emotional Scottish woman and a fine scholar with a master's degree in classics and honours in German. Louisa's older sister, Bella, was one of the first women doctors out of the University of London. Sydney was far behind Britain; there was yet to be a female graduate despite permission for women to be 'admitted to all privileges' over a decade earlier, and Louisa still had to smooth over the great concern in the colony that women would serve as a distraction in lectures and that the subjects would have to be changed in case damage was caused to their delicate sensibilities. Such fears were allayed, slightly, when a reporter from the *Herald* described Louisa's arrival in March 1892: 'Miss MacDonald despite her great attainment, has nothing of the typical blue stocking in dress and manner. With a fine vigorous frame, handsome face, a ringing unaffected voice, she confesses a liking for nice clothes and ... a due sense of what custom demands in the attire of a gentlewoman.' It was a lesson on impressions, well learned by a young woman who changed into her 'prettiest dress' after her climb of Mount Cook, in order to quell any rumours that women mountaineers were unfeminine.

Another influential friend of Emmeline's was Miss Rose Scott, founder of the Women's Literary Society, from which the Womanhood Suffrage League had evolved, and to which all the women in Emmeline's circle belonged. Country born, Rose had moved to the city at the age of 35 and quickly turned her sharp brain and social connections to the creation of a salon in her home in Woollahra, where every Friday evening, men and women, the influential politicians, artists, poets and intellectuals of the city, gathered. Outwardly sweet and refined, Rose was politically very astute and not afraid to give her opinion. She fought openly with anyone she disagreed with, including members of the League and later the English Suffragettes over their militancy. There was plenty to fight about. The demand for suffrage had been taken up quickly and by the mid-1890s had become the subject of upper class dinners. The wife of Edmund Barton, Australia's first Prime Minister, was president of the League at one point but many wealthy women had little understanding of the real issues and loathed the idea that working women and prostitutes could have the same vote as them. Working-class leaders were naturally offended by this view and generally strove to achieve equality with men in work as well as in law, but it helped having the power of the upper classes behind them. Eventually meetings had to be held in the neutral ground of the popular refreshment rooms run by Quong Tart, gatherings which the Du Faur women could also attend. There, beneath intricate gilded woodwork, ferns, palms and surrounded by fountains under which golden carp leisurely swam, ferocious arguments ensued over the education of the poor, the treatment of women in prisons and the rights of women in law in regard to property, care of children and financial support, all of which they lost if they were deserted or divorced. The factionalism may well have undermined the drive for the vote; New Zealand women received suffrage in 1893, whereas women in New South Wales didn't claim theirs until 1902.

The vociferous exchanges were exciting and the ideas enhanced, for an impressionable girl, by a warmth absent from the Du Faur household and a daring absent from a female and somewhat conservative school. Through Miss Scott and Aunt Emmeline, Freda heard of and obtained a copy of the *The Subjection of Women* published in 1861 by the British Member of Parliament and philosopher John Stuart Mill. His re-evaluation of what women should expect from life enthralled her and the tract was to become her 'Bible'. Even when completely familiar with it, she carried it with her. Fifteen years later, when trying to convert a skeptical, mountaineering friend, Otto Frind, she wrote, concerning the treatise, 'I humbly recommend it to any seeker of the plain facts and fine logic and would like to see it as a list book for seniors in every school.'[9]

At the age of seventeen Freda was beginning to clarify her attitudes to her future lifestyle and her rights as a future woman. She may have been intolerant of weaknesses in both sexes, aware of her own place in society and proud of her family history, but she would believe in the equality of women all her life. She also became increasingly comfortable with the idea that women, not prepared to forgo success and a career for marriage, could find support from other women, although the question of lesbianism did not yet arise. It is highly likely Emmeline and Ethel were lesbian, as Louisa MacDonald may have been as she brought a lifelong female companion, Evelyn Dickinson, out with her from Britain and would comment that Evelyn 'practically shares the work of this place although is nominally my guest'.[10] But what Freda actually understood and saw was, rather than sexuality, the support the women gave each other. If she had any doubts about the way they sustained each other, Ethel's death dispelled them.

The young woman was dying of cancer. It had been a long excruciating process. As early as 1895 when Ethel was only 36, Louisa MacDonald had written to a close friend in England, outlining the struggles she had in her work and the help Emmeline Woolley gave to the college. She mentioned that 'Miss Pedley is on the way to recovery but is still feeble … She [Ethel Pedley] and Miss Woolley are in the country together, the latter exhausted from the effects of trouble and anxiety as much as looking after her friend.'[11]

Ethel went into remission long enough to risk a trip to England with Emmeline to investigate setting up a system of local examinations through the Royal Academy and Royal College of Music. The trip was successful but the optimism premature and on 6 August 1898, Ethel Pedley died. She was buried in the Waverley Cemetery, on a slope facing the ocean. It seemed such an oppressive way to finish a life, weighted with earth, instead of dissolving into the heavens as smoke. However, despite the suffering, for Freda the care her aunt lavished upon her friend and their closeness, would be a 'verification of life – a chosen life shared'.[12]

It was a situation in which she would find herself later in her own life.

At the end of 1899, Freda's schooling came to an end and she went back to Flowton aware of mortality and that youth and talent could not stop death. The pudginess produced by institution food, reduced exercise and the remains of childhood was still there; mourning had not produced, as exercise and intensity would, the small-boned face and determined mouth that would appear in her late twenties. She wore her hair twisted over her ears to disguise their size and then put it in a roll on top. She had clear skin, always wore hats and tried to keep out of the sun. Some of her school friends were already earning themselves the title of 'young matron', by returning to the country to marry into the squattocracy, or to marry majors in the army, or under-secretaries to the Premier or, even like one school friend, Midge Caird, to become Lady Bruxner, wife of the Premier of New South Wales. Some returned to their old school as governesses and became devoted to the next group of girls or went to finishing schools in France and Europe. Others left Australia to serve God and Morality, as missionaries in Asia, New Guinea and Africa. Most would still be called 'girls' when they were paying the old girl subscriptions and sending their own daughters to the same school.

Freda did not know what she wanted to do. University was out of the question. There were no prizes given during her first two years of school but Freda won nothing in 1898–99. She was not the rare intellectual star that 'should go on' despite her parents' optimism. She would remain distantly attached to the school and be grateful for all she had gained there. Until 1912, she paid subscriptions and expressed a desire to keep in contact, she donated money regularly for the Old Girls' Prize but was too much of a loner to go on the Old Girls' Committee. Instead she sent in chatty letters of her activities and eventually articles on her climbs.

There were more pressing needs at Flowton. Blanche had become dispirited by both Ethel's death and the sudden demise of her younger sister, Charlotte Courteney. Fortunately for Freda, who had begun to fear that she could well spend the best years of her life as housekeeper to unmarried brothers and elderly parents, Blanche's sisters revived the companionship of their childhood. Emmeline began staying out at Flowton, Charlotte's grown children, Claude, Ivor and Agatha, began to visit and Constance arrived with her twin sons from New Zealand. Constance energised everyone and, despite her hardships, the death of her husband and the disappearance of her eldest son, Reginald (who was still in England and a dissolute), was as vivacious and dominant as ever. With the help of her Harry and Lance, as Ralph was more commonly called, she had taken over a farm in the rough hilly country centred on Manakau, north of the capital Wellington and close to the west coast town of Otaki. The work of clearing the bush had been an enormous task, quickly turning teenage boys into young men. Up to fifty acres had been cleared, which were burned each winter to provide future pastures. Timber was sold to finance the farm in the years before their flock was fully established. At times the Bacchus family had had to rely on food from the gardens of the local Maori.

Now that the five-year gap in their ages was not so apparent, Freda became friends with her cousins. Both were big, handsome men with strong, shaven jaws, brown hair and intent, brown eyes under straight, low brows. They had few pretensions, were hard-working, good humoured, and desperately supportive of their mother. Harry was already courting a beautiful local girl, Sabrie Ruth, so Freda took Lance with her to tennis, to social evenings at the Edwards' and Gerards' and to the frequent parties held by the Abbotts or the Harnetts. At one of these gatherings Lance met Enid Harnett.

Freda was not entirely impressed at suddenly feeling less important in both the lives of her cousin and her good friend. She was somewhat threatened by the situation especially when Lance asked for Enid's hand and she actually agreed. When the Bacchus family left for New Zealand, taking Enid with them, Freda was anxious that she would lose both her cousin and her best friend to that repressive institution of marriage, that the one person she could rely on to be bold and to embolden her would become a simpering wife. Freda was wrong: marriage would make Enid even more headstrong; they would always remain close friends.

After their departure, it was Freda and Eccleston who were thrown together. Blanche rested and played her piano, made calls and received calls, Guy was busy in the orchards, which were maturing and needed tending, and Bertie was back at his engineering studies. Eccleston, at nearly seventy, had, on the contrary, not slowed down. He had become involved in the argument for the use of myxomatosis as a way of ridding the colony of the plague of rabbits, was devising solutions to the poor transportation around the harbour and was still running the Du Faur and Gerard Pastoral Company, although on his own until 1901. As well he held the post of treasurer, and actively so, of the Art Gallery while, in effect, was still the financier, engineer, contractor and overseer of Ku-ring-gai Chase.

The building of a houseboat, an oil-fired launch that could sleep six and would be useful for exploring the waterways, taxed more of Eccleston's energy and his family. It created more money problems. He wrote to the NSW State government and his bitter complaints about their reliance on him succeeded in extracting a grant of £1,000 for the boat, which became a base for meetings and useful when conducting photographic and scientific forays. It was also used by family and friends, with some trips lasting up to a week out into Pittwater, then into the open sea and round to Manly at the head of Sydney Harbour. The park was Freda's father's fiefdom, the boat a royal yacht. He would stand at the helm dressed in a black frock-coat, white duck trousers, and top hat. His body was wiry and still upright, his beard a continuation of his long pale face and hooded eyes.

The madness continued and the vision widened. Eccleston wanted a golf links, a rifle range, a resort. There were ultimatums to the government: 'I have given up fully one third of my time ... and some amount of money ... to keep things going. I am no longer in a position to do either.'[13] As always his family were dragged in. If there had been any intention of Freda going to Europe or to finishing school, there was not a chance now. Money and Freda were needed elsewhere, at first on clerical work until, under the guise of helping catalogue wildflowers and trees, she ventured out as much as possible into the mainly unexplored ridges and valleys of Ku-ring-gai Chase. She might not have extended the knowledge of the flora in those valleys but she did over 'five years of scrambling' gain 'a very considerable knowledge of rock climbing'.[14] While promising to be out for only a few hours, she continued to perfect the art of escaping and cast off the layer of city plumpness and lethargy. She never kept to the track, that was pointless, and never doubted her ability to get out of any situation as she learned to balance at an angle, keep momentum long enough to scale a face that had little more texture to it than sandpaper and to manoeuvre over the plates of sandstone that jutted out over the valley. Finally, after a successful climb, there was a reward of wonderful views, enhanced by the romantic notion that she was the only human being to have ever been in that exact spot. So she continued to roam for miles while Possie barked at the birds in excitement and 'deserted [her] whenever so inclined, to chase iguanas, possums and native bears'[15] or had to be carried over really difficult terrain.

It was an unusual way for a young woman to spend her time. 'Besides rock climbing, I developed a love of exploring and adventure and self-reliance which caused my parents some alarm. However the expected never happened, I neither broke my neck, sprained my ankle, nor was bitten by a snake.' Freda's parents, by allowing such freedom, were daring in their own way, although they might have been less so if they had seen 'some very pretty problems' she had to face.[16] Eccleston Du Faur could not have suppressed what he had admired most in himself as a young man. And Blanche? Blanche wanted Freda to do more with her life than she had. And neither parent had any better suggestions.

Freda described herself as 'ignorant of both mountains and mountaineering', and as roaming with 'neither the moral or material support of either a rope, or a companion'.[17] In the Chase, Freda expected nothing more out of life than to ramble during the limbo between childhood and womanhood.

5 HEAVENLY BODIES

'The joy of life in steepness overcame,
And victories of ascent and looking down
On all that has looked down on us and joy
In breathing nearer heaven.'

Tennyson

By the end of the century, when Freda was eighteen, the depression had come to an end and there was a sense that a new life, or any change, was entirely possible. Moves had begun during the last two decades to create a federation from the separate colonies of Victoria, New South Wales, South Australia, Western Australia and Tasmania and to cast off some of the old links that meant that Australia was little more than a provider of raw materials and agriculture for Britain. A large number of English-born and even those born in Australia of English parents, referred to England as 'Home' and felt that such a move was unwise and ungrateful, but there were many who felt, as Louisa MacDonald did, less than a decade after arriving in the country that, 'Surely leadership means danger and responsibility, not privileges and wealth and position. The Australian Colonies suffer from the way in which men from the old world come out and use the new as a Tom Fiddlers ground and pick up what they want and go home to spend it.'[1] The Du Faur family were entirely in sympathy. After a referendum in June 1899, the Bill for the Constitution was carried and the four States were joined by Western Australia. Eccleston became a member of the committee to organise celebrations for Federation Day planned for 1 January 1901.

On 15 December 1900, the HMS *Royal Arthur* arrived carrying Australia's first Governor-General, the Earl of Hopetoun, who would eventually select Edmund Barton, leader of the federal movement as Prime Minister of Australia. On New Year's Eve, Sydney lived up to its wild past. Eccleston and Blanche joined the official Federation Ball. On that night, there was a clear view from the upper verandah of Emmeline's house across the layers of narrow roofs, to the city buildings decorated with electric lights, flags and lanterns. Occasionally firecrackers shattered the sky, then faded in a trail of green, red or white. The populace was out celebrating Federation and the creation of a new country.

By 10.30 a.m. 1 January, Proclamation Day, overcast skies and drizzle had been replaced by one of Sydney's humid uncomfortable days as the procession set off from the Art Gallery through the city to Centennial Park. The Du Faurs, as family of the Committee, were provided with comfortable seats from which to view the parade of floats and bands, gleaming fire engines and official carriages all decorated with banners and flags, and, at the end, the high stepping cortege of the new Governor-General, like something from the British Raj with his medals and plumed hat and surrounded by lancers on horses. The officials and their families were then whisked by waiting transport, ahead of the 150,000 that would swarm into the park. At one o'clock, heralded by a volley of gunfire, the Governor-General was sworn in and the Commonwealth of Australia was proclaimed. Ten thousand children sang. It was a day of dancing, celebration and hope. The break was emphasised for

Freda's generation by the death of Queen Victoria a few weeks later and the succession of the younger, urbane King Edward. They were now Edwardians, an age that epitomised Freda, with its less onerous lifestyle and unfussy clothes as they climbed 'out of the dark woods and valleys of conventional tradition and gained the fresh invigorating air and wider view-point of the mountain top'.[2]

It was so easy for Freda to think optimistically, especially when surrounded by such optimism. It was as easy to record such a thought when those mountain tops had been gained. But at the beginning of the century, beneath her cheerful veneer, Freda's world was full of doubt. She did not know what she was going to do. She could not ask advice because she was proud that people seemed to have such high expectations of her, yet she hated drifting. She also feared she could become anti-social, was in fact beginning to suspect it was a defect in all the Du Faur children and that, if she did not do something, she could become almost a hermit like Guy or the loner Bertie was on the verge of becoming. She had been educated too well by women she wished to emulate. She wanted to do something but what? A social conscience was a black hole in a person who did not know how to use it, especially as Sydney was filled with injustices which she felt powerless to rectify. It was clear other women had found interests, or even careers, but Freda could never imagine joining those charitable groups. She loathed the way women of her background dressed in similar clothes and talked too much about the same things, regardless of their intelligence. She felt sure she was special yet could not pinpoint a single special talent and was reluctant to commit to anything, especially a group that might swamp her yet to be discovered excellence.

Diversion was provided by Enid's return to organise her wedding, the later arrival of the Bacchus family and the marriage, on 17 April 1901, of Lance and Enid at St Clement's Church, Mosman. It was a big wedding; the Harnetts were back in the money and in their old stamping ground, and were determined to do it in style. Then, as quickly, Enid was gone only to be back again early in 1902. There was to be no midwife or local farmer's wife for a pregnant Enid. On 11 April her first child, George, was born in a private hospital, The Marcellan, in Mosman; then, as soon as Enid and the baby were able to travel, they sailed for New Zealand. With them went Freda and Blanche.

Travel, Freda hoped, might give her life purpose. She was less inclined to such an opinion after five days of seasickness but her attitude improved on her brief viewing of the capital of New Zealand, Wellington, with its charming timber buildings and homes built higgledy-piggledy down the steep hillsides. There was no time to explore; Enid was never one to sit around doing useless things such as sightseeing and soon had them bundled onto the train that would take them north over the hills surrounding the city, into the yellow tussock land between the foothills of the Tararuas and the west coast town of Otaki. From there the line turned inland to stop a short time later, literally in the centre of Manakau – the railway line neatly divided the town. Two dusty roads bordered either side of the line and along them were single-storey, wooden commercial buildings, all with iron verandahs and behind these were small private houses, a two-roomed public school and a large 29-roomed hotel. Although the Bacchus farm primarily stocked sheep, the town was thriving on the wealth derived from the rich dairy pastures, a number of dairy factories, flax mills and sawmills. The wives of well-off farmers tended cows in the byres in the morning and callers in the drawing room in the afternoon.

The Bacchus homestead at Mount Olympus in South Manakau Road had begun as a few rooms and gradually with time, money and the pressure for privacy, had been extended. The rooms lacked grace, velvet hangings and dim chandeliers struggled to disguise cracked whitewash but the verandahs were pleasant to sit on and

created shelter, as did the thick walls, especially when snow drifted down from the Tararuas in winter.

It was a quiet time when Freda arrived. The stock had been
culled and there was a break before shearing and lambing. Most of
the work by then involved caring for the small dairy herd and clearing and burning the dry scrub after summer. When evening came
the women joined the men and their Maori workers to dampen
down the newly cleared patches when all but the most solid stumps
had turned to ash.

It was easy being in such an environment. There was company
when Freda wanted it but no one questioned her or confronted her
with newspapers filled with women's stories or opinions that
nudged her fragile conscience. The heavy farm work helped. Freda
took over some of Enid's chores which she reluctantly gave up to
look after baby George. Even collecting wood was important as it
was the only source of heat, and the camp oven had to be kept
going day and night. Freda learned to cook the popular local foods
of roast meats and wild pork and 'sea-pie', a mix of meat and vegetables with a lid of suet pastry. Sometimes, she and Enid took the
punt out down the slow, reed-lined river where they could discuss
the trials of Enid's life and how to solve them. Enid felt an outsider,
a townie and didn't like being dominated by her mother-in-law so,
as it seemed to her she was always on the back foot, she had decided to behave as everyone expected: outrageous and self centred.
Occasionally everyone took the day off and drove over the rough
road to Otaki and the ocean. The beach is actually a continuation
of a much longer one, curving from the town of Waikanae in the
south, toward Wanganui in the north. Freda, when she stood on
that sand, used to strain her eyes 'to see Mount Egmont and, on a
clear morning, was sometimes rewarded by the glimpse of a white
pyramid across the sea', that perfect conical volcano, usually with a
cap of snow. It had first been climbed nearly fifty years earlier by a

white woman, Jane Maria Atkinson, but Freda did not know this; for her it was 'too ethereal and far away to wake my ambitions'. [3]

Instead she sat on a rug with the others after a swim and listened to her cousins' stories about pioneering in the area. They admired the activities of the warrior-chief, Te Rauparaha, whose stronghold had been on Kapiti Island, a long khaki coloured strip of the land, visible off the coast.

When times were particularly tense between the Maori and the Pakeha (European), Te Rauparaha had been arrogant and successful enough to dare threaten Wellington. Interest in the chief took Freda to the Rangiatea Maori Church where, after his death, there had been an attempt to bury him, but his body was taken by his people and returned to Kapiti. Freda was fascinated by the church; there was nothing like it in her experience. It was a strange mix of 'heathen' and Christianity – a perfect example of noble savagery with a traditional altar frontal, created in needlework reputedly done by Queen Victoria, yet the building was carved out of a native tree, the totara, and decorated in panels of ochre that depicted *mangopare* (the hammerhead shark) in the rafters and the *purapura whetu* (stars in the heaven). A star in the earthly heaven, that was what Freda desired to be, but wrote back to her old school magazine like any young socialite of her year: 'Freda Du Faur has gone to New Zealand for a trip and is thoroughly enjoying herself.'[4]

She and her mother would return again to New Zealand for the summer of 1902–03 but these stays were more complex than her letter inferred. The trips were opportunities for them to be together as adults and during these times some of their misunderstandings were set aside. Blanche wished she had been stronger but it wasn't in her nature and above all it was too late and Freda came to see her father as a flawed human being, to be admired but not necessarily emulated. She knew his intelligence mingled with his generosity but began to see how good works could disguise selfish passions. The sympathy she began to feel for her mother improved their relationship but did not blind her to the possible traps in her mother's experiences and she was impressed by the urgency of finding something to give form to her life. To work was the only way she knew how.

Freda was ready to commit herself to becoming a useful human being and to do it perfectly. In the SCEGGS magazine of March 1904, Freda was recorded as one of the old girls who was doing something with their lives. Several old girls had gone into nursing, and Freda as a probationer had gone to the Redfern Homeopathic Hospital.

The Woolleys had always been supporters of homeopathy as it was not only popular in England when they were there, but particularly so in Norwich where, even in the 1850s, there had been a number of dispensaries. In Sydney, one of Dr John Woolley's close friends was the homeopathic doctor John Le Gay Brereton. As a poor-law surgeon in the north of England the doctor had observed outbreaks of diphtheria and typhus and the inability of regular medicine to deal with these diseases. He recognised that poor health fostered such epidemics so looked for and found another approach which had hygiene at its base and the natural system of the body as its defence. Once in Sydney he began to foster these ideas.

A homeopathic dispensary had been set up in Sydney in 1858 but it made little impression on a city where quick cure-alls could be obtained at the local shops or from itinerant quacks, and children could buy lozenges containing morphine, chloroform, cannabis indica and prussic acid over the counter. Public health was almost as bad. There was little awareness of aseptic techniques; doctors would not believe that they were the carriers of the blood infections that killed so many of their patients, hospitals were breeding grounds for disease, and sewerage was rare. By 1900 conditions had barely improved in Australia, where approximately one in a thousand died of tuberculosis and there were persistent outbreaks of diphtheria, typhoid and scarlet fever, savage illnesses such as influenza and, in the year of Federation, the dreaded bubonic plague.

With a push coming from Le Gay Brereton, it became clear to the practitioners and their adherents that, if homeopathic practices and good hygiene were to make any kind of impact, a hospital was essential. A board was set up. Supporters were primarily well-known businessmen, academics and social figures but also included a Mrs Du Faur and her friend Mrs Sulman, both of Turramurra. The institution was, according to the first superintendent, Dr Field Deck, intended 'to act as a centre for the propagation of the knowledge of Homoeopathy and will link together all those who sympathise with its views and are anxious for its advance'.[5] It was hoped that it would function all day and every day as a dispensary with outpatients, as well as being a hospital. There was to be a small charge for those who could afford it but, because the Government refused to allot any money to the project on the basis that only a minority demanded the resource, money had to be raised by such groups as the Ladies' Aid Association and the Sydney Comedy Club. Finally by 1903 a large, three-storeyed terrace at 301 Cleveland Street, with a pleasant outlook over Prince Alfred Park and the city, had been rented for £75 per annum. A smart brass plate on the door announced the 'Sydney Homeopathic Hospital'.

A matron, Katie Hopcraft, was employed at £52 a year and free board and lodgings. Hired also were two experienced nurses named Black and Bradley. As well, there were scullery maids, a cook and cleaners. Probationer nurses were expected to work for free and parents were expected to make a donation to cover their costs. In

September, Probationer Edith Sulman was hired after a two pound donation from her mother. In December 1903 the superintendent reported that outpatient numbers for the month numbered 162, with 32 newcomers. Eight were admitted to the wards, ten discharged cured, one died and four were still in treatment and the services of Probationer Du Faur had been engaged. She would begin immediately with a two pound donation from Mrs Du Faur.[6]

Freda had just turned twenty-one. She was put straight to work. The small wards were immaculately clean with gleaming floors and fresh linen that attested to a never-ending slog. Infection rates were kept remarkably low and there was joy in seeing patients get better, although there would always be other patients to replace them, but gradually the long hours and erratic shift-work began to undermine her. After less than two months' training she was expected to be on her own with a seriously ill patient for sixteen hours straight. Much of the time she and Edith Sulman were little more than scullery maids who cleaned up vomit, emptied toilet pans or washed bodies, both live and dead. Support staff left regularly, there was always a shortage of nurses and with patient numbers doubling and no financial security there was no spare cash for niceties. There was no time to read or think or imagine or socialise. In the beginning, if she and Nurse Sulman were not on duty, there had been a chance to compare notes and buoy each other up but pressure soon kept them apart. Freda, with a growing feeling she would fail, began to distance herself from her colleague who seemed to be handling the situation. Edith would in fact survive as a nurse.

There was no Christmas break that year.

In early January 1904 Matron Hopcraft took a three-week holiday, an event that aggravated the stressful working conditions as did the death, soon after the matron's departure, of one of the few experienced nurses, Nurse Bradley. Patient numbers doubled but there seems to have been little money to hire qualified staff.

With the desire for perfection that was to suit a mountaineer but debilitate a nurse, and with all the skill she had perfected as a child at hiding her weaknesses, Freda struggled on. She was obviously regarded highly because on 9 February, she was promoted to full nurse status. Freda was already on a wage of one pound a week while, the previous December, Nurse Bradley had to threaten to leave just to get ten shillings a week. Soon Freda did not have the energy to take a proper break even when there was an opportunity.

The ideals that had brought her to the hospital were now a fermenting ground for crazy thoughts and fears, but she could not accept she was unsuited to the grinding work she had taken on. Her growing feeling of failure was oppressive as was the continuing patient demand with apparently no replacement of staff. Finally, on 17 March, Freda asked 'through ill health to be released from her duties'[7] and, as a failure, went home to Flowton. Her mother continued to donate until July 1905.

Freda remained in her room and shut out the hopeless world beyond the house. Even if she had wanted to talk about her feelings there was no one she felt would understand her. She could not put a greater load on her mother who had troubles with Eccleston, whose role at Ku-ring-gai Chase was coming to an end. Freda's breakdown may have been the final straw as he also resigned in March 1904, although resigning from one interest meant there was more time available for others. It was too late for him to change and become a 'Papa'. Instead he became the scholar his father, his grandfather and his great-grandfather had been before him. He translated Homer from Greek to English and his beloved *Quatraines de Pibrac* from French to English. He began to follow an interest in Antarctica and the development of weather patterns in the region. The National Art Gallery benefited too, although there was growing resentment from some of the younger artists that the gallery was becoming staid and new ideas were not being allowed to filter through.

In October 1904 Freda once again went to visit the Bacchus family. The boat trip, although hateful, served to create a break from bad memories, but it was still a very different Freda from the young woman who had left Manakau the previous year. She might have been uncertain then but had believed there were exciting things ahead; now she couldn't go back to what she felt had been a charming period of her life and had no direction forward. Tenacious in her contemplations, she helped out at the farm but with little interest and even the antics of Enid's latest child, Barbara, born a few months earlier in June could not please her, although she did get enjoyment out of walks with curious George.

Eventually, dragged out by her cousins to go horse riding, her old competitive instincts and her need to do something strongly physical finally began to ease away her sense of hopelessness. A point-to-point race of the kind that she described later as galloping 'in and out of flax-bushes, the horses swerving and dodging all obstacles with the ease that becomes second nature after a few seasons'[8] always worked, even if the men won and side-saddle and a lack of practice held her back. Over the next few months out in the natural world, once again she felt that inner call to use her body, keep moving and ignore the darkness in her mind. She returned to Sydney at the end of summer in 1905 with a somewhat more philosophical approach to her first attempt at a career and the hoped for self-sufficient life.

The following summer saw her again back at Manakau, then she returned home for the winter of 1906, where it was cool enough to enjoy being out in the Chase and continue her 'scrambling'.

But if young artists in Sydney were grumbling about her father, Eccleston's interest in art finally gave Freda the chance to finally discover where to place her frustrated passions. Eccleston was going to the New Zealand International Exhibition of Arts and Industries to be held in Christchurch in the South Island. His intention was to show off the photographs he'd commissioned from Ku-ring-gai and the Blue Mountains, and to view an extensive exhibition of British art. Most of the paintings were on loan from private collections, but Eccleston and other representatives had raised £4,000 with which to buy any works that could balance the present collection at the Art Gallery. He set out early in November 1906 with the intention of departing on 14 December. Freda joined him in early December.

It was her first trip to the South Island. The ship from Sydney brought her into Lyttelton, the harbour for Christchurch, set in what was originally a series of volcanic craters, the sides of which had blown out letting the sea flood in. The port was not unlike a tiny Wellington, with steep hills, and the wharf was crowded with neat wooden houses with tiny crow's nests set into their roofs. It was a busy place as exports were expanding out of Canterbury and there were always squat bales of high class wool and frozen meats ready to be stacked into holds to be exported to Britain.

Christchurch was different again. On the other side of the Port Hills from Lyttelton, it spread over flat land and was exactly how someone from the antipodes might imagine an English town to be: full of Gothic spires, half-timbered houses and large gardens with exotic trees of the kind that Blanche loved in Mount Wilson. Initially a Church of England settlement, many of its wide streets were named after English bishoprics and the squares after famous bishops, but although only founded 56 years earlier, the bustle of a large influx of visitors to the International Exhibition and the use of dark, grey stone gave the city an air of long-settled tranquillity.

The Du Faurs, father and daughter, stayed in a small hotel between the main Cathedral Square and the Avon River, but their time in Christchurch would do little to enhance their relationship as Eccleston was spending, as he put it, 'a large part of the day in the picture gallery [obtaining] as thorough a knowledge of its contents as those in our own'.[9] Fortunately, Christchurch was a safe city for a young, single woman so Freda was pleasantly free to follow her whims. She joined what seemed like half the town on the short walk to the Exhibition Buildings, any doubt about direction dispelled by the noise of side-show jingles, marching bands, the chants of Maori concert parties and sound of the enthusiastic hymns sung by the Salvation Army, formal and overly warm in their woollen suits.

In 1903 Richard Seddon, the Prime Minister of New Zealand, had decided that an International Exhibition should be held 'if full justice is to be done to the settlement and the development of the colony, its resources and manufactures, its commerce, its grand unique and beautiful scenery and its arts and products'.[10] Not without a struggle, he secured a £1,000 for preliminary expenses and eventually fourteen acres was set aside. It was an impressive effort and although predominantly organised to promote New Zealand, there were also exhibitions from all over the Empire. The pure white building, turrets and buntings of the Exhibition were built on the banks of the Avon, a river swept with summer green willows brighter than any in Australia, on which ducks floated and punts drifted by, the occupants as English as Oxford itself, in boaters and striped jackets, The main entrance was marked by a dome, with the Maori welcome of *Haerae Mai* over the top and a tower on each side. At the beginning of December, when Freda was visiting, the focus was on a 'highly spectacular ceremony ... the forgathering of three great tribes of the Pacific—Maori, Cook Islanders and Fiji, who greeted each other with poetic and emotional singing and fear inspiring dances of warriors'.[11] Other exhibitions were of varying standard, among them bronco riding, which she later compared,

75

unfavourably, with the riding skills of a Maori porter on the west coast of the South Island, who put on, 'as fine an exhibition of horsemanship as I have ever seen and put the professional buck jumpers in the Christchurch Exhibition altogether in the shade'.[12]

Beyond the side-shows were the state exhibitions. The entrance to the rather austere New South Wales Court was through an arch held up by three massive columns and flanked by a Corinthian colonnade, more in keeping with the International Exhibition buildings than the life and style of Freda's home state although, once inside, the impression improved. The roof was festooned with an arc created from unprocessed wool, there were displays of wood and a section contained Eccleston's photographs of Ku-ring-gai and the Blue Mountains. Although charming and familiar, they were no match for the dramatic paintings in the West Coast Hall. *The Official Catalogue* described the vision:

> To begin with a general idea of the enormous size and extent of the great Southern Alps and the endless sierra of ice peaks was contained in a long panoramic picture ... showing the whole central stretch of the dividing range, with glaciers gleaming in deep valleys and sublime Aorangi's tented crest rising white and supreme more than 12,000 ft above the artist's viewpoint on the sea front. Then came picture after picture of alpine gloom and alpine glory.[13]

As well, photographs, produced with primitive equipment, went far beyond the usual impressions of mountains as black rock and dead white ice. Freda understood photography, although she had only a couple of months earlier bought her first camera, but she had never seen anything like these mountains nor the techniques used to get such clarity. What she could not anticipate was that her life would soon be entwined with two of the photographers, Dr Ebenezer

Teichelmann and Rev. Newton, men who knew their subject as pioneering climbers and the first to encourage the later famous Graham brothers to begin mountaineering. On Teichelmann and Newton's ascent of Mount Cook in 1905, one of their two guides was Peter Graham; on the ascents of a number of other mountains it was Alex Graham.

As Freda's interest in the mountains grew, the Exhibition began to pall and she knew she had to go there, to the mountains, knew she must touch that rock and fill her 'snow-starved Australian soul',[14] – simply that, nothing more. She spoke to the people manning the show and collected brochures on how to get to the 'Ice Region of New Zealand' where 'The Grandeur of the Scenery of this District has No Parallel outside the Polar Regions.' First class return fares from Christchurch were four pound ten shillings, second class cost four pound two and six, expensive for two hundred miles, but Eccleston paid for the trip and without argument left for Sydney on 14 December, alone.

All the torments of possible careers, a guilty conscience and self-deprecation were left behind as Freda set off for the Southern Alps. The train travelled south down the coastal Canterbury Plains through expanses of open farms, across wide gravelled, meandering rivers, past sheep the colour of the wheat fields that were divided by gorse hedges with windbreaks of slender poplars, essential defence against the infamous nor'wester. This is a similar wind to the fohn in Europe or the chinook in the USA. It drops its rain on the western slopes of the Southern Alps, blasts hot and dry across the eastern plains and creates the weather patterns that make mountaineering so treacherous.

At Timaru, a charming seaside port, there was a half-hour wait before connection with the train inland to Fairlie, where there was an overnight stay and the opportunity to get to know her fellow travellers. Among them was the perennially boyish Heinrich Von

Haast and his wife, Nellie. A self-styled explorer, the lawyer was the son of Sir Julius Von Haast who, in 1862, was the first recorded explorer to get up into the Mount Cook range and describe in detail 'the magnificent pyramid' of Mount Cook (the Maori name is Aoraki or Aorangi.)[15] Heinrich Von Haast faced difficulties that Freda could readily comprehend – a famous father who had significant landmarks, the Haast River, Mount Haast, and later the Haast Pass named after him – although he would never have the ability, as much as he desired, to make a name as Freda would. He would in time, however, take care of her New Zealand affairs.

The next morning the travellers rose to the fresh mountain air, a clear sky and fortunately dry conditions as rain could have made the ninety-mile coach trip along the dirt road, into the vast lonely landscapes of MacKenzie country tussock, impossible. The route on that dry day took them via the small turquoise lake of Tekapo where they stayed another night, and from where a message was sent via pigeon to the Hermitage, the only hotel at Mount Cook, detailing the numbers arriving. Freda, although enjoying the trip, as usual hankered for more; she would have loved to have been there twenty years earlier, when the railway had just been put through to Fairlie, when travel was haphazard and crossing rivers was a daring event. In those days the rapids of the Pukaki River had to be crossed on a ferry consisting of two old whaleboats joined together with plank decking. That would have been real adventure. But such romantic hankerings did not survive the visual splendours of the 'wonderful chalky-blue' of Lake Pukaki which reflected and foreshadowed the mountains, 'that long silvery line of snow-clad peaks breaking the blue of the distant horizon'.[16]

The Southern Alps were everything Freda had hoped for. Even more. She was in love for the first time. It was a first passion that nothing else would ever come close to again. Her reaction was as purple as that of a heroine discovering love and convincing herself that fulfilment could only be obtained through her lover. Oblivious to this she wrote: 'From the moment my eyes rested on the snow-clad alps I worshipped their beauty and was filled with a passionate longing to touch those shining snows, to climb to their heights of silence and solitude and feel myself one with the mighty forces around me.'[17]

There was the Mount Cook Range dominated by the great cloud piercer itself, north was the valley of the Tasman Glacier, one of the largest glaciers in the temperate world, from which flowed the freezing waters of the Tasman River. Beyond and about the glacier were the peaks of Malte Brun, De la Beche, The Minarets and Hochstetter Dome. The road veered round the Ben Ohau Range and turned at Sebastopol to follow the Sealy Range into the Hooker Valley, which had been created by the convergence of the Hooker and the Mueller Glaciers, where the horses, scenting home, picked up their gait. Ahead was Mount Sefton and, beyond the southern flanks of Mount Cook and the Hooker Glacier, the higher mountains of Tasman, Dampier, then the virgin peaks that Freda would one day call Nazomi, Du Faur, Pibrac and Cadogan.

Finally could be seen, at the foot of the lateral moraine of the Mueller Glacier, a long, low thirteen-room building, the Hermitage. So isolated was the area that it had been impossible to transport materials in so the foundations had been created out of blocks of concrete set in kerosene tins, the framework was held together by No.8 fencing wire, the clay for the sun-dried bricks had been excavated from the front yard and the hole left had formed a small lake. There were also separate buildings including a bakehouse, storerooms and a dairy.

Outside the Hermitage the resident manager, Mr McDonald, and his family always waited for the new arrivals. According to Peter Graham, McDonald was a handsome old man with white hair and beard, who met every coach and saw off every visitor. Mrs McDonald,

a pleasant Scottish woman, with an attractive accent, made the butter and special cheeses. The eldest daughter, Miss Molly, did most
of the cooking while the second, Miss Nettie, 'the Madonna', very
good looking and clever, helped the visitors and kept the books.
Duncan, the son, looked after the cows, stores and firewood.

Waiting with them was the chief guide and star of the
Hermitage, Peter Graham. Freda's travelling companions had
already told her about his brilliance as a guide and mountaineer
and she knew that if she was to get the most out of being there he
was the one to befriend. Never afraid of demanding what she wanted, that evening, after he'd greeted his old friends and she'd been
introduced, she took him aside. She was hoping, she explained,
that he would understand her 'craving for nearer acquaintance' with
the mountains.[18] She wanted to know what, as a novice, she could
attempt. He wanted to know what kind of walker she was, then his
answer was simple: go out on an easy climb and just find out.

For Peter Graham a woman approaching him about climbing
was not new. A tall, tanned, dark-haired man with a wide, cheerful
mouth and dark liquid eyes, he was skilled at handling the delicate
role of being both in charge of the climb and yet keeping to his
place as an employee. His job, above all, was to keep his clients safe
and, as a single man, safe from himself as well, no matter how
encouraging a woman might be. Determined to make his own mark
during this first year in command, his way was to encourage people to climb and enjoy the countryside; an excursion was a failure
if a client had no wish to go out the next day.

Freda's first trip out was up the Sealy Range with a party guided by Peter. Although the beautiful sunny day, on 'a long, long snow
slope' soon became 'toiling in a burning sun, never seeming to get
any nearer to the top, such tortures were soon forgotten and nothing could dispel her delight in being out there. She 'joyously played
in it while wiser members looked on'[19] with resultant sunburnt

hands, but it soon became apparent to her that it was not just snow she wanted to touch. As soon as they set off again the heights above were so tantalising that she could not wait for the others so 'struck out for herself' instead of following in Peter Graham's footsteps and climbed on her own. With hints of what was to come she 'stood alone on the crest of the range and felt … for the first time that wonderful thrill of happiness and triumph which repays the mountaineer in one moment for hours of toil and hardship'.[20]

She was hooked and was already likening herself to a mountaineer. It was cheeky but she did not care. Freda was caught in her dreams; in the dreams of her father and those before him and her need to be someone, to conquer her brothers and the limitations of her womanhood. To conquer them all, and her own fears. Freda called it that: to defeat, subdue, to vanquish. That was what she wanted to do, like a knight of old, not a frail, flighty lady. She knew already that she 'could never be content to worship the mountains from a distance' and at the end of the day, she wrote, 'I returned to the hotel, fully convinced that earth held no greater joy than to be a mountaineer.'[21]

Peter Graham had no idea of her plans then. It was a reasonable climb, she had achieved it surprisingly well and he was diverted by the arrival of others from Australia: Leonard Lindon, headmaster of the famous Geelong Grammar School near Melbourne, and his wife, Annie, also a teacher. Lindon had done a number of trips to Fiordland and the Lakes District and the couple had already been to the Southern Alps when Annie had been the first woman to cross the Barron Saddle. Travelling with the Lindons was their great friend, Professor Walter Baldwin Spencer, a famous biologist and explorer, usually to be found wearing a huge overcoat and with a pipe tucked under a droopy white moustache, stained yellow from the habit. He was another of the eccentric older men Freda would befriend.

Peter would remember Freda on the day for the fun she'd had and her endearing enthusiasm rather than for a great commitment. She was, according to him so 'thrilled' with a glissade down the snowslopes that she climbed up to do it again, despite the fact the slope was steep and the first run had left her upside down and filled with snow.[22] That night afraid, not of the heights but of failure again, Freda lay in bed and the question came like a fearful weight: did she have the 'physical strength, courage, endurance and perseverance without which nothing worth doing could be accomplished?'[23] Only she and time could answer that.

The next day a trip up the Tasman Glacier to Malte Brun Hut was planned which involved a long walk up the valley, onto the dirty lateral moraine and then on to the clean, glacier ice to reach the small wooden hut which would become one of Freda's favourite places. She always revelled in the views and isolation and never tired of sleeping in the hut, with its corrugated-iron roof and tiers of wooden-framed bunks and canvas mattresses. The ladies' section had the luxury of a wooden floor and a felt-lined roof. At every opportunity on the trip up Freda plagued Peter Graham with questions. To many visitors sitting out in the sunshine, surveying the magnificent views from the verandahs of the Hermitage, Freda would be viewed as rather too bold, but to Peter Graham, who eagerly sought knowledge and style, women as outgoing and able as Freda were always a welcome release. 'In those early years at the Hermitage', he wrote in his autobiography, 'it was rather rare to meet a woman travelling without a companion of any kind and if one did so she was invariably looked upon by other guests as eccentric – perhaps more so than was the case. I usually found after taking such women on excursions that they had travelled extensively and could give such descriptions of their travels that to act as a guide to them was a privilege.'[24] Being with Freda was that privilege.

Peter came from a family of five boys, dominated by a much loved and respected mother, and had an exalted vision of the female so he was eager to admire and assist when a rare woman arrived who focused more on climbing than on leisurely scenic trips. He was grateful for his position but his life as a guide could be frustrating and very different from that experienced by his counterparts in Europe, who could purely guide and climb. In New Zealand, in those early years, guides were often little more than hired help, required to repair buildings damaged by winter snows, build tracks and erect new huts with timber and iron they had to backpack into the mountains.[25]

Freda's arrival, as that of other solitary women, provided Peter Graham with the opportunity to make decisions about the way they climbed, something he could not usually do with men of any experience. Patient and skilled, he enjoyed the role of mentor and the control implicit in that. He also knew it was only a matter of time before women arriving at the Hermitage would make big climbs. He wanted the kudos of those successes.

But Freda would be prevented from following up any plans. When they arrived back at the Hermitage, weary and ready for a hot bath and food, a grave-faced Mr McDonald handed over a telegram.

Telegrams meant one of two things. Congratulations or bad news. No one was yet ready to congratulate Freda. The telegram informed her that her mother was very ill. She must return to Sydney immediately. It said too much and yet too little. The trip to the Hermitage, the climbing, the elation combined with the shock, caught up with her. Immediately the protective women tourists, who one day would try to protect Freda from her own spirit, enveloped her. Peter Graham also had great sympathy, not only because of her potential but her plight was a fear he and his brothers always lived with, that something would happen to their mother, who was a three-day trip away on the west coast. Having to go to Australia during such a crisis would be unimaginable. When Freda left the next day, he was up, with the ubiquitous cup of tea ready, along with the McDonalds and Professor Spencer, to see her off.

6 Non Omni Moriar

> 'I shall not wholly die! of me
> The greater part shall 'scape Oblivion's wrong;
> In future praise, I'll ever be
> Renewed ... '
>
> a translation of an Horation ode by Eccleston Du Faur

Freda would not find out what had happened to her mother for over a week. Previously, after five days at sea, there had always been welcoming sights when arriving home: the sandstone cliffs; the way the sun caught the slight harbour waves; Manly and Mosman, the Nest and the 'Mirror Castle'; little yachts with loose white sails in a weak breeze and the old SCEGGS buildings; but this time there was no delight. It was time to put on mourning

Blanche had died on 3 December at the age of sixty-two. What she died of was not accidental or so irregular that an inquest was necessary. Her death may have been caused by a heart attack or stroke as neither Freda nor Eccleston would have gone for an extended trip if she'd had a long-term or terminal illness. For Freda, Blanche's death was made more difficult by the introverted nature of Bertie and Guy and especially her father's reaction. He had placed a notice in the *Herald* on 1 January, 1907. It was remarkable for its austerity and omission of his children's names. It defined Blanche in terms of the men in charge of her life.

> Du Faur, at Flowton, Turramurra.
> Blanche – wife of Eccleston Du Faur.
> Second daughter of John Woolley.

The funeral was held on the following Tuesday, before Freda returned. Unlike most death notices of the time, there was no mention of 'beloved wife' or 'dearly loved mother', nor was there a 'kindly invitation for friends to attend'. Blanche was the sociable one. But Eccleston's restraint was not through lack of feeling. He could hardly deal with the loss. Blanche was buried in the Gordon Cemetery at the historic St John's Anglican Church on the Pacific Highway, Sydney. Over the grave was placed a large concrete cross and under that her name, then the words Eccleston had chiselled on her headstone: *Non Omni Moriar* from the last line of the third book of the *Odes of Horace*. It meant that nothing would entirely die – that there is always hope.

The death of a mother, leaving an elderly father and unmarried brother, usually meant one thing for an unmarried woman but Eccleston did not expect Freda to stay and look after him. He knew she was not another Blanche, nor did he want her to be. Nevertheless, there would be at least a year of mourning ahead and the 1907 climbing season would have to be forgone.

Always the practical man, life went on for Eccleston. He was back to work within a few weeks of the funeral. A letter, in response to criticism of the expensive trip made to Christchurch, was sent to the *Herald*, with an apology for not responding sooner, 'but circumstances since my return have prevented me addressing you earlier'.[1]

In February 1907, *Horace: The Odes* was published. Bound in soft, burgundy leather with gilt-edged pages, each copy included a pen sketch of the author and a list of subscribers, literally an 'who's who' in Australia, including the Governor-General and Prime Minister of the day. With such a list who needed close friends? Freda did, but just as she began to get closer to her aunt, Emmeline's time was taken up with her brother, Captain Severin Woolley, who had been hospitalised in a coma from a stroke; it was feared he would not survive. Ruth Gerard had moved out of Sydney with her parents, the Edwards girls left home and Edith Sulman was still nursing.

Freda made one new friend, a woman about her own age, Muriel Kirkpatrick, who lived at Lynister, opposite Flowton. Muriel was looking after her niece, Marjorie, who was recuperating from an illness. She was a keen skater, so the two women began taking her on day trips into the Glacerium in the city. They would drive to Turramurra Station, leave the horse and buggy at the livery stables there, then catch the train into Milson's Point and the ferry across the harbour. Skating in the Glacerium was the nearest thing to a vast, cool world Freda could get to in Sydney.

Letters arrived and were received with both joy and torment. Some were from Peter Graham who, over winter, was working at the head office of the Tourist Authority in Wellington. The letters, in theory, were to arrange the best times for Freda to climb in New Zealand but in reality moved an acquaintance to a close friendship. Peter wrote openly about his nostalgia for the Southern Alps although he could still see value in being in the capital. One of his greatest supporters was the Superintendent of the Department of Tourist and Health Resorts, Mr Thomas E. Donne, who had discovered the young man on a trip to the west coast. Despite his lack of education, and the labouring jobs he was working in, at 25 Peter was a perceptive man and had intelligent ideas about mountaineering and the bush. The minister recommended him to Jack Clarke, then head guide at the Hermitage, who took him on as a guide. In

1903 Peter made the first of many trips through the Copland Pass into the eastern side of the Southern Alps; moraine and tussock were something he had to learn to love but he was immediately impressed with his new boss. Although their backgrounds were similar, Clarke had spent time climbing overseas and gave the appearance of a well-educated man with his ' fine rather cultured voice'.[2] It was a style Peter wanted to emulate and Wellington was the perfect place to learn it. There he was invited to the homes of some of the people he had guided, particularly the Von Haasts and the widow of the former prime minister and west coaster, Richard Seddon. They introduced the country boy to everything from opera to the popular songs of the time. He described his introduction to music as passionately as he would the Mount Cook region: it was 'magnificent, stirring, beautiful' and he enthused that it was 'not easy to come down to earth' after such an experience.[3]

When Peter returned to Mount Cook at the beginning of the 1907 season he continued to communicate with Freda. He was particularly taken with the new arrivals, Mr Murray, the biologist, and Mr Mackay, the medical officer, from the Shackleton Nimrod Antarctic expedition.[4] He also mentioned the arrival of another keen mountaineer-explorer, Jim Dennistoun, a young farmer and one of the few from the Canterbury area interested in climbing. His sister Barbara and her friend Ada Julius would later take up the sport.

That season Annie Lindon did not seem to be as active as her husband, although she was prone to a knee problem and it may have limited her activities. Leonard Lindon, Professor Spencer and Peter Graham went over to the west coast, via the Tasman Glacier and the Graham Saddle, named after George Graham, one of the three men to first climb Mount Cook. They struck a storm and were confined to Malte Brun Hut for two days. When it cleared, a sharp frost had coated the glacier in slippery ice, requiring steps to be cut, then it became too hot, tiring the climbers. Professor Spencer had, according to Peter Graham, 'a most telltale moustache – it normally stood out firmly on each side of his upper lip, but when he was tired the two ends hung down limply, a sure sign a rest was needed'.[5] They returned via the Copland Pass where Annie Lindon met them.

Freda's year continued to revolve around family, thoughts of climbing and such letters. Bertie and Wynifred married in Mount Morgan, Wynifred's home town. It required a two-day train trip as far as Rockhampton, Queensland before changing to the small, efficient branch line built primarily to service the mine. Mount Morgan epitomised the worst demands of civilisation over Nature's perfection. There was nothing untouched by the mine's activities: the nearby Dee River was muddied by the vast diggings and tailings left after the gold and copper ore had been extracted; dust, waste and heat were unavoidable but had not encouraged anyone to plant shady trees or take pride in the appearance of the wide-verandahed buildings with their corrugated roofs scoured to the colour of the soil. Life revolved around the pubs and store, the local hall and the school. But there Bertie was making his own life; his job as an engineer had given him responsibility and he was respected for his hard work and leadership abilities to the extent that his fellow workers composed a poem about him. The theme concerned a miner caught in machinery and no one knew how to save him.

> But another then came to the rescue,
> And released him – 'twas Mr Du Faur.
> And when freed fro' his awkward position
> His coat dropped in rags on the floor.[6]

But black crepe had hardly been cast off before it was time to put it back on again. It was Emmeline this time. She had never picked up after Blanche's death and now had cancer. At 65, she had only just retired from the St Cecilia's Choir, was still on the board of Women's College and on the committee to set up a Sydney Orchestral Society, but it was soon clear that she would not have the years that Ethel had to battle with the disease. Freda helped to look after her, a duty that was as much Freda's need as Emmeline's, who was financially well off and had many friends to assist her. For Freda her aunt was the last of the Woolley women in Australia, the line that had come out with such optimism from England. It was the end of the pure 'angels in sisterhood', of the unrealistic hopes, of the romantic dreams of 'Papa' when at 5.30 on the morning of 18 March 1908, Emmeline Woolley died in her Darlinghurst home and she too was buried in the Waverley Cemetery. Obituaries and photos of her appeared in all the papers.

When Emmeline's will, made on 10 January of that year, was eventually read, at first there was amazement at how much the dead woman owned, then at how she'd bequeathed it. Freda had been left £2,000, (in a period when two guineas per week was regarded as a living wage and Members of Parliament earned six hundred per annum), Guy received £1,000 and Bertie £750. A note was made in an attempt to assuage Bertie on the grounds that he had already received £250 for his education and therefore could not expect as much as his siblings. Claude, Ivor and Agatha, the children of Emmeline's deceased sister, Charlotte Courteney, and the three Bacchus brothers received a £1,000 each. Smaller amounts went to Constance and Severin. The surprise was Emmeline's personal estate: two houses in Burwood known as the 'Russell Street investment' and four cottages in Rowntree Street, Balmain known as the 'Buckle investment' which were to be divided equally among Guy, Bertie and Freda. As well, Emmeline's considerable residual savings were to be divided equally between Guy and Freda, another sore point with Bertie. It is highly probable that Emmeline felt that he, as a mining engineer, had financial prospects whereas Guy's and Freda's were limited. Emmeline wanted Freda to have the financial freedom she had thrived on. Bertie was not impressed but that was not Freda's concern; she was independently wealthy and could now look over the Tasman to that long line of white peaks.

The Lindons and Professor Spencer, this time with his favoured daughter, Alline, whom he nicknamed Chappie, were intending returning to the Hermitage in the 1908–09 season. At first there was some doubt Freda could join them as she did not like to leave her father, but he was encouraging and was already immersed in another project described in a letter to his sister Frederica in London. He wrote that he was so invloved 'in calculations and writing for the press on the burning questions of our communications with Sydney by Bridge or Tunnel across the harbour on which our future so much depends, that I cannot turn my thoughts just now to Genealogy and Heraldry'.[7] As well, like many who worry about their own health, he was overly concerned about the health of his daughter and did want her to get back to her broken holiday of over eighteen months earlier. There was still some uncertainty over Severin Woolley but by the beginning of September he was, according to the same letter, 'still in much the same state but a little more conscious and endeavours to articulate' and at least was reasonably stable.

Freda decided to go to New Zealand. Her plans gave her, what she thought, plenty of time before Christmas to investigate climbing so she promised to join her adored Professor Spencer and Chappie on a trip from Mount Cook through to Milford Sound. Chappie, who was 17, her older sister, Dorothy, and their mother, Lillie, had just returned from two years away in Europe and the Professor was concerned that his beloved daughter would be bored with just him for company. As well, he thought Freda an interesting woman and felt she would counteract, what he regarded as, the shallow interests of his wife.

The Professor had been in an unhappy marriage for many years. His wife Lillie loved the social life in Melbourne while the Professor loved his work, art, bushwalking, dynamic men and interesting women. During their marriage he was often away on anthropological field trips to the Aboriginal tribes, primarily the Arunta in Central Australia, and in 1912 he would be made Chief Protector of Aborigines. His enthusiasm, intelligence and skill was marred by his paternalistic approach, but it was a role he loved, and advised his own daughters, 'Above all, if I were a child, I would like to have my parents as my friends and to be guided without knowing it to a love of nature and things beautiful.'[8] He loathed it when his wife took his girls off on one of their long, frequent trips back to England. He was desperately lonely when they spent months in France for further education. To him it was all so pointless; they had made their life in Australia, they were Australians – which was exactly what Lillie was afraid of.

Then, just as Freda's plans were finalised, her Aunt Connie Bacchus decided to visit. Freda had to put back her trip and, unwilling to let the Spencers down by cancelling going to Milford, was left with only two weeks' climbing. The truncated stay at the Hermitage was a disappointment, but it would at least give her time to discover whether mountaineering was more than just a passion that had sustained her through great sadness and long days. After the first breath of mountain air, all doubt was gone.

After one day's rest they went up to Ball Hut and the day after that to Malte Brun. Freda took things cautiously in the beginning but found she could not only keep up, but was the most enthusiastic and, once again, the fittest, according to both her and Peter Graham. She was well aware the guide was impressed and enjoyed the fact that he responded to her – he in turn didn't at all mind her admiration – so the entire period was one of great delight. She said she was, 'fortunate in always going out with the chief guide and [on climbs] which usually included no other woman'.[9] However, a more appropriate description of her outings with Peter Graham may well have been 'well planned'. Freda may not have wanted a man all of her own but as a climber she wanted Peter Graham and had no intention of sharing her chosen one with any other.

Despite what probably amounted to hero worship of the chief guide, formalities were consistently observed. Freda was always referred to as 'Miss Du Faur' and she called Peter Graham, 'Graham'. Even in her book, *The Conquest of Mount Cook*, Freda rarely called him Peter, although she called Alex Graham (referred to as Alec by his family although not by Peter in his biography) by his christian name perhaps because they met initially as friends and their client-employee relationship was never inhibited by government rules. But there were general standards of etiquette all had to follow: any successful climb was regarded as the client's, not the guides', although the latter usually led, had the heavy work in the days when crampons were a novelty rather than a regular tool, and cutting steps in the ice was the norm. The guides ensured routes were suitable and carried swags containing enough to furnish suitable living conditions for a client.

Despite these restrictions, Freda and Peter soon had an understanding. As well as being fit and self-reliant, she was outspoken, so despite their different status he knew what she was thinking, up to a point, and was quick to return the banter they both enjoyed. She was careful about how she dealt with 'her' guide, went after what she wanted but never confronted him while others were around. Eventually, finding she was being held back by weaker climbers, she asked him to look out for another strong climber to make up the customary third but the only suggestion he had was Hugh

Chambers, a farmer from Hastings in Hawkes Bay on the east coast of the North Island, but he would not arrive in time. There was no one else as the Hermitage was not yet a Mecca for mountaineers of all levels.

Considering Freda's lack of experience, it was a great compliment as Chambers, although young, was regarded by Peter as one of the country's best, apart from guides, who did not count.

While others in the group rested, Peter took Freda off to practise. After climbing in the Chase, she handled all the rock work he put her up to, but she did not explain her competence, preferring Peter to think it was all natural ability. By the end of the first week, with this kind of attention, she was able enough to climb with him up to a point below the third peak of Mount Cook, probably Ball's Pass. It was the highest level she had ascended to. She vowed then to be a real mountaineer and become the first woman to climb Mount Cook, writing later: 'When I made this decision I was half afraid of it. I knew the history of every expedition hitherto undertaken, knew how trained men and guides had been beaten back time and again and how fierce was the struggle for those few who had succeeded.'[10] It was presumptuous but she thought of nothing else until, all too soon, she was off again, as she had promised, with the Spencers, to Milford.

Despite the frustration, leaving then may have been timely. Freda needed to digest her commitment. Staying, attempting climbs prematurely and failing, or being put off by an accident could have destroyed everything. As she was leaving she warned Peter Graham that she was coming back to do high climbing, if he considered she was fit for it and would undertake to train her in ice and snow work. He eagerly agreed. A pact was made. Freda knew her goal, Peter Graham appeared not to, but he was astute and had his own ambitions. Training a woman to climb Mount Cook was among them.

7 A PLACE

*'A man hates a mannish woman but, when a slight girl equals him at
his favourite sport and yet retains her womanness, he readily admits
her claim to a place on the rope and admires her greatly in consequence.'*

Lady Chorley
A LADIES' WEEK AT WASDALE

Freda went home finally optimistic that she had a chance of conquering Mount Cook, although well aware that an experienced
woman mountaineer from the Northern Hemisphere could trump
her. From Australia she clung to the hope that any who did come
out would be like the dilettantes or naive women Peter had to deal
with and had told her about. One, a member of the English Ladies'
Alpine Club, had styled herself as one of 'the greatest women
climbers in the world' and made a triumphant progress on foot
from Fairlie to the Hermitage, dressed for the part in climbing costume and carrying a rucksack and ice axe. Within a few days the
guide longed for a woman who would admit she knew nothing, as
his client persisted in coming up with climbs, none of which she
would attempt once faced with the reality. Perfect climbing days
were wasted. Bad weather finally saved him and she departed south

on another walking tour. Another, Lady B, claimed to be an experienced European climber but, when he suggested her clothing might not be appropriate, she was scornful and ended up falling on the moraine then glissaded down 'with her legs pointing skywards'.[1]

But not all the women who pretended to be better than they were did so out of pride; one the guide took a great liking to was determined to go everywhere despite fatigue and obvious fragility, and only later did he discover that she was 67 years old.

Despite these anecdotes, women in the Old World were well ahead of those in the colonies. In Britain and Europe there were far greater numbers ready to break the rules, a wider variety of acceptable lifestyles and attitudes, and more money to finance climbing. The first woman reported climbing in Europe was as early as 1808, although the 18-year-old, stall holder, Marie Paradis, was reportedly 'hauled' up Mont Blanc by the local men. (Freda would be accused of being a token climber and being hauled up herself.) Marie hated climbing, was cold, unfit, and never climbed again, verifying the common opinion that women were not physically suited to such exertions. But she did prove mountaineering for women was possible and survivable and her ascent, however it was achieved, set a precedent decades earlier in Europe than in New Zealand, and mountaineering gradually began to take off.

In 1822 a Mrs and Miss Campbell crossed the Col De Geant, a difficult pass in the Mont Blanc Range. In 1838 Henriette d'Angeville encountered the kind of opposition Freda would, when weeping friends implored her not to climb Mont Blanc. D'Angeville found the going exceedingly difficult and suffered, what is believed to be, altitude sickness: 'palpitations of the heart' and 'lethargic drowsiness'. She told her guides to 'drag her body to the top if she died before she got there' but the successful ascent revived her; she was heartily kissed by her guides and recovered enough to continue climbing until she was 61 when she quippd that she 'dropped the Alpenstock before the alpenstock dropped me'.[2]

In 1871, after thirteen years of mountaineering, an English-woman, Lucy Walker, climbed the Matterhorn and newspaper columns and poems turned her into 'the Heroine of her Generation'. She would make 98 expeditions with either her father or brother as chaperones and always with the guide Melchior Anderegg. When asked, much later, why she never married she replied, 'I love mountains and Melchior and Melchior already has a wife.'[3]

Even when Freda arrived at Mount Cook as a fledgling feminist and with so little knowledge of mountaineering that all she wanted to do was play in the snow, women had already ventured out of Europe. Fanny Bullock Workman, in 1903, with her husband and three guides, climbed the Pyramid Peak in the Karakoram, and in 1906 the Pinnacle (22,000 feet) in Kashmir. A great supporter of women's rights, in the Himalayas, Fanny brandished a banner bearing the device 'Votes for Women'. Few women mountaineers would have disagreed with her as they boldly climbed, in increasing numbers, to a relatively great age – Annie Peck, climbed Huascaran in Peru when she was nearly 60 – and by the turn of the century, no great scandals had ensued from their activities, they had not broken down, nor had the men from their presence, although great care was taken not to offend against the 'codes of etiquette of the time or [to] take undue risks on the mountains that would bring women climbers into disrepute'.[4]

In New Zealand the small number of early women adventurers who went into the mountains tended to be there because of their husbands and are usually mentioned in relation to their men's achievements. The first woman into the environs of Mount Cook, Joanna Harper, mother of the later famous mountaineer A. P. Harper, camped with her surveyor husband, Leonard, near the present day Hermitage in 1873 and travelled to the face of the

Tasman Glacier and onto the ice of the Mueller Glacier. She was followed by others interested in visiting the glaciers, but they came as tourists rather than climbers, and the first real woman climber did not arrive until 1883 when Anna Von Lendenfeld, whose name is marked by the Anna Glacier on the eastern slope of Mount Elie de Beaumont, arrived with her husband. His name is marked by Lendenfeld Peak. Both in their early twenties, they ascended the Hochstetter Dome where, while he sketched in fading light, she provided food and assistance. They became lost on descent, scrambled through crevasses and over ice all night and eventually reached bivouac after 27 hours out. There was no hint that she was unable to cope.

Similarly, the game and intelligent Forrestina Ross, after whom the Forrest Ross Glacier is named. It helped that she had money and her husband was Malcolm Ross, a well-known mountaineer, but she made a number of expeditions, including the partial climb of Mount Earnslaw and was climbing again within eighteen months of the birth of her son. So involved was she in mountaineering that she wrote articles on the subject and briefly edited *The NZ Alpine Journal*.

In 1903 the first group of women, which included Jane Thomson, who would later go on to traverse Mount Cook, crossed the Copland Pass causing 'quite a sensation' particularly to Peter Graham as they passed him and Alex working in the bush. One of the women, Miss Constance Barnicoat, an experienced English climber, was actually wearing a man's suit apparently supplied by the chief guide, Jack Clarke.

Freda may have been somewhat envious to discover when back in Australia that, while she'd been playing at Milford with the Spencers, Annie Lindon climbed the Nun's Veil with her husband and Peter Graham, and then became the first woman to cross the Graham Saddle (9,000 feet). She described the trip across the saddle with a similar passion to Freda, as 'the most wonderful day and night I have ever spent for no one could hope to describe the magnitude of that scene of snow and ice'. The sound of cutting steps was music to her ears. Despite a long haul through melting snowfields and after eighteen and a half hours of constant work, a hot bath and clean clothes was enough to leave her 'quite refreshed'.[5]

In later years Annie and Freda would be described together in the newspapers of the day in a manner that would have pleased them both: 'They put up athletic records by the size of which the policemen-kicking feats of the London Suffragettes are very small potatoes.'[6] London Suffragettes actually were smashing the windows of shops like Liberty's at the time and went on to fire houses before the vote was given. Annie Lindon was impressive and Freda envied the freedom the support of her amiable and admiring husband gaver her, but when Peter had a choice of pupil, Freda's youth would give her an advantage over the older woman along with the skills she had developed in the Chase, her extraordinary inherent fitness and his claim of Freda as his own. Peter could work directly with her and Freda pushed him to teach her with a determination he had never encountered in any other client. He wrote urging her to come over early in the season before the Christmas rush of tourists made serious demands upon his time. Freda had been out in the Chase, practising what rock climbing she could and trying to reinforce the brief lessons she had, especially what she had learned on snow. She increased the amount of practice she was doing in the hope that that would be enough.

As ready as possible, after only climbing on sandstone cliffs, on 6 December 1909 Freda departed Sydney on the SS *Marama*. After disembarking at Lyttelton, she stopped in Christchurch to buy top class equipment including hobnail boots of English leather, a rope of manila hemp, a new haversack and thermos, a warm sleeping bag, a Swiss ice axe, and knee-length puttees. All real equipment for a climber, not toys for a tourist. The shadows of the deaths in her family and the demands were gone. The train trip south denoted freedom, power and adventure. She was alone, fit and, in a way she had never anticipated, financially free, fully adult and confident. She rapturously 'perched on the box seat' of the car, which now meant a ten-hour trip in one day from Fairlie to the Hermitage, as they left behind 'all the worries of everyday life', refreshed them- selves at a 'crystal stream flowing over gray water-worn pebbles … dashed over a narrow bridge … then away across the long stretch- es of brown tussock grass which undulate for mile after mile'. Every turn, every view was a marvel, as was the garden at the Tekapo Hotel where they had lunch, 'gay with poppies and cornflowers, the beds edged with a brilliant border of tulips and sweet with the scent of two great bushes of lilac', and Lake Pukaki where the waters 'rip- pled silver under the sun's rays'.[7] Freda was never afraid of the hyperbole, especially where nature was concerned.

They arrived at the Hermitage about 5.30 p.m. although, dis- appointingly, Peter Graham was away with a party up the Tasman Glacier. When he returned the following evening, Freda, anxious about her intentions and whether she had lost any of her skills, was ready to talk about plans. He suggested an introductory course to 'put her in touch with the mountains again'[8] so their first day out was a minor excursion, a traverse across Mount Kinsey and Mount Wakefield. With them came a young engineer, Mr Hopkins, so the talk was mainly between the men, of the changes that had been made at the park over the winter months, what huts had to be cleared of snow and reprovisioned, and how long it would take for the Hooker Hut to be finished. Freda had little interest in Mr Hopkins but might have been keener for him to stay on and be the 'congenial climbing companion' Peter believed he could be for her,

if she had anticipated what lay ahead. What she had, in the innocu-
ous Mr Hopkins, was a chaperon.

After his departure, Peter and Freda planned a climb of Mount
Sealy. Too far from the hotel to attempt a direct ascent, they decided to set off late afternoon then bivouac overnight. It would be real
mountaineering. When Freda cheerfully announced this intention,
she was suddenly up against what she called 'all the cherished conventions of the middle aged' – mainly women fearing she would
lose her good reputation. She complained angrily that 'there was
not the ghost of a climber on the premises, only women who found
a two-mile walk quite sufficient for their powers'.[9] She pointed out
that she had come to the mountains to climb, not to sit on the
verandah and admire the view, a rather scathing comment that
antagonised her opponents. She may well have been egged on by
her ratbag Professor, who described them as 'school ma-ams some
of them very weird. Heaven only knows why they come up here.'[10]

Freda's appeals and assurances were of little use, for it was just
not done for a single girl to stay out overnight with a man and she
was implored by one little old lady, with tears in her eyes, not to
spoil her life for so small a thing as climbing a mountain'.[11] Freda
always considered Peter a highly moral man. There were rumours
of affairs but there had never been real proof of this and such talk
may have originated from the guide's ease with women. His reputation, according to Freda, years after they first met, was 'one at
which the most rigid moralist could not cavil'.[12] Sexual liaisons
would have been difficult anyway. More often than not there were
large numbers in the few huts, with separate quarters for women,
and most were exhausted anyway after hard climbing or tramping.
As well a bivouac, in a tiny tent in the snow, was hardly conducive
to passion. Most women travelled with husbands, brothers and
chaperons. Freda was rigidly watched over by Professor Spencer,
who was always prepared to give his opinion on what was good for

her. Flirting was one thing but most women were not generally open to casual sex. 'Lady Chatterleys', willing to commence a liaison with a definitely lower class employee, were rare, and there was only one reported case, but any guide with a reputation for seducing clientele would have, at that time, been useless as most female clients would have been nervous about being alone with him and husbands and fathers would not have put up with it. Peter Graham knew all these arguments. He loved his job, he liked the respect he gained from his position; womanising was not something he would have engaged in lightly.

Freda thought she had left such moralists in the drawing rooms of Sydney and remembered her response perfectly: 'If my reputation was such a fragile and useless thing then I'm better off without it': but she was sufficiently the daughter of Victorian parents to hesitate. She knew she was doing no wrong but was used to the conventions the other women were trying to defend and was not yet assured enough in her new role to break them. She joked bitingly that she wished she was the possessor of the 'useful appendage to a woman climber, a husband'.[13] She appealed to Peter for advice. He, as usual, suggested the compromise of hiring a porter at a pound a day, an easy solution for a guide who believed any woman travelling had money to spare. It did not please Freda. Indignant at the injustice, she was furious at herself for not ignoring the women, furious at Peter Graham for not making her ignore them, then furious that she had to pay an extra pound a day. A man wouldn't have had to. But she realised she was up against limits imposed upon her by the mere fact that she was unfortunate enough to be born a woman. She now fully understood what that league of women, the Rose Scotts, the Louisa MacDonalds and her own Aunt Emmeline had been railing against in Sydney, and what women were up against if they wanted to change their lot in life. She fumed and sighed, then gave in because there were no women like them to support her. So, hiding her outrage behind that practised calm, she dealt with the situation graciously. As Peter Graham said, she 'had a rare sense of humour and later saw the funny side of it', and threatened to send the extra bill to her 'tormentors'.[15]

It was agreed. On 18 December, Peter set out with 'chaperon porter' Tom, while Freda, familiar with the route they were taking up the Sealy Range, remained behind for the weekly arrival of Australian letters. An hour later she followed and caught up with the men who were carrying heavy swags and together they climbed the next five hundred feet or so where they bivouacked for the night.

Sleep was hard to come by as she was excited and drizzling rain meant she had to be aware enough to ensure her belongings did not touch the canvas and get wet; cold weather was bad enough, wet clothes as well could be lethal. Eventually she fell asleep, to waken at 2.30 a.m. to the billy boiling. They sat out in the cold, eating breakfast, amongst the tiny mounds of tents and haversacks, observing the mountains around them. Freda wrote later in her diary:

> their summits stood out clear against the deep blue sky in which innumerable bright stars twinkled and flashed. As I watched, the stars faded one by one and the first streaks of dawn lighted the eastern skies. Brighter and brighter grew the colours, and soon a patch of rose lit up the dead-white snows of Mount Sefton: onward and upward it crept until the whole summit flushed to glowing crimson. One after another the light caught the surrounding peaks edging their cold snows with glittering gold.[16]

Visual splendour was something she, and Peter Graham, for that matter, never tired of.

With the 'gold' now glimmering on their chilled skin, they set off across the vast snowfield of the Annette Plateau (named after Annie Lindon) before the sun softened the snow and the way became a slog. Freda, despite good spirits, had not entirely forgiven Tom the chaperon. Once she had an impression of someone it was rare for her to change her mind. According to her, Tom was 'depressingly slow and stolid' although he had been carrying the heaviest rucksack the previous day, likely to have been over fifty pounds. As they began to climb poor Tom became 'a novice on rock and consequently rather unhappy. He was short in the limbs (and breath) and had visibly not been intended by nature for a mountaineer.'[17] It is unlikely he was completely incompetent but he had been hired only as a porter, and as a chaperon he certainly had his uses. But he was a convenient scapegoat for Freda's own inability to deal with the 'petticoat brigade'; in fact, he was as much a victim of convention as she was.

Roped, they set out up a steep and frozen face above a 3,000 foot drop to the Mueller Glacier below. Peter, as he cut steps, kept an eye on her as this was her first experience of this type of climbing, but she said she covered any anxiety 'with my cheerful grin', and once on the steep rock face beyond, her only problem was her inexperience with the rope, which seemed to be 'considerably in the way'. But soon, when Peter Graham turned to check on her he usually found her proudly at his heels. 'Did not know I was taking out a blessed cat',[18] was her mentor's comment.

Although she later felt that this, her first real climb, was not as difficult as she had expected, she was delighted by Peter's praise for her work and their subsequent decision about her future. On the summit, while Tom napped, they sat on the rocks in the sun and Freda brought up the 'plan that was hatched long ago', that of climbing Mount Cook. The guide liked Freda's cautious approach combined with her eagerness and potential, and promised to help her but made it clear she had certain obligations to fulfil, in particular that she continue to do well and train patiently. She might be able to complete the climb right then, but to do so meant she would not enjoy it as much and there would be far more danger. He had a theory he wished to put into practice, and Freda could give him this opportunity, that to give minimum risk and maximum pleasure, climbs should be gradually increased in difficulty, a process that should increase mental and physical fitness. In that way the climber was always ready for whatever difficulties might appear. He explained to her that she 'would stand to lose the best of a wonderful experience because [she'd] have tried to grasp it before being ready to appreciate it in all its fullness' and would gain nothing, except the 'mere notoriety of being the first woman to climb it'.[19]

Freda called it 'wise training', well aware that in mountaineering the greater the challenge and the harder the climb, the greater the risk. In 1909 crampons were not in common use, there were few tools, only one type of rope and woollen clothing; but even with improvements in equipment and styles of climbing, and with greater ease of travel to the mountains, events still occur outside the control of logical decision making. Disasters can occur in a myriad of ways when human beings climb into high mountains where the oxygen is thin enough and the cold severe enough to damage the brain and destroy the body. Sometimes, in the case of avalanches or storms, it can be a matter of sheer bad luck, of being in the wrong place at the wrong time. But, with all the cautions and plans made, they packed and began to descend. Freda then had a lesson on why a rope was a useful encumbrance when Tom, still nervous even without Freda's impatience, fell and began to slide. She immediately jammed her axe in a crack, twisted the rope round it, and brought the porter to a standstill, much to the surprise of both herself and Peter Graham. It was an unconscious movement; the instinct of a climber.

The following afternoon, 20 December, with the weather still holding, they were off again, this time accompanied by a real climber, the guide Jim Murphy. The intention was to ascend the Nun's Veil, so called for the crisp sweep of glacier that descends from the summit. After a long haul on horseback and a difficult crossing of the Hooker River, which was swollen with melting snow, they left the animals at the shepherd's hut at the bottom of the steep slopes of Gorilla Creek or 'Griller' according to Freda; presumably she had misheard the name of the creek, but as it was so hot she felt she was being grilled all the way up. On the grass slope at the top they camped the night and sat long into the evening around the fire as 'The red flames lit up the brown faces and gleaming eyes and teeth of the guides ... and the whole made a picture worthy of Rembrandt.'[20] All this stirred Freda's excitement. After broken sleep, at 2.00 a.m. the next morning she roused the guides and within two hours they were toiling up the last of the grassy slopes and into the climb. Unexpectedly Freda's greatest difficulty was in dealing with the monotony of snow work on the long smooth sweep of snow and she yearned for the diversion of pure rock climbing which the Southern Alps would rarely provide. On the Veil there would be only one real climbing challenge, a wide schrund, which is a gap between glacier ice and rock, near the summit.

Peculiarly, despite feeling she had climbed well, Peter Graham practically ignored her afterwards and stalked away ahead of her down Gorilla Creek. She recalled '[I] followed in the rear with protests in my heart that I never got near enough or [had] breath enough to utter.' As a guide, used to keeping to the pace of the slowest member, it was an unusual thing for him to do. He may have just been anxious to catch up on duties at the Hermitage, but it is more likely that he was testing her fitness and tenacity, perhaps concerned too that she was overly cocksure after the first climb. If this was so, they were already moving away from an employee–employer relationship. At the end of the ride home, he lifted the weary Freda off her horse, with what she saw as 'a commiserating' smile, although it could well have been a guilty one.

Freda slept until noon the next day but, while she slept, sunburnt skin that she hadn't been aware of began to peel on her face. She hated it happening, partly out of vanity, but primarily because it undermined her stance that mountaineering could do nothing but good. When she came in for lunch, her appearance verified for the other women that climbing wasn't worth it and if she was a good girl she would admit it. She dismissed their pointed comments airily telling them that the damage was 'only a temporary evil and as nothing to the joys I had acquired at the same time'.[21]

By Christmas, tourists had arrived in great numbers so the Hermitage was overflowing. There were parties at night, the old kettle piano was moved into the dining room, the rugs rolled back and everyone danced. Freda savoured all this, her enjoyment in climbing, the pleasure she gave playing the piano and with Peter Graham's warning not to rush still vivid in her mind, she took the time to enjoy the company of old friends, particularly Professor Baldwin Spencer. It was mutual. His frequent letters back to Chappie had much to say of Freda's activities interspersed with his own.

The Professor (he was later to be knighted) was everything Freda thought she would have loved in a father. Eccleston and the Professor did have much in common as explorers, being Fellows of the Royal Geo-graphical Society and prime movers in their own states in the formation and security of National Parks. Both loved art but the Professor was a patron and close friend of successful artists such as Whistler, Streeton and Roberts and had grand collections of their work whilst Eccleston Du Faur was much more interested in helping painters to work rather than buying what they produced. It would have been very painful for him to have read a letter from Sir Julian Ashton, a renowned Sydney artist, who wrote to the Professor: 'Consider my dear Spencer that here there has been no one like you to take any interest in art. To talk about it in season and out of season. To travel five hundred of miles to see a collection of water colours.'[22] But at 50 years old the Professor seemed more in tune with things that were happening than Freda's elderly parent. He had a natural understanding and interest in different generations, he was fun, intelligent, witty, she could say whatever she wished without offending him and their friendship was without the pressures of trying to prove herself worthy. The Professor was the first to appoint women as lecturers and associate professors to his Department of Science at Melbourne University but, despite this liberalism and his fascination with the human condition and unlike Eccleston Du Faur, he had a stubborn narrowness. He thought the classes should know their place and despite extensive anthropological surveys of the indigenous people of Australia he held the view that 'Australia is, at the present time, a refuge of creatures often crude and quaint, that have elsewhere passed away and given place to higher forms. This applies equally to the aboriginal as to the platypus and kangaroo.'[23]

This narrowness raised Freda's ire at times, especially when he tried to dissuade her from doing something he disagreed with. He genuinely believed that mountain exercise was not for young women and Freda would turn stringy instead of plump and pleasant as all young women should be. But the sparring over their different ideologies was something they both enjoyed, and in fact brought them closer.

After New Year, with a crowded Hermitage but clearing weather, Freda easily persuaded the Professor to join her and Peter Graham on a trip to Malte Brun Hut with the intention of climbing the great rock ridge of Mount Malte Brun. Also joining them was the experienced English climber Lawrence Earle who, on 23

December had ascended Mount Sefton, a severe exposed mountain towering 10,359 feet over the Hermitage, with Alex Graham, Captain Bernard Head, another Englishman, and Jack Clarke. After the descent the guides recommended against crossing the Copland back to the Hermitage for Christmas but their clients ignored the good advice, were caught in a blizzard and had a very uncomfortable time. As Jack Clarke had injured his foot on the trip he was no longer available for Earle, who was then happy for the opportunity to continue climbing with Peter Graham and his client.

When they reached the hut on the 7th, the Professor was intimidated by the mountain, considering that it 'held too many thrills to the square inch for his constitution' but promised to keep house and have a delicious meal waiting on their return.[24] The others made plans for the following day without him. Immediately another problem arose, one that was entirely unexpected.

Mr Earle approved of the selected climb but he did not approve of Freda's apparel. A strange argument that ensued, one that reveals as much about Freda's defensiveness, at the time, as her poilitical beliefs. She had permanently and proudly shortened her skirt but Earle refused to climb with her dressed like that. Freda didn't see what was wrong; her clothing was radical but practical, and safer than the current practice of wearing long skirts pinned up with safety pins supplied by the guides. Her clothing was not immodest, her legs and knees were covered by puttees and she had knicker-bockers underneath.

Mr Earle may have been her senior in every way but Freda was the more stubborn. She pertly told him that if he didn't like her costume, he needn't climb with them. Without disclosing why, she asked Peter Graham what he thought of her skirt. He joked, 'Skirt? I call that a frill', but when Freda appealed for his support, he was too wily to be trapped into siding with one client against another. With the problem still unresolved, she retired 'to the ladies compartment with dignity and a determination that was worthy of a militant suffragette to stick to [her] rights'.[25]

But the whole episode seems to have been based on a misunderstanding: the Englishman's preference was not that Freda should go back to a long skirt, but that she should wear trousers which were safer and warmer. He considered traditional wear to be impossible, long proved when the first attempt on the Matterhorn by a woman, Félicité Carrel (it had only been climbed two years earlier and then four of the party had been killed on the descent) was halted 300 feet below the summit, when strong winds blew her crinoline over her head. Nevertheless, confusion of opinion, between a polite, kind Englishman and a feisty Australian was understandable, when even so-called liberated women in Europe, confronted by conservative attitudes, resorted to wearing breeches with a skirt over the top which could be removed once away from civilisation. As late as the mid-1890s, Lissie Le Blond, when climbing in Switzerland, left her skirt at the beginning of a traverse and returned for it rather than dare to scandalise the local village.

Freda won whatever battle it had been as on 8 January they set off on a new route devised by Peter. Freda wore the 'despised dress', and Mr Earle 'wisely refrained from objection'.[26] Ultimately the English climber was more interested in his climb than defending principles. He was certainly more mature about it than Freda, who was still simmering.

Initially the rock on Malte Brun was everything they could have hoped for but difficulties soon arose. By keeping off the lower part of the arête, they found better rocks but any time saved was lost during a half-hour manoeuvre over an aiguille, a small sharp rock tower. They finally reached the arête, where they climbed easily until they were confronted by, what Freda euphemistically called, 'quite a fine bit of rock-work'; the ridge dropped about ten feet and then stretched out in a narrow, straight line of rock for about seventy more feet. Freda referred to this ridge as 'a cheval' as it was so sharp and narrow, with sheer drops on either side, that crossing it required them to straddle it as if on a horse for the entire length. Peter, unperturbed, shuffled along about halfway, to the end of the rope where he perched then called back for Freda to follow. She hesitated. Behind her was Mr Earle. Sitting astride the ridge with her short skirt hitched higher was going to expose more than her knees (how useful trousers would have been) but she lowered herself gingerly down onto the ridge where, wishing insanely for a cushion between her legs and knowing that would hardly prevent the 'some slight danger of being halved'[27] she crossed with short, awkward movements.

On the upper slopes they encountered loose crumbly rock. Only one climber moved at a time as care had to be taken not to dislodge the rocks until they reached the summit at midday. Once there they all shook hands then, using Freda's hat pin, they inscribed their names and the date on a whitebait tin and placed it in a small cairn of rocks. It was a ceremony that made Freda feel 'inclined to whoop' with pride that she had really accomplished a first-class climb, which only three other men had achieved, embellished by the added praise from the gracious Mr Earle of, 'Well done young one', which she felt 'wiped out all old scores and left me with the feeling that at last I might count myself amongst the elect'.[28]

Now that Lawrence Earle was her friend she could confess that she and Peter planned an attempt on Cook, if things went well on Malte Brun. Earle had made the ascent the season before and it was his route, primarily on rock, that Peter planned for Freda. Ever generous, the Englishman assured her that there was nothing as bad as the cheval and if the day was as good as this one she'd 'go up like a bird'.[29]

There were still plenty of lessons for Freda on a different route down, primarily that a descent is usually more difficult than ascent,

as once muscles are tired, adrenalin gone and excitement at
achievement has evaporated, lack of sleep and the strain begin to
show. Ropes get in the way and ice axes, awkward at the best of
times, catch on rocks, jab into ribs and threaten balance on the long
haul down precipitous cliffs. Mr Earle was rising more and more in
Freda's estimation. What she initially saw as irritating pedantry was
now care and patience, something she was grateful for when she
dislodged a pebble which smashed his pince-nez and left him with
limited vision. Later she slid on a patch of ice, cutting her hands,
although Peter held her on the rope. By 6.00 p.m. they were finally
down and, after a short break, reached the hut by 7.00 p.m. where
the Professor had everything organised. While the men smoked,
Freda could relive the day, photographed safely in her memory
dreamily weaving together 'the hopes, fears doubts, despairs and
joys that make up the rainbow tale of a day in the mountains'.[30]

The following day, Sunday, was a day of 'loafing about' as the
Professor put it. It was a cheerful time. Freda actually mended, of
course poorly, her own clothes and patched the Professor's pants so
badly in unmatched tweed that 'merely to contemplate it from
behind, even in the most serious climbing crisis, put new heart into
me.'[31] She and Earle even cooked a meal together while Peter went
out to reconnoitre the Professor's choice of climb, the nearby
Minarets (10,058 feet), which had been climbed only once before,
thirteen years earlier.

Next morning, wind rocked the tiny hut, threatening to send it
down the mountain although by 5.00 a.m. it had abated and the
dreaded moment of getting out of warm beds into the cold clothes
and stiff boots was upon them. What followed was a very difficult
day. Freda's lack of experience on ice was multiplied when they
reached a difficult maze of crevasses, narrow yawning spaces and
frail ice bridges that revealed great blue chasms. Beautiful and terrifying, she wrote how 'backwards and forwards we dodged

amongst great blocks and pinnacles of ice which sagged and leaned at drunken angles as if they meant to fall and bury us for ever more'. At the moment she thought things would get easier, it suddenly felt as if 'there wasn't a solid yard on this horrible mountain strong enough to bear my modest weight'.[32] Then, when they thought they were over their difficulties, they had to face a steep icy wall which fell away into a schrund. There was great pleasure in beating these obstacles but success for Freda was always bound up in seeing beyond, to what she could aim for: 'you know the thrill of victory and achievement in its fullness, a feeling so subtle and soul-satisfying as to defy analysis and which is absent, no matter how great is your achievement, when you conquer and see nothing, leaving only a bitter sense of failure and disappointment.'[33]

So when cloud blotted out everything by midday, there was no such reward, no heavenly view to make it all worthwhile. They even had to take Peter's word they were on the summit. It was 'an ordinary sized table top', according to the Professor who was suffering far more than Freda.[34]

The return trip was as abysmal, coloured by the failure to see anything and aggravated by the heat, eerie mist and the boom of avalanches caused by softening snow. They had to move quickly to cross ever-dwindling ice bridges that dripped into ever-widening crevasses. At the last one, with great caution, Peter tapped the slender strip of ice with his ice axe and as he withdrew, the spindle of ice collapsed, leaving a vast cavity with smooth unclimbable walls. This forced them to backtrack over unstable ground and take a route Peter had spotted the previous day and rejected as unsuitable.

Freda now had her rock climb; a steep overhang that required each climber to be lowered by rope. It was misery for the poor Professor, who faced a climb far worse than the one he'd refused to go on up Malte Brun. Mr Earle went first, followed by the two less experienced climbers, then Peter Graham at the end, who had to climb down without a rope while the others watched anxiously below.

Finally, when they thought they could reward themselves with that favourite time of recounting the climb in front of a fire, they were to be disappointed again. Another guide, Darby Thomson, with a large group were already in Malte Brun Hut, so the next morning they tramped through pouring rain to the Hermitage, finally arriving in sunshine at 5.30 p.m.

For the next four days of glorious summer, while Peter went off guiding tourists, Freda played the well-brought up and charming girl and pleased everyone. She wore straw hats to protect her skin, picnicked with the Professor and some of the other guests from the hotel at a small tarn halfway up Mount Sebastopol and played the unruly tomboy up there, doing better than any brother, indulging in 'the never-failing joy of rolling down huge boulders, watching them bound from rock to rock, hurling themselves over a precipice and shatter into a hundred pieces below'.[35] Her patience and apparent contentment were an illusion. Freda's Professor wrote to Chappie, a few days after the Minarets climb describing the adventure as 'magnificent' and adding 'As to Miss Du Faur she is capable of anything in the way of climbing and next week, if the weather is fine, will get up Mt Cook with Graham and Murphy.'[36] It wasn't easy for someone like Freda to be idle when dominating every view was that mountain waiting for her, as perfect days passed.

8 PIERCING THE CLOUDS

*'No rock so hard that a little wave may not beat submission in a
thousand years'*

Tennyson

When Peter Graham still hadn't returned from taking two ladies
over to the west coast, Freda began to worry about the weather and
bitterly begrudge the four perfect climbing days he'd been away. As
she had feared, when he finally returned on the evening of 16
January, the glass in the foyer had begun to fall and their second
guide, Murphy, had poisoned his arm. Again the shortage of guides
and good climbers was apparent. With no one to climb as a third,
their only solution was to take a porter, leave him at the last
bivouac, then she and Peter would go it alone.

Conservative forces rallied once again on the now windswept
verandah of the Hermitage. Two climbers, especially when one was
a woman, attempting Mount Cook was madness, an unjustifiable
risk. Even Jack Clarke tried to talk them out of attempting the
climb without at third as 'against all mountaineering rules'.[1] Peter
Graham owed a lot to Clarke, had deferred to him in the past but
he wanted the climb, so he claimed ingenuously that his client Miss
Du Faur was an independent person; accordingly, he could not

interfere in her private affairs.

But Freda, with a long year ahead in Sydney, and tired of the polite dithering, was not so diplomatic and challenged Clarke, arguing that the rules on numbers had been set down for ice and snow but the route they were taking, up the Hooker, was mainly rock. Clarke hadn't seen her on rock, and the speed with which they had climbed Malte Brun, on a new and more difficult route, proved she was capable of attempting Mount Cook.

The experienced Jack Clarke had no answer. The aggression that had taken Freda to this point was turned on the senior mountaineer. She loved such moments of contention although she was not always adept at recognising when she had made her point. Mr Earle supported her unequivocally and swung opinion her way. Whether or not this moment was the cause, she and Jack Clarke would never be entirely comfortable with each other and she preferred not to climb with him.

Jack Clarke had reason to be concerned as Mount Cook was not just the rock climb Freda was claiming it to be. The experienced European climbers, the Anglo-Irishman Reverend William Green and two Swiss men, Emil Boss and Ulrich Kaufman, making a first attempt up the north-eastern side on March 1882, managed to reach a few hundred feet from the summit, but were beaten back by the weather and in particular the late hour. They were forced to bivouac overnight at over 10,000 feet. With avalanches falling around them, they barely made it through to morning. But as Freda's attempts and successes would make high climbs seem possible for local women, the men's attempt issued a challenge to local men. Such were the changeable conditions, it would take twelve years before success. The nearest to come to it was a climb by the New Zealanders, George Mannering and Marmaduke Dixon, who, climbing too early in the season, never got that perfect day as Freda did and were beaten back close to the top when they too ran out of time. Finally on Christmas Day 1894, New Zealanders Tom Fyfe, George Graham and Jack Clarke then only 19, reached the top of Mount Cook.

A decade and a half after the first ascent by men, the weather was holding Freda's attempt up. After four days of rain, and with avowals of pending doom from their skeptics at the Hermitage, she and Peter, with Tom the porter, who was braving her again, were on their way. It was 21 January. Freda was optimistic and relaxed as they followed the narrow path cut out of the cliff alongside the rocky white water of the Hooker River, then cut up through grassy meadows studded with clumps of beautiful white mountain lilies and veronica. To the west, Mount Sefton's 'white wall towered above' and straight ahead, seemingly close enough to touch, stood the 'centre of all our hopes, Mt Cook'.[2] They bivouacked for the night in makeshift tents, using ice axes as posts and alpine rope as the ridge poles, high enough to sit up under the canvas, creating enough space for three. At five o'clock the next morning they tramped to the Hooker Glacier and climbed down the moraine wall to the ice. However, because of deep crevasses in the ice fall, they were forced to climb up the rocks at the side, something of a slog for the men weighed down by four days' supplies. By half past nine they were resting before tackling, what was expected to be, the smoother glacier above the ice fall.

Rarely are expectations fulfilled in such a landscape; the ice was badly broken up and the crevasses impossible to cross. Again and again Peter searched for a possible crossing while Freda and Tom waited, muscles stiffening in the cold. Twenty minutes later Peter returned. He had found one possibility, an apparently bottomless, green-blue pit with a fragile ice bridge, so narrow it was impossible to walk upright on it. Bouyed by Peter's opinion that if

they could just get across this they'd be on their way, Freda agreed
to the crossing and a few moments later, tied only to Tom, with an
ice axe firmly wedged in the snow for extra protection, Peter lowered his twelve stone frame onto the ice bridge 'as lightly as a cat'
and carefully worked his way across. Once he was secure, Freda,
anxious that he might have weakened the bridge, lowered herself
down. Hand over hand, abyss below, ice between her legs, she finally reached the shimmering white bank ahead. Then swags were
hauled across and Tom followed.

From then on the sun burnt down on them on the glacial ice;
it was 'almost unbearable' with no respite, even when they reached
bivouac at 8,000 feet, an area only big enough for the two tents and
covered in tiny sharp stones. As soon as Peter left to reconnoitre
and kick the steps necessary to give them a good start the next day,
Tom begged Freda to persuade Peter to let him climb as well. Freda
had some empathy with his position, but rather pointedly 'felt
inclined to remind him of his feelings on Mt Sealy' and pointed out
that he was untrained and this attempt was regarded as 'rash', as it
was.[3] When Peter returned Tom's request was quashed immediately, although it hardly mattered as Peter was not optimistic about the
weather.

As he'd anticipated, next morning they woke to the sound of
rising wind and the tent flapping. They waited and when the wind
seemed to be subsiding, at 4.45 they set out across the snowfield,
following Peter's frozen footsteps, kicked in soft snow the previous
night. Behind them, the tiny bivouac and sleeping Tom disappeared
into a jumble of rock, ahead the endless curve of snow they were
traversing to reach the head of the basin. Again there were problems. They reached a huge schrund; climbing into the lower lip
wasn't too difficult but, when they searched for a way up and out,
there seemed to be only one possibility over icy, snow-covered
rocks. Once on these Peter found himself in one precarious position

after another and Freda, watching below, began to understand why Jack Clarke had warned them about the need to take a reliable third, not only because her small size and lack of strength might fail to get Peter out of difficulty, but what he needed to get up over the upper lip was a pair of strong shoulders to stand on. Freda, at eight stone, could not hold him. Nor would he allow her to take the lead by standing on him. It was doubtful she could have balanced on the tiny foothold above the schrund and taken his weight anyway. Whatever the arguments and possibilities and regrets, they had to retreat.

Peter could reassure himself that, as a guide, the care of his client was paramount but Freda could find no excuses. She felt she would never get over the failure she felt was caused by her lack of strength; she called it years later 'one of the bitterest moments I ever experienced'.[4] There were two consolations: it was too late for another woman to climb Mount Cook that season and, as the day turned grey and cold, she was sure there wouldn't have been the wonderful view that she so coveted.

As it was still only 8.30, Tom was still sleeping when they returned. They ate breakfast, retreated to the first bivouac and caught up on some of their lost sleep. The disappointment, combined with her lack of sleep, was debilitating and the return trip, which she had imagined would be covered in glory, ignominious. They 'plodded' down the Hooker with Mount Cook still pristine above them. To make things worse, she was caught by Professor Spencer and his friends down by the Hooker River, looking a mess, with sunburn, hair awry and her 'exceedingly abbreviated climbing costume none the better for having been slept in for two nights'.[5] There were questions and condolences which Freda, when she was well, always found irksome. She managed to tidy herself up enough to look civilised and defend her stance on women mountaineers.

A couple of wet days gave her respite to get her energy back then she, Peter and the Professor attempted a crossing of the Graham Saddle to the west coast, intending to return via the Copland Pass but, after four days of rain cooped up in Ball Hut, they gave up. The Professor, running out of time, favoured a trip to Lake Wanaka, south from Cook through the wild MacKenzie country, so Freda joined Peter and a client, young Canadian Otto Frind, who intended crossing the Copland Pass to the west coast.

Frind, at 23, was an eager, extremely wealthy young man, on a world trip with his grandmother and he began climbing for the first time in New Zealand. He was the first mountaineer Freda could climb with as an equal in the Southern Alps, a relative novice, but keen, able and in her age group. His boyish way and lack of imagination could irritate her but the competition between them was stimulating and there was a great deal of banter particularly concerning male–female roles, about which he was quite conservative.

Leaving at the same time, on 2 February, but for the Tasman Glacier, was Mr Earle, his cousin and a now healthy Jack Clarke. The Professor got up 'in scanty attire' to see them all off and by 7.00 a.m. they had walked up the Hooker. Freda was relaxed, all thoughts of what might have been were at the back of her mind, as she enjoyed everything around her, at least until they reached the rocky parapet of Copland Pass, from where she had a clear view of Cook. From that position she could only 'sadly' look ahead to where she was really going, the beautiful west coast which she was sure 'could never excite that passionate thrill of exultation and devotion which lured me to battle on the icy heights of the great mountains'.[6]

They moved from the Pass into the snow basin below, onto slippery snow grass slopes that took them to the head of the Copland River, into dense bush, narrow streams, silver rapids and boulders across which sure-footed Freda happily leapt. The trip necessitated an overnight stay at Douglas Rock, an overhang that was almost a cave with a fireplace in the middle of the opening, a necessity as smoke was the only protection from mosquitoes and sandflies. There they made beds of fern and used sleeping bags left behind by others.

The next day they set off through miles of extraordinarily beautiful bush but deep crossings of wild water. Peter, despite Freda's objections, insisted on piggybacking her while Otto photographed them. Freda 'wisely confiscated this interesting negative' of her 'wildly waving limbs and large nailed boots'.[7]

Again they were in bush, until reaching the hot springs at Welcome Flat where, unfortunately for the swimmer in the group, the four pools were either bubbling hot or covered in sulphurous scum. They did not linger, and on reaching Architect Creek, a few miles futher down, picked up horses organised for them as part of the trip. Freda was initially put out by having to use a man's saddle rather than a side-saddle she'd been trained on but, as soon as they reached open ground, a canter developed into a full gallop as she and Frind raced each other to their overnight lodgings at Scott's farm and accommodation house at Karangarua.

The next day, as Peter was making 'a triumphal progress' stopping for 'yarns' with everyone, his impatient and competitive companions raced each other wherever possible. Freda, on a favourite horse and side-saddle borrowed from one of the Scott daughters, finally had an advantage, and kept challenging Frind until eventually he announced he would have to 'take his meals off the mantelpiece for the next few days'.[8]

Without their guide, they reached Waiho (which would later become Franz Josef), a 'populous settlement' Freda jokingly called it, consisting of a hotel, three bark humpies left from the goldmining days and one cottage with a post office and store attached set in a garden full of flowers. This was the Graham home. Peter's widowed mother, Isabella Graham, then over seventy, sat them down to afternoon tea until Peter, and then Alex Graham, arrived. This was

Alex and Freda's first meeeting. Based primarily on the west coast, and without the demands of full-time guiding, Alex had the freedom to explore the western flanks of the Southern Alps with his close friend, Dr Teichelmann. Alex was a shy man, whose quietness carried as much authority as his brother's ebullience. He was also less aware of the impact he had on others and more at peace with himself.

Mrs Graham was one of those rare people whom others naturally gravitate towards and Freda, conscious of her own losses of older women in her life, adored her. The elderly woman was interested in everybody and told wonderful stories of the old gold-digging days in Australia and New Zealand, all of which Freda avidly took in. Born in Dublin, into a medical family, her parents died when she was three, so she was adopted and well educated in London by her uncle and aunt. The author Charles Dickens was a close family friend. At the age of fourteen she migrated with her family to Australia where her uncle practised in the inland town of Bendigo. She married there, was soon widowed, then trained as a nurse in Melbourne before moving on to New Zealand for her health, and reached Okarito, then a town of four or five thousand people. She thrived in the cooler summers on the west coast and revelled in the demanding life. She enjoyed an autonomy out there that she could never have experienced in the city and she was thrilled by the physical challenge involved in getting to patients in outlying mining and farming settlements. In 1869 she married David Graham, who worked as a baker and grocer, until taking on a tiny farm and the job as ferryman at Five Mile Beach, south of Okarito. These jobs and occasional goldmining bought few riches so Mrs Graham's nursing skills helped to provide for the family of what would be five sons, David, John (Jack), Jim, Peter and Alex. The only daughter and eldest, Margaret, died in her early teens.

The greatest disappointment for the Graham parents was the

impossibility of providing education for their children in such an isolated area, especially when Mr Graham had a stroke which disabled him until his death, eight years later in 1900. Although the elder boys were already working, Peter, then about twelve, also had to leave school and turn his hand to whatever work he could find, at first around the house and ferry, then goldmining, clearing the bush and working on the roads. Later the three older brothers left the farm and transferred their share to the two youngest. Neither Alex nor Peter were very good farmers but the land provided vegetables, milk, meat and butter and was useful later when Alex, Jim and his wife, Rose, established the Franz Josef Hotel.

That evening Freda, Otto and the Graham brothers went across to the nearby Batson's Hotel to join Leonard Lindon and Dr Teichelmann, who were waiting for the right conditions for Alex to guide them across the Graham Saddle back to the Hermitage. Then aged 50 and Superintendent of Westland Hospital, Ebenezer Teichelmann was tiny and deceptively frail looking, with a 'Captain Cuttle' beard which was already white, deep grey eyes and a 'squeaky sort of voice'.[9] He wore a sports coat, knickers and stockings, and wide, welted boots which made his legs look even skinnier. Freda was immediately taken with him; he was not unlike the spirited architect Horbury Hunt. The Little Doctor, as the Grahams called him, rarely travelled anywhere without his photographic equipment. With the generosity of spirit that characterised the coasters, even those of Austrian extraction and born in Australia, he freely gave photogaphic advice so others need not make the errors he had. For a time his photos, one of which was reprinted in Freda's book, *The Conquest of Mount Cook*, were regarded as the finest in New Zealand.

During those clear, sunny days Freda really relaxed, both in her surroundings and with her companions. Her friendship with Otto Frind continued to evolve; there was little they couldn't tease each other about and they had a similar sense of irony. She adored teasing the Grahams as well, and claimed to cease to 'be a scoffer at the beauty of this wonderful Westland except now and again to tease some proud West Coaster to defending it with all the ardour of a true son of the soil'.[10]

There were long walks particularly with Frind, good food and bathing in the mineral pool behind the hotel. Almost oily, the water repaired her sunburnt skin and soothed her muscles aching from riding. The only disturbance was the return of Mr Lindon and Dr Teichelmann, who had been beaten back on their third attempt to cross the saddle. This time Teichelmann had a touch of frostbite. Freda and Otto had no inclination to attempt the same route.

On 7 February, as Freda was booked to leave the Hermitage within the week, they left Waiho to return the way they had come. The weather was fine although there was some concern that the earlier rain that created waterfalls off the crags and rapidly rising rivers could cause a problem but the nearest to a disaster occurred when Peter's horse caught a foot in a rabbit hole, rolled down an embankment and pinned the guide by his leg. He wasn't hurt so Freda suggested she sit on the horse's head to prevent it rising and perhaps hurting him. It was the right thing to do but she could never work out why both men found the suggestion so amusing.

Driving rain forced an extra night's stay at Scott's farm but they made it over the Copland to clearer weather, stopping only briefly at the site of a new hut, the Hooker, which they hoped would eliminate one night's bivouac on their next Cook attempt.

The ship left Lyttelton for Sydney on 12 February 1910. Freda had been away from Ku-ring-gai for three months. She had left with some apprehension about becoming a mountaineer but was returning with confidence albeit without her prize. She was forging a place for herself, distinct from the Du Faurs of Sydney and the du Faurs de Pibrac. In the Southern Alps, the Du Faur name meant Freda, not Eccleston. There, too, she had been able to choose compatible brothers. That knowledge would carry her through the low months ahead. She need only plan for the future.

Out in the Chase, with winter coming, the leaves had dried out and rustled underfoot. Otherwise it was quiet. Guy was engrossed as always in the gardens and orchards. Horticulture had given Freda's eldest brother a purpose, but it was not a career and he would describe himself only as a 'gentleman'. He'd made a close friend in one of his father's connections, Mr Maiden, curator of the Botanic Gardens, who provided him with advice and interesting plants. The Flowton gardens, in which Guy was assisted by a caretaker, Clarence Buisst, supplied most of the household's needs, although civilisation in its most benevolent form had arrived with a baker calling in three times a week, a milkman twice daily and a butcher turning up in his cutting cart, a fairly unpleasant activity in the heat of summer, peak time for flies. Buisst's wife, Gertrude, looked after the house, which was still lit by candles and paraffin lamps and would not have water mains until 1914.

Barely had Freda arrived at Flowton than a letter from Peter Graham reached her. It would have had to have been written soon after Freda left the Hermitage. Inside was the disturbing news she had feared. New Zealand male mountaineers were determined that an 'outsider' would not make off with another prize in their mountains. Neither Peter nor Freda said who the well-known guide was, who stated he would 'get the lady in question to the top if he had to carry her there',[11] but the push is assumed to have come from Jack Clarke, who had every reason to take the climb from Freda. There was no one else, apart from Peter Graham, with the capability. Jack Clarke, at the time, was sweet on the beautiful Nettie McDonald, who was conveniently staying at the Hermitage. It is assumed she was the 'lady'.

It was easier to write rationally later about the news than at the time, although it did become obvious to Freda that the New Zealand team could not attempt the Hooker route as it was already closed, so the attempt would have to be from the Tasman side, not easy for men, let alone an inexperienced woman. Freda considered that an experienced woman would have refused to attempt it. A number of years later the experienced Austrian guide Conrad Kain commented:

> Climbing Mt Cook is hard work for guide and Tourist. I personally do not consider it a difficult mountain compared to mountains in the Swiss Alps and that is from a technical point of view, but where bad weather conditions are concerned there is no doubt Mt Cook keeps pride of place. Mt Cook would only allow a man to stand on his head when in his best temper.[12]

Mount Cook was rarely in a good temper and the New Zealand team was turned back by bad weather. The attempt probably said as much about the men and their attitudes to women's abilities than anything else. The idea of dragging a woman up a mountain shows contempt, not only for women, but for the skills required to climb at all. No one attempted it with an inexperienced woman again, although it would be a long time before such opinions subsided. The charge of being carried up was one of a number levelled at Freda. Even her success on traverses that men hadn't tackled would not change every poor opinion of her, although the situation was confused in that so much was done by guides especially in carrying, step cutting and kicking.

There would also be claims from various quarters that Freda

bought not only her guides but her climbs, by hiring the best guide over a season and thus preventing anyone else undertaking them. Freda was never that rich, the costs at the Hermitage were not cheap and there were many times when she and the weather were ready but Peter had been hired out by others. Climbers such as Annie Lindon, Ada Julius, Jane Thomson and, what Otto Frind would later call, 'Peter Graham's Ladies' Admiration Club' could have financially matched Freda in hiring Peter Graham at any time. Freda's main difficulty was finding suitable climbing companions. Nevertheless, she must have been exceedingly nervous for a period of time and pleased when winter ensured that no one else could attempt the climb before her.

She was acutely aware, though, that her next attempt might be her only chance. It was quite feasible another woman mountaineer could turn up. Although she commented that the New Zealanders did her 'the honour to imply that I would not fail on my next attempt'.[13] Freda was not so confident. She knew she could not afford to waste time getting into condition when she returned the next season. She had to begin immediately. She had to be as fit as a man and as strong as she possibly could be.

9 VENUS

'It takes an intelligent, trained woman, who thoroughly understands
the weaknesses of her sister to guide her with absolute accuracy ...
and from this will be realised a type of womanhood, new in history,
undescribed in fiction, from which there shall proceed, a majesty,
more pure and tender than anything which poets have sung.'

George Dupain

It did not take Freda long to realise she had absolutely no idea how
to build up her body and stamina and that it would be almost
impossible to do so on her own. Through the Backhouse boys she
had heard of an unusual organisation for the time, a fitness studio,
named the Dupain Institute, which had its premises in the Royal
Chambers on the corner of Castlereagh and Hunter Streets. It did
not immediately appear promising. The rooms, above solicitors and
accountants and reached by a rickety lift, were expansive enough
but the courses offered boxing, fencing, ball punching, weight-lift-
ing, wrestling and treatment for everything from' 'Chest and Lung
Deficiencies' to 'Abdominal and Bodily Reduction'. Moreover, the
walls were covered with pictures of men who resembled a cliché of
the nineteenth century, the strong-man, with handlebar moustache
and a large chest partially covered in a striped suit.

The founder, George Zepherin Dupain, was not easy either. A highly energetic fanatic, he had commenced his working life as a wool classer but, in the process of perfecting his own body, had become fascinated with the perfect classical form. He began to study the muscles and skeleton of the human being and then founded 'The Tabernacle', an institute for amateur gymnastics. So popular was his approach that physical fitness was a science that could be controlled and explained by a scientific formula and then applied to the individual, that the institute had to move into larger premises in the city. There'd been nothing like it before nor for a long time after.[1]

At least Dupain did allow women to attend some classes. On Thursday nights young women, dressed in loose tunics, not unlike soft gym slips that dropped from a square neckline into folds at the knee, could train in rhythmical, graceful exercises, designed to develop fitness, to get rid of the corset but never to inhibit childbirth. George Dupain summarised his concerns in his treatise *Exercise and the Woman*: 'The whole training of women should be related to her special function in life, that of motherhood and anything which may interfere with or jeopardise this attainment should be cast aside without sentiment.'

He believed that the physical characteristics of women could not cope with too much exercise as it would tighten the ligaments and muscles of the pelvis, making a woman's ultimate role very difficult. As well, 'periodic fluctuations' meant that 'her nervous system was more or less unbalanced'. He recommended a number of activities from running to ballet, as long as they weren't competitive. Mountain climbing according to the Dupain theory would be a near impossibility and the concept of Freda taking her own weight, let alone that of a man, unthinkable; but he did advocate exercises for women and encouraged them to look after themselves and to free their bodies and minds from the rigid constraints of the time. He truly believed that his rational approach could lead to romantic perfection, that of a beautiful, well-formed and nourished classical body. As well, he was prepared to tailor his generalities to the specific needs of an unusual situation. A man could know the theory but it took an intelligent, trained woman to fully understand 'the weaknesses of her sisters to guide her with absolute accuracy'.[2]

To this end, George Dupain trained two 'Lady Experts', one his sister, Jeannie Dupain, and the other, her senior, Muriel Minnie Cadogan, a strong clear-eyed woman with a swath of thick brown hair who was put in charge of Freda. She made it clear to the instructress what she required and, in the process of explaining the mutual dependency of two people, thousands of feet up on a cliff of rock and ice, she began to tell of her failure to take Mount Cook and she did not have to put on a brave face. Muriel was sympathetic and was not so sure Dupain was entirely right in his theories. Keen to put some of her own ideas into practice, she devised a spartan regime based on hard work, concentration and baths to keep the skin clean and free and 'active by mild sweating and strong shampooing'. Warm baths only were recommended, as cold baths, according to Dupain, were inefficient cleansers and were apt to become a fetish. Freda's diet was checked, her intake of fresh foods increased. Special exercises were developed to strengthen her arms and abdominal muscles, and increase flexibility and stamina. Muriel taught her to build up her lungs through the 'art of proper breathing', a form of aerobic training, well ahead of its time.

A strong friendship developed. Muriel began staying at Flowton so they could go out on the cliffs and she could assess the economy and strength of her pupil's movements. Their efforts were succeeding. There were no winter flus and colds to set Freda's fitness back that year. She was clear headed and less prone to depression and found she could climb for longer periods and was more agile. The gap Enid had left in Freda's life began to be filled. Muriel was a more kindly and sensible woman, but a rebel all the same; she proudly claimed: 'it is nothing for me to be uncorsetted because I do not care for public opinion'.[3] A year younger, but more worldly than Freda, she had held a full-time job for ten years, was an expert on a subject she loved, was not intimidated by anyone and had a sure grasp of her clients, George Dupain and the institute. She loathed the way women did not support each other. Real women wouldn't have discouraged Freda from climbing and carped about her reputation. Freda was wrong to have caved into them.

Everything was simple to Muriel: being physically fit was enough in itself. If Freda was in love with mountains, Muriel was in love with the perfect female form. A healthy body to her meant a healthy mind, 'just do it, think it, say it, believe it, follow it'. With such simple maxims, Muriel could write confidently about her own 'feminine theories' which Freda soon took up. Muriel's idealised woman was Venus, 'a transcendent embodiment of mature feminine beauty ... her magnificent womanhood affects us like a strain of exquisite music. She is both great and tender.'[4] Hardly how one would describe Freda, but at least she never needed a corset, which was fortunate as one article Muriel wrote on the evils of the corset took up fourteen pages of the *Dupain Quarterly*. She felt that when 'we compare this ideal with the shape moulded by the corset what do we find? ABSOLUTELY NOTHING which can bear any comparison with the beauty of Venus.' Muriel was very good at talking in absolutes even if she put women down in the process of changing them. Women who wore a corset, she considered, were either ignorant of the ridiculous damage they were doing or were 'unmoral' as they only wanted the artificial hourglass figures to titillate men. Muriel felt with great passion that, 'women have often been called fools but it is hard to imagine any nearer relationship to the imbecile class than these adherents of the latest fashions. Is not this a deplorably oversexed condition that would make women descend to these depths of immodesty in order to attract the attention of men.' Not that she hated men. In fact she felt that blaming them for corsets was 'a libel on the majority of mankind' as most of the men she knew preferred women without them. Men who thought otherwise, Muriel regarded as 'wanting in enlightenment and who have neither sense nor understanding of the truly beautiful'.[5]

Surprisingly Eccleston enjoyed Muriel. She was chatty and lively and enlivened his daughter. The theories Muriel expounded were interesting even if he considered them unlikely and he went out of his way to lend her art pieces and organised some from the National Art Gallery to be photographed as illustrations of classical beauty in the *Dupain Quarterly*.

Freda soon began visiting the Cadogans, which required a trip out on the double-decker coach from the city to the upper middle-class suburb of Marrickville. Unlike Turramurra, the suburb was lively, with traders in their horse and carts all advertising their wares in sing-song voices, selling anything from rabbits to clothes props. Hamilton Court in George Street, the Cadogan home, was a large, two-storey brick buiding with attics, set in expansive grounds surrounded by a wrought-iron fence. Stone lions, as was the fashion of the time, guarded the front steps. At the back was an enclosed courtyard, kitchen garden and poultry run.

There were seven children in the Cadogan family. Muriel, at 26 was the eldest, then came Nell, Beryl (nicknamed Queen), Irene (Tiss), Hilton (Mick), Sylvia, and the baby, three-year-old Max. The family was an unusual mix of German and Scottish. Muriel's maternal grandparents, Heinrich and Emily Metzler, had five girls and two boys of whom Muriel's mother 'Min', short for Wilhemina Sarah, was the eldest. The Meltzers were a hardworking, close family who would remain, even when married, around the Marrickville area.

Muriel's youngest brother, Max, said of her: 'She wasn't pretty.

She was … I can't describe her. She was an ordinary sort of woman',[6] but what made Muriel extraordinary was her extravagant energy, her thick auburn wavy hair, her freshness and her distinct, uninhibited movements. She had inherited her robust practicality and loyalty from her mother but it would be her father's relatives that would eventually dominate her life.

Muriel's paternal grandfather was a Scotsman, George Callum Cadogan, who married her grandmother, Marianne Frances Moss, in Sydney in 1855. Their son William, Muriel's father, was born on 6 September 1856 but three years later George died in the wreck of the SS *Royal Charter* off the coast of Wales. Soon after Marianne Cadogan began a relationship with a Yorkshire man, Charles Shaw and, although they did not go through a formal marriage, she took his name. In 1861 Marianne had another son, Alfred Moss Shaw. Four daughters followed over the next ten years.

William Cadogan, brought up as part of this new family, was always the interloper, the fatherless son never adopted into the Shaws. He began his working life as an accountant for a commercial pottery, Bakewell Bros, obviously a successful enterprise as the china on the family table had his initials, W.H.C., baked into the rim of every plate and dish – a gift when he left to go into partnership. The firm he set up, W.H.Cadogan, Stewart and Co. Accountants, at 12 Castlereagh Street, Sydney, worked in the lucrative local government market and did well, but William could never match his younger half-brother. The family doted on him. Alfred, much to everyone's pride, trained as a lawyer, then married, had a son, Cyril, and set up the legal firm with a junior partner.

By 1899 all appeared well at the firm of Shaw and Jagelman of 108 Pitt Street, Sydney, but before the year was out, clients were becoming nervous. Trust account money, in one case cited as £ 900, had disappeared. Recent trust cheques had been cashed and money, drawn to pay Jagelman, were kept by Shaw. Mortgages supposed to have been arranged were never carried out as Alfred began absenting himself from the office until, on 25 February 1900, he was made bankrupt and went into hiding, apparently in Melbourne, and then in New Zealand. Seven months later, he was struck off. It was discovered he had been insolvent for ten years.

Unfortunately William Cadogan, according to Muriel, had invested £20,000 with Alfred. As only one trust book was ever retrieved, this figure cannot be verified but there seems no reason to distrust Muriel's claim; and her brother, Max, did agree a large sum of money was involved. Despite this, it was not William Cadogan who put Alfred Shaw into court, for he thought it pointless to pursue money or seek revenge, and a public fight would only have bought more problems for his mother.

Whatever the loss, the Cadogans were never as well off as they should have been and Muriel would always feel it keenly. When the fraud was uncovered she was sixteen and well aware how her family life changed, particularly the opportunities she had lost in furthering her education. The house was sold and they moved into a rented, although pleasant, house, Rolwyn, in Mosman. William coped by living to the hilt, spending any money as it arrived. Muriel left school, as did Nell, and went to the Dupain Institute. Mrs Cadogan, with the added problems of the loss and the effect on her husband, as well as five younger children to care for, let Muriel take over the running of the household, a role she would never entirely relinquish even when overseas.

All the Cadogans would work. Mick, in time, went into his father's office as an accountant and eventually took it over, Tiss and Sylvia became secretaries, Beryl became a nurse at Crown Street Women's Hospital and Nell became a housekeeper.

Training continued on Freda's muscles, heart and mind, right up until she left for the 1910–11 season in New Zealand. Over that time she came to rely intensely on Muriel's good sense and her energy. Not for Muriel, the doubts nor the bouts of ill health that dogged Freda. She kept an emotional consistency and balance, in contrast to Freda's competitive nature and emotional highs and lows, and opened Freda up to many possibilities: of women working; of living away from the family; of making decisions about behavioural standards, regardless of upbringing. Her views and knowledge about women's physiology and health were useful too, although Muriel was also very fond of turning generalities into specifics and this Freda indiscriminately picked up. After some of her great climbing successes she would be confident enough to advise (or rather lecture) young women, à la Muriel with a dab of Peter Graham and wrote: 'The men and women who develop physically, mentally and morally are surely worth more to the race that those who attain maturity at twenty-one and at that advanced age settle all life's problems and then live in bovine placidity to a green old age.' She advised women who did not wish to be so cow-like, to take up mountaineering but to do so sensibly: 'First be sure that you are sound of heart and lungs, and then work up from small beginnings to climbs of increasing difficulty and you will gain health, strength self-reliance and poise.'[7] Freda would enjoy immensely a role as a 'lady expert': she would become a defender of mountaineering for women and in turn would encourage other young women to take up the sport.

But, as her trip to New Zealand grew closer, intellectual rationalisation became no match for the highly strung imagination. Freda had been in contact with Peter Graham, who assured her that he would be waiting for her, but still she began to worry that he would change his mind. There were times when she doubted her fitness, or was sure that an international woman climber would get there before her, or a freak early summer would allow 'that New

Zealand woman', or some other New Zealand woman to try before her. With Muriel planning to meet her later at the Hermitage early in November 1910, Freda, by then 28, sailed for New Zealand, determined that any unfounded fears would be well hidden behind a cheerful, confident face.

Freda was obviously, as Peter put it, 'trained to a hair' but always cautious, and with no sign of rivals, he suggested minor climbs to get back in touch until Mount Cook was ready to climb. They would then wire Alex, whom Freda, not willing to be left without a second guide again, had hired for a month. On the 14th she and Peter set off for a leisurely day on nearby Mount Annette and by 6.30 they were back at the Hermitage where rain kept them in for the next few days.

The time wasn't entirely a loss as there was interesting company in the form of a member of Captain Robert Falcon Scott's planned expedition to the South Pole. Peter had been ordered to give him any assistance he required so as soon as the weather improved, Freda joined up with them to go to Ball Hut, from where they climbed Mount Mabel (7,150 feet), all an apparent lark for Freda with glorious glissades and complaints about the heat as a diversion from her underlying serious intent. The next day her Professor arrived among an influx of tourists.

On the following day she and Peter went up the Mueller Glacier with the intention of climbing to the Barron Saddle. It was a joyous energetic outing and she was delighted to compare her work now to when she had last been on the glacier as a 'scared little novice who had hated stepping over a two foot crevasse'.[8]

Unpressured, she took the time to experiment with her camera, a Kodak 3a, and a yellow screen she'd brought with her from Sydney, with the intention of working out how to filter out glare and how to create shape and shade out of what could seem like a pure white vista. Bad weather days would give her time to develop her photographs and discover what techniques worked in the varying conditions that arose. She grew, in a few years, from 'bitterly regretting that she was the merest amateur'[9] to a skilled photographer who could dramatise and highlight her climbs, as well as draw attention to the fact she was a lone woman up there. In time, she supplied her work to newspapers, magazines and even to the memoirs of other mountaineers.

Deciding that the Barron Saddle was not exciting enough she and Peter decided to look for some good rock work, so targeted one of two virgin peaks at the head of the glacier, although Freda later discovered that it may already have been climbed by Tom Fyfe and George Graham in 1894.

Carelessly chatting and unroped, first Peter went into a crevasse to his waist, then Freda followed. She recalled: '[I found myself with] my toes dangling in space and [I] was only supported by clinging to my ice axe which was fortunately wedged firmly above me.' Peter could barely see her head above the snow and only after he had 'ingloriously' hauled her out and they were roped did he dare joke that it would have been 'awkward' for him if he'd lost her altogether.[10]

In the end the rock climb they had hoped for was impossible, so they turned to another route up a steep snow couloir (gully) which, because of the heat of the last week, was ready to avalanche. To drop a thousand feet 'rolled in a giant snowball' was more excitement than either required, so traversing became a tense progress as small avalanches hissed away on either side. The only difficulty after that was a buttress of rock, almost smooth, with few hand or footholds. Their rope was not long enough for Peter to climb up to a secure position so, after trying hold after hold, he swung along a crack, his hands taking his entire weight. Freda, helpless to hold him if he fell, waited. '[I had my] face turned to the rock, my feet on a ledge and my hands stuck in a crack above my head, for what seemed like an eternity.' As the rope was too short he had to wait until she moved before he could brace himself properly and take her weight. Not liking the idea of hanging off the side of the buttress she decided to climb over. It was the hardest rock work she had undertaken, but an easy half-hour rock climb took them to the summit and the superb view. Later she wrote: 'Other peaks were ahead of me of greater name and fame, but I wondered if any of them would inspire me with the utter happiness, satisfaction and peace of this unknown peak, climbed on the spur of the moment and conquered only by strenuous effort.'[11]

On 23 November, now sure she was fit and ready, Freda and Peter decided to go to the head of the Hooker Glacier and inspect the state of snow and ice on the summit of Mount Cook. Freda invited a young Christchurch man who had been out with them on Mount Mabel a week or so earlier, and a Christchurch woman, a botanical artist, Mary Murray Aynsley, to join them. Guide Murphy, still working on the new Hooker Hut, put together temporary bunks for the women, then they all sat outside, having a party, eating and talking until the sun went down and it became too cold.

At 4.30 a.m. the next day, she and Peter left the others, and five and a half hours later they had a clear view of Mount Cook. Peter's opinion was that another week of hot weather should free the top rocks of ice then everything would be ready. Freda was slowly learning patience, which was needed as there were three wet cold days to follow. However, on 28 November, a wire arrived at the Hermitage from Alex to say he was leaving the next day and would reach the Hooker Hut on the evening of the 30th.

Freda, restless and determined to remain in her highly trained condition, pushed for action so, despite a hot day, she and Peter went out to Mount Wakefield, although they seemed to spend more time admiring the spectacular moraine ice in the Hooker River and observing recently released chamois than climbing. Finally, on the evening of 30 November, Freda and Mary Murray Aynsley set off for the Hooker Hut, leaving Peter to follow with the packhorse.

Mary Murray Aynsley was one of seven children of an influential Canterbury man, Hugh Murray Aynsley, a sheep station owner, director of the New Zealand Shipping Company and a member of the Provincial Council for Lyttelton, so there was enough money for her to do pretty much as she pleased: which was to paint, particularly, flowers and plants. Her interests had fostered a friendship with Peter Graham: he admired her skills, her knowledge and her quiet classiness. In his autobiography, he went into detail about his activities with her: 'She painted alpine flowers and berries most beautifully. I was greatly attracted to her work and would bring her back from my trips different species of flowers to paint … In the evenings … I would join Miss Murray Aynsley with my book and we would endeavour to work out the names of the flowers she had painted.'[12] Despite the Du Faur family interests in art and native flora, it would be some time before Freda could comprehend how Mary could go so close to the mountains, enjoy the outdoor life, walk for miles, yet never climb with great enthusiasm. Their friendship never seemed to advance beyond a general acquaintance and Freda never commented on the other woman's personality or her work, despite the considerable time they spent in each other's company.

When Peter, then Alex, finally arrived they discussed plans with what Freda described as 'rabid enthusiasm' that is 'boring and unintelligible to the outsider',[13] who may have been Mary. But it was an exciting evening as everything felt organised. She not only had guides she trusted, but two of them for a change. She would rhapsodise that 'No woman ever had two more kind, considerate and trusty companions'[14] and she felt everything they did for her was done 'in a spirit of pureminded chivalry, that would not have shamed a member of King Arthur's "table round"'. Nor would they have 'shamed' Tennyson, her grandfather Woolley, nor her mother. But even the guides took a distant second to Freda's real objective as they lay outside the hut, long into the chilly evening, and watched 'the after-glow creep up peak after peak, till it lit the topmost crest of Mount Cook with one triumphant wave of scarlet, which overflowing, spilled down its flanks in runnels of fire, lingering longest in some rocky cavern, where it glowed orange, crimson and red, till the very heart of the mountain seemed aglow.'[15] But the beautiful night preceded bad weather from the west which shook the raw, as yet untested, timbers of the hut. By daylight two things were clear: they would not be blown clean over the moraine and there would not be an attempt that day as the westerly was not going away.

On the following morning, 2 December, all was clear as at 5.15 a.m. Freda and the Grahams, laden with 50 pound swags containing all the comforts they believed their client required, set off. Too much the gallants, they could not change their ways, even when Freda pleaded with them to leave the luxuries behind. Before the snow and ice could melt they were clear of the Hooker Glacier and easily reached the bivouac site by 11.00 a.m., where the brothers set up tents and later left to kick steps. This time they passed the schrund that had defeated Freda and Peter the season before and found a clear run, up a thousand feet of snow couloir, which would save time and energy the next day.

When the sun went down, a low mist lifted, but it was still extremely cold. Freda, alone in her tent, felt such 'icy aloofness' was ridiculous and that not to share a tent with honourable men was an even more ridiculous convention than the ones she had already broken. So, without interference from prying conventional eyes, she suggested the brothers join her. All three curled down in her tent and went to sleep surrounded by the comforts they'd brought up for her.

Freda woke, just after midnight, to that smell of the meths spirit stove and food. Two hours later, roped together they left their tiny camp. Peter was in the lead, carrying a lantern, while Alex trudged at the rear, carrying another. They were a strange sight: three people in the middle of nowhere, in swinging shadows broken by the abstract angles of hard snow, the only sounds, the crunch of boots and the dry rasp of breath cutting the air.

Halfway up the couloir, there was enough light for the lanterns to be snuffed and by the time they reached the top, at 4.00 a.m., it was dawn. Their chosen path, up the western buttress directly below the peak, was all shadow and freezing so here was no time to linger and admire views; the only warmth would come from their exertions. On they went.

Freda and her two guides, Peter and Alex Graham, succeeded in climbing Mount Cook in the record time of six hours up, two hours there, and six and a half hours down. On 3 December 1910, Freda's climb was the seventh ascent and the first by a woman. She had found her strengths, found her path, found the joy of being, momentarily, at one with the universe, at one in companionship and was finally famous, more famous than her father had ever been.

In New Zealand, to her surprise, she was feted. Telegrams and congratulations in every shape and form 'came in from all over the country' from 'members of the Government and the Admiral of the Fleet to unknown and unheard-of admirers in out-of-the-way towns'.[16] But Freda had not lived in her father's household, where organising journalists and photographers and writing letters to the press were everyday events, without having learned to publicise herself. Well aware that 'the average person's idea of a woman capable of real mountaineering or any sport demanding physical fitness … is a masculine-looking female with short hair, a large voice and large feet', and as someone delighting in 'personal daintiness', she went straight to her room and changed her clothes, before confronting all the well-wishers waiting for her. The impact was perfect. She paraded around the lawns of the Hermitage, a charming and civilised contrast to the backdrop of Mount Cook ,and made wonderful copy. The journalist Douglas Cresswell wrote about her in his book *Canterbury Tales:* 'Skirts were to the ground and she wore one of pink billowy tulle. She looked fragile and small enough to put in your pocket.'[17] The Graham brothers' 'smiles grew broader ... proud trainers of a prize pupil'.[18]

In such circumstances even her past failures could be lightly dismissed. When questioned about her inability to finish her nurse's training, she was reported to have 'smilingly' said, 'There's a world of difference between holding a delirious patient down and conquering a crevasse, isn't there?'[19] Everyone wanted to photograph her. Two photos taken by the mountaineer and photographer George Mannering have become classics. One is the well-known posed photo of Freda looking towards those distant mountain tops. She is wearing the notorious cut-off skirt, the cheeky puttees and a demure lace blouse with a cameo at the high-necked collar. Her face and body are lean and eager, her hair loosely tied back. In the other photo, taken at the same time, Alex and Peter Graham stand on either side, holding their ice axes. They all look directly into the camera.

Articles about her appeared in every newspaper. The Attorney-General of New Zealand, Dr Findlay, was quoted as admiring not only the attractions of the Hermitage area, the ease of getting there now the journey had been reduced to twelve hours with the advent of the motor car, but also the appeal of the area to Australians and in particular to Freda Du Faur. He did not mention he was a good friend of one of Freda's supporters, Professor Spencer.

It was somewhat different in Australia. Perhaps if Freda had gone straight back she might have made more of a splash in her own country although *The Sydney Morning Herald* was not particularly adept at reporting news in depth anyway. Most news, apart from local calamities and parliamentary matters, was supplied directly from Britain and the United States. Freda's achievement was listed in the 'Personal Column' on 6 December 1910, between a note about the outgoing Mayor of Camden who had been presented with a bag of sovereigns and a Mr Lynne who was about to join the parliamentary reporting staff. It stated: 'According to a telegram received in Sydney yesterday, Miss Du Faur of Turramurra has succeeded in climbing Mt Cook in the Southern Alps of New Zealand. She is the first woman to reach the summit.' A telegram was also received by Muriel. She immediately wrote an article praising Freda for the *Dupain Quarterly*.

But not all was good publicity. In her enthusiasm, Freda, out of love of mountaineering, occasionally went too far in her pronouncements and could be unjust. She may have meant well but few women would find the following comment endearing: 'The time has passed when the majority of women could, even if they would, lead the life of an animated jelly fish.'[20]

Never one to find a good balance, Freda was also over-modest when she described herself as a 'nine-day-wonder'. She was at least a five-year wonder and of great interest and inspiration to climbers, particularly women, then and to this day. Soon after Freda's ascent the young New Zealander Ada Julius made a strong attempt on Cook and made the first ascent (by a woman) of Elie de Beaumont. On 12 April 1912, Annie Lindon became the second woman to climb Mount Cook. Later, on 13 December 1915, Muriel Graham, Peter's wife, after a narrow escape from an avalanche on the Linda Glacier, became the first New Zealand woman to climb Mount Cook.

Freda, with her guides, would be the first ever to complete the

Grand Traverse, which requires crossing the three peaks that make up Mount Cook, and was subsequently delighted when in 1916 Mrs Jane Thomson guided by Conrad Kain completed the climb. These two were also criticised as Freda and Peter had been, not because of the moral risk, but of the physical risk in not taking a second guide. There were women on three of the next six successful Grand Traverses of Mount Cook.

It may have been an accident that Freda became a champion of women's rights, but in hindsight she felt great pride when she wrote:

> Five years after my first fight for individual freedom, the girl climber at the Hermitage need expect nothing more than raised eyebrows when she starts out unchaperoned and clad in climbing costume. It is some consolation to have achieved as much as this, and to have blazed one more little path through ignorance and convention, and added one tiny spark to the ever-growing beacon lighted by the women of this generation ...[21]

Muriel couldn't have written it better if she had written the paragraph herself.

Freda still had a lot to learn about tolerance and generosity of spirit but she was still young and much of her insensitiviy came out of her love of mountaineering. Everything that had occurred in her life had been preparing her to become a climber and anything else was a side-show compared to this real event.

10 STEPPING STONES

'So try man's foot, if it will creep or climb,
Mid obstacles in seeming, points that prove
advantage, for who vaults from low to high
Makes of the stumbling-block a stepping stone.'

Robert Browning

Getting away from the Hermitage was the only way to find space to savour and come to terms with everything that had happened. Consequently, after five days of fame, Freda with Alex as her guide, headed out to Ball Hut. With them went her Australian friends, guided by Peter. Finding the hut was also crowded, full of snuffling and snoring sleepers, the smells of bodies, feet and damp clothing, Freda enthusiastically volunteered to sleep outside in the 'dog box', a low tent not unlike a stretcher with a hood. However, instead of enjoying a peaceful night, she had to lie worrying that one of the untethered packhorses roaming about might put a large hoof through her head. It would have been an ignominious end to a glorious beginning and good reason to be first up the next morning.

That day, on 9 December, she and Alex and Peter with his group left to go up the Tasman Glacier. Freda was enormously happy and recorded the trip in rapturous detail: the ice forms; the sounds of trickling water and cracking ice; the cliffs and valleys, satin,crystal, translucent, dazzling blue-green and white. The sun came out once they reached the hummocky ice, melting the snow and opening chasms, so it became a struggle up the last steep 300 foot path to Malte Brun Hut. Once rested they took in the superb vista, then made for the couloir at the back of the hut, where giant buttercups with 'shining painted faces' were growing through the snow. Freda did sweeping glissades with her friends to end at times 'head over heels ... like a snow covered hedgehog, amidst a chorus of friendly chaff and laughter'.[1] Being laughed at! Success had given her the confidence to admit to seeing herself as a small, vulnerable animal, and a prickly one at that.

When Peter led his band away the next morning, Alex and Freda were alone. It would have been strange for her to be on her own with a different guide – especially as Alex was so gentle and quiet that his expectations would have been harder to anticipate. Freda would have been apprehensive that she might not measure up or, without Peter as a buffer, they wouldn't get on, but when the grey day turned into a snowstorm, the enforced stay gave them time to get comfortable with each other.

The next day, in settled weather, they set off for the 'snow-and-rock cone' of Mount De la Beche, via the saddle between it and the Minarets to the north. When they got through broken ice, they assumed it would be 'a romp' to the summit, but icy slopes necessitated intensive step cutting. All was fine until, on the sharp steep curve of the final arête, Alex doubled over with cramp.[2] Freda was entirely responsible for his safety yet could do nothing to help, other than wait for the cramp to ease.

Freda wanted to turn back, fearing another attack in an even more difficult situation, but Alex insisted they should continue. Fortunately there were no more problems and, on the descent, Freda finally took the lead. It was momentous. At times all she desired was the security of being in the middle of a party of three, especially 'crawling over doubtful bridges' but, by the time they reached the hut, she felt she had done well. She was immensely proud at leading, and doing it well, and from that time on her self-confidence in her ability and her judgment grew.

Freda and Alex could climb as partners from then on, with one partner being more experienced and one able to pay the bills. She made the transition to leading more quickly with Alex as he was, generally, an egalitarian man, less precious about defending his status than his older brother, and did not expect Freda to live up to any particular expectations other than her own. He allowed her her opinions and did not just give lip service to them. She would find that Alex's quietness was not reproof, that there was freedom in his uncritical manner.

Peter was her hero; she was careful not to appear a fool in front of him, but with Alex she was able to be more open emotionally. Various mountaineers, from a later period of Alex's life, reported that the guide did not like Freda. This is not possible. He would not have admired her feistier moments and her aggressive stances, but he had too much integrity, and there was too much for him to do elsewhere, for him to bother to climb with someone he disliked. Later Freda talked of Alex going to Canada as her guide. She was always aware how people felt about her and would have had no desire to take him with her on sufferance.

The night after De la Beche, they decided Mount Tasman was a possibility. This was ambitious as, at 11,475 feet, it is the second highest mountain in New Zealand and reputed to be a more difficult climb than Cook. No one had attempted it since the 1895 ascent by the Englishman Edward FitzGerald, his Swiss guide Zurbriggen and Jack Clarke. Wisely, unwilling to try the climb without a third, and particularly without Peter, Freda and Alex went down to Ball Hut to send a message to the Hermitage but the weather changed and it was they who joined Peter and the tourists.

Wth time on her hands, she was easily persuaded by a photographer from the Government Tourist Department to take part in, what she described as, a 'cinematograph drama' in which she played the 'heroine' by playing herself. In a series of photos, she balanced carefully between sending herself up and her real pride in being regarded in such a light. There she was 'plucking' lilies or exiting from a tent in climbing costume, or climbing 'in a manner to thrill an excitement-loving public'.[3] The bad weather provided another useful benefit. By the following Wednesday afternoon most of the tourists had departed, leaving Peter suddenly free to attempt Mount Tasman with them.

The first part of the planned route would take them up the Haast Ridge, north-east of Mount Cook and south-east of Tasman, so they set off on 16 December, for the Haast bivouac. After a climb beneath the Hochstetter ice fall, a 'wonderful hanging glacier, 3,000 feet of jagged white pinnacle, riven with crevasses and caverns of vivid colour', they climbed up the right-hand side on moraine, then another 3,000 feet up a rock ridge to their destination. The bivouac was a tiny rocky ledge, barely big enough to pitch a tent on, with a two-foot shelter from the north and an overhanging rock protecting it from falling stones.[4]

After setting up, the men as usual went out to reconnoitre and kick steps. By six o'clock they were back, ebullient over the possibilities for the next day (a Tasman climb would be a coup for them as well) and by the time an orange moon rose, exaggerated by a thin mist, they were in sleeping bags, again sharing the same tent, with the expectation of a 12.30 a.m. rise.

Freda rose to the chill routine of breakfast, 'a weird sequence of food made bearable only by the hot tea', and the 'deadly struggle into frozen boots and the endless winding of putties'.[5] By 1.30 a.m., they were following the path of the now golden moon on their route, which would take them to the ridge above. During the hour to the top of Glacier Dome, the slope grew steeper and steeper but eventually, from the ridge, they could see, stretching below and ahead, a pale sweep of shadow and gold-tinged mist, the Grand Plateau.

As they moved down into the plateau, the moon dropped away behind Mount Haast. In poor light, staved off by weak candles, they made a near blind descent into cloud and snow. In this eerie and isolated space they plodded while all around them 'loomed vague shadow-mountains, whose great height but increased the awesome depths that fell away to nothingness'.[6] Only the snow that crunched underfoot and their own steady hard breathing broke the silence, as they followed the steps, tramped in during the previous day, down into the Grand Plateau and across to the Silberhorn.

At the base of that mountain the three climbers rested as the sun rose and lit the mountains, one by one, with rims of gold and scarlet, until the entire sky was a 'pea-green'. A peculiarity of the southern skies, it was theoretically a harbinger of bad weather, but the green gradually merged into the deep blue of a summer's day which provided them with a clear view of Mount Cook and a very tempting north-east face.

Ignoring the possibility of trying another route up Cook, they pushed on up the Silberhorn, which required step cutting in ice and the crossing of two nasty schrunds before they reached the top at 7.15 a.m. From there they intended crossing a sharp connecting arête to Mount Tasman which, from the Tasman Glacier, had seemed a softly inviting slope. At closer quarters though, it reared, 'a knife-like edge for a 1000 feet' at an 'appalling angle'[7] with patches of ice and sheer drops to the Linda Glacier south of them and north to a great schrund, itself a problem as it stretched around the south-eastern face of Tasman, across the path they were to take.

As well, the ice-covered ridge they had to reach to get to the summit looked just as appalling. And if the ascent seemed bad enough, contemplating the descent was even more unnerving. Freda was not alone: to Peter Graham Tasman looked bad, to his brother it was as 'bad as can be'. Faced with these conditions they decided to at least cross the linking saddle between the two mountains until they reached the schrund and could assess the situation again. Once there, they managed to climb down and cross to the other side but were then faced with cutting steps up a twenty- foot perpendicular wall of, what turned out to be, solid ice.

Peter refused to give up. Again he began the slow process of step cutting. For an hour and a half he worked while, beneath him, Alex and Freda waited, bruised and cut by sharp ice sprayed by the ice axe, and slowly freezing from inactivity and the deteriorating weather. Cloud came down, icy 'wind moaned eerily past'; they had progressed only two hundred feet with four hundred to go. Fog suddenly blanketed everything, the wind became a gale. It was madness to go on; the summit could be reached but the return would be unlikely.

In great disappointment they edged down the arête. At times, wind blew snow into the painstakingly cut steps, the ice became too hard for the point of an ice-axe, and the wet rope froze into an unyielding, near-useless lump. In a later newspaper interview, Freda stated that she had nerves of steel and would give up climbing if she didn't, but she had forgotten the strain of climbs such as this.[8]

She was so aware of her comparative lack of skills and intensely aware of the drop beneath her, and that any false move could cost everyone their lives. But the men trusted her, gave her occasionally 'a quiet word of advice', although there was 'a worried line' between Peter's eyes. At one place Freda couldn't face looking down so let herself down backwards straddling the ridge while Alex waited below 'his face a mixture of horror and amusement'.[9]

So difficult was the descent that it took them longer than climbing up, even without all the step cutting. They did check another route on the north-east face but the summit was covered; it was windy and icy, so they gave up and crossed back to the Silberhorn. There they immediately realised they should have taken a photo of the arête when they had the chance so they could analyse it later.

The descent of the Silberhorn was just as difficult, especially where steps had melted and there was rotten ice. By then very weary, they had to plod through now soft snow in the Grand Plateau to reach bivouac at 5.30 p.m.

The next morning, in light rain, with the barometer dropping further, they hurried down to Ball Hut. Light snow filled the treacherous couloirs and made the going easier and with this ease came philosophical spirits and a chance to rekindle their optimism. It was the weather that had defeated them, not their incompetence. It was only halfway through January, Freda still had a few more weeks to take Tasman before the season was out. Two years later she wrote, in an article for the *Otago Daily Times*, that she believed it was the thought of the descent that really turned them back: 'coming down from one slippery step to the another with no help from one's axe ... with slender support from the rope ... a slip from such a ridge meant probable death for all'.[10]

Eventually they came to regard the Tasman climb as 'a more interesting and finer piece of work' than Mount Cook. It did her reputation no harm with other climbers and satisfied most of her critics that her climb of Mount Cook was not a fluke. Privately, however, she considered that despite the experience it gave her, to achieve what she wanted to she needed to feel as confident on ice as she was on rock. Being able to admit this to herself meant she was developing the analytical clarity of someone confident and experienced in their chosen profession.

Although in a 'cheerful state' over her achievements, Freda did not make the most of Alex's presence, nor find another guide for the ten days before Muriel's arrival. Despite her avowed satisfaction, it was still surprising that she didn't do more intensive climbing, as she intended to cut back when her friend arrived. Instead, Freda decided to cross the Graham Saddle to the west coast for Christmas. It was the lure of the brothers, their mother, and the family. It could also be that the failure on Tasman, despite her cheerfulness and later rationalisations, made her uncertain: there was always part of her character that wanted to run and hide from difficulties and fail-ure, a part that she had to battle with as much as any difficult schrund or cliff face.

On Wednesday, 21 December with Mary Murray Aynsley, Hugh Chambers, who had recently arrived from Hawkes Bay, and the Grahams, Freda set off first to Ball Hut and on the next day to Malte Brun Hut. Expecting a fairly demanding day, they left at 2.00 a.m. for the pass as it was anticipated to be a trip of fifteen to twen-ty hours but, by dawn, a raging blizzard ahead made it impossible to go on. No doubt mindful of Dr Teichelmann's and Mr Lindon's experiences, and with prudent guides, they turned back to Malte Brun Hut where they were joined at first by a Mr McDonald and his guide, George Bannister, and later by Jack Clarke, Ada Julius and the keen Canterbury climbers George, Jim and Barbara Dennistoun.

In theory, with the hut almost full, the newcomers shouldn't have expected accommodation but, with snow falling heavily, it was impossible to turn them away. An uncomfortable couple of nights followed: there was not enough space or blankets; the roof and walls leaked as the snow piled up against the hut; wind blasted the corrugated iron and the timbers doors creaked. To talk over such a din was almost impossible. On Christmas Day, when they should have been in the comfortable family surroundings of the Franz Josef Hotel, they were still snowbound. Their only Christmas present arrived, late that afternoon, when the storm abated and they managed to escape outside and get rid of the oppression of living in such cramped quarters by lobbing snowballs and taking photographs.

Freda missed, what would turn out to be, her one chance to cross the Graham Saddle and to explore the extraordinary Franz Josef Glacier, as it was too late to get to the west coast and back in time to meet Muriel. Instead she returned with Hugh Chambers, who was meeting his cousin, Hugh McLean, back at the Hermitage. Once there the pair, deciding mountaineering experience could be equated with guiding skills, took on the new arrival. On the way to Malte Brun Hut, the inexperienced McLean did not complain about the odd routes as they searched for landmarks and the excessive enthusiasm of his guides, although he 'mournfully' requested rests.

The next day was spent learning to ski and the day after, on 30 December, with Guide Murphy, Freda and Chambers climbed the nearby Mount Green, a peak of 9,325 feet, which had only been climbed once before. Freda, although finding it strange not to be climbing with at least one Graham, found a growing ease on ice. The rope, which had once been awkward, she now handled easily and without thought. She found also that she could be supportive of less experienced climbers. And from the peak there was a great view over Westland. A hot descent followed, as the sun was radiating off the ice slopes, then a 'joyous whiz' on skis to the hut. The next day she was back in time to meet Muriel, who arrived in the evening.

On New Year's Day, despite terrible weather, Freda was eager to show Muriel everything she adored in her world; so she cadged a lunch from the kitchen, and dressed in oilskins, they set out. Most of the time was spent under an overhanging rock up the flat Hooker Valley. It was pointless to do otherwise as there was little to see. It was privacy they were really after, a quiet time, to savour the good times as Freda so liked to do after her successful climbs, and to share every moment with Muriel whom she absolutely adored, and who had been so instrumental in training her. Freda wrote of her friend, that 'Her sympathetic understanding was all I expected it to be, and I felt infinitely the richer by a thoroughly sympathetic companion, the first in all my seasons in the mountains.'[11] It is clear that Muriel was favoured over all the men, Peter and Alex, Otto Frind and Hugh Chambers.

Eventually a clear day arrived on the 3rd. As it was a good initial foray for Muriel, they climbed the steep rocky path up Mount Sebastopol. Freda was now checking on Muriel: was she enjoying climbing and did she love the mountains as Freda did? She was even concerned that Muriel wasn't handling things physically because mountaineering had very different requirements to a gymnasium. The next day Freda and Hugh Chambers took Muriel and some tourists up the Sealy Range where Freda could teach Muriel some of her skills, especially the thrill of glissades. They boiled the billy at a small tarn from where there was a superb view of Sefton and Cook and when the others returned to the Hermitage for dinner, the two women remained behind and lay on the grass where they 'drank in all the beauty of the ever-changing sky as the stars finally came out and the universe was ours'.[12] It was an idyll, although they would discover the next day that at some point Muriel had damaged her knee, so they had to take it easy. Freda seemed to be peculiarly suited to climbing and never reported physical damage unless it was caused by something external, like a rock hitting her.

Freda had intended spending the last week or so showing Muriel about and not climbing at all but, under pressure from Hugh Chambers and from Muriel, who didn't require sacrifices to prove loyalty, she gratefully succumbed. On 10 January, with Murphy as guide, Freda, Muriel and Hugh left for the Ball Hut the next morning. Once they reached the hummocky ice of the Tasman Glacier, Muriel went on up to Malte Brun Hut with other tourists, while Freda, Chambers and Murphy made for the grass slopes at the foot of Mount Chudleigh, which was essentially two peaks connected by a small ridge. It had never been climbed and promised good rock work, something in short supply in a season of frequent snow storms.

Freda's role as coddled client was coming to an end and all were carrying swags, difficult in areas of deep crevasses with sharp ridges and drops which they had to cross before toiling up the slippery slopes to bivouac at 5,700 feet. While the men put up the tent, Freda wandered off to follow a nearby stream which eventually became a deep icy pool where she stripped off and dived in, a fairly extravagant thing to do and not to be compared to the hot pools over the Copland or at Waiho. Such impetuosity was part of her growing feeling of invincibility, that everything was controllable and bearable. The shock of the freezing water only served to make her feel more alive and in touch with herself.

But the next day was miserable. Freda felt dull and heavy, her shoulders hurt from the pack and it is possible she was ill. A long zigzag grind up snow and scree was followed by precipitous ice along an arête of rotten and dangerous rocks. Then, even what had appeared to be good rocks at the summit turned out to be rotten as well. Hugh Chambers grew increasingly uneasy and, according to Freda, picked on her, fearing she would be careless or kick rock down on him. Freda was outraged; the Grahams thought her as 'clean a climber on bad rock as they had ever taken out'.[13] Guide Murphy sympathised with her but was not in a position to caution the other climber. The bickering did not stop, even on reaching, what they hoped, was the summit. Freezing winds deterred them from crossing to the other peak, so they returned the way they had come. Good glissades on descent assisted in wiping out any tension

155

and they began to enjoy themselves until, on the lower slopes on their return to Malte Brun Hut, Freda was almost swept away by tons of boulders that hurtled down near them.

Muriel had also encountered disappointment. Well on the way up Hochstetter Dome, the other tourists either weren't able to go or were unwilling to wait while the guide took her to the summit and she had to turn back. Freda was rather elated by this disappointment as it appeared to her that Muriel had 'every sign of her catching the mountaineering fever badly'.

That night, they shared the three-foot-wide top bunk in the overcrowded hut, an event Freda described as an 'exciting experiment but hardly restful'. The 'hardly restful' was understandable, in a three-foot bunk, but exciting? It was ingenuous rather than a brazen comment. Confessing to lesbian tendencies in a book would not have endeared her to anyone in the climbing world, even if she had been aware of them herself. This comment has never been interpreted in such a context. Freda was then still just another breathless heroine with a 'best chum'.

By the time they returned to 'a taste of civilisation' at the Hermitage the old piano had been put back out of the way in its usual position but the place was still overcrowded. So on their last night, 16 January, looking for privacy and wanting to make the most of the glorious surroundings, Freda and Muriel camped out by the lake on the Sealy Range. It was full moon, the skies were dark beyond the mountains and the snow on them was crisply delineated, but it was warm enough to lie outside. If the inhabitants of the Hermitage were not curious about why two young women should seek privacy local keas, those rough sabre-beaked New Zealand parrots, certainly were. Here was entertainment, food and toys all laid out for them. Freda was initially impressed when one bird in particular would 'gravely sit down opposite us and stare steadily for a few minutes with his head on one side and an air of incredible wisdom. Then he would advance with ridiculous side-long hops and make a dig at the nails in our boots, he would hop onto us, if we lay still and pluck at anything with his strong sharp beak.' But he also made sleeping outside impossible so the women had to take turns on watch, ridiculous only to anyone not familiar with the inquisitive and destructive nature of the birds. Finally it was the humans who were 'routed' into their tent and 'reluctantly tied over the flaps shutting out fresh air, moonlight and their tor-mentors'.[14]

The next morning, with no sign of the feathered voyeurs, Freda took the billy to the lake to get water. There an unusual shape in the water caught her eye: her good 3a Kodak, which weighed some-thing over three pounds. The top of the thick leather case was gnawed through and the camera half pulled out, leaving the metal underneath exposed. The film was soaked. At the Hermitage she was assured that the camera would be repairable, but in time Freda would wish those keas had demolished her camera completely.

For a two-month trip, Freda had climbed surprisingly little. Despite some good expeditions she had, in effect, spent a month at the Hermitage waiting for Mount Cook to be clear enough to climb and had not seriously considered what else she might attempt. Heavy snow and Muriel's presence, although delightful, had also been a deterrent. But the trip had cemented two things: her ability as a climber now that she was confident on ice and was capable with the rope and of leading; and her trust in Muriel whose 'love and sympathy' would never fail her.[15]

11 A Delicate Balance

'What have we come to conquer? Only ourselves.'

George Mallory

Mollified by Muriel's company, Freda spent most of 1911 at Flowton keeping as fit as possible, but she also used the time to analyse the season. Clearly money and time had not been efficiently utilised; she had to be more organised.

As Bertie and Wynifred were coming from Mount Morgan and climbing conditions were better later in the season than earlier, Freda booked to go to New Zealand after Christmas. She may well have wished she'd gone before 25 December as her relationship with her brother had not improved. His work in the mines and his habit of disappearing into the outback on surveys had widened the distance between them. As well, Bertie had given her too hard a time in the past for her to forgive him easily and, unlike Guy, he was never aware of the need to create a new, adult relationship with his only sister.

Wynifred was different; she and Freda had a lot in common, were of a similar age, outgoing, outspoken and interested in events in the world and in particular women's rights and roles. Wynifred had lived in a mining town for most of her life and was used to a

158

certain amount of freedom of opinion usually restricted by middle-class life in the city. She was well educated, something insisted on by her physician father, she was blunt and proudly liked to say that she had 'no desire to sit around drawing room tables, eating cakes and talking about the price of eggs'.[1] Wynifred preferred to use her well-modulated voice for reading her own poetry and spreading the benefits of elocution and knowledge of the great poets at the classes she took in her home. But she was also used to taciturn men, absent men, too busy to interfere in her daily life. It gave her control.

As soon as Christmas was over, Bertie and Wynifred left but, on the night before Freda's boat sailed, Eccleston had, what Freda described as, a serious accident. As it was at night, it probably occurred in the house and was some kind of fall, perhaps resulting in a severe break, common to people his age. At that time of the year, with so many people away, it was almost impossible to find someone to nurse him so Freda, with her few months' nursing experience, was the obvious solution. It was difficult enough for Freda to nurse a stranger sixteen hours a day but now she was completely at the mercy of Eccleston's demands, although no doubt he felt he was at hers. Father and daughter gave each other a miserable time. She discreetly and passionately described the situation later. 'I have nursed friends and relations and I know nothing in mountaineering so trying as being solely responsible for a delirious patient whose very life may depend on your ability to persuade him to do the thing he does not wish to do.'[2]

Eventually, once Eccleston was convalescing, getting away from that house of sickness and its demands became for Freda a matter of survival. Freda had become so low-spirited with her frustrating role as nurse that Muriel's attempts to get her to look after herself went completely unheeded: she was on the edge of another nervous breakdown. When a private nurse was finally obtained, the doctor ordered a holiday. Freda recalled that there were 'strict instructions to leave serious climbing alone until I was thoroughly fit once more'.[3] This loss of fitness happened in one month.

In the second week of February, much later in the season than was customary, Freda arrived at the Hermitage, clearly severely depressed and unconfident, and spent her time convincing everyone she was not 'in the pink of condition', from which she seemed to gain a warped sense of importance. She had not the slightest desire to climb. Instead of taking up 'very tempting propositions' to join climbers of the calibre of Hugh Chambers and his private guide, she went on a leisurely trip to Malte Brun Hut led by Peter Graham, with tourists not climbers. Freda found, with a certain pride, that even that five-hour trip was very hard going and a number of times she '[I] would cheerfully have cast myself down on the glacier and said I was incapable of further exertion.'[4] Giving up was not really an option, for Freda had arrived at the mountains with the intention of climbing but she had to somehow break out of her terrible sloth. So contrary was she, that she of the poker face was happier when her companions knew she wasn't 'merely adapting her pace to them' but was struggling. She said that she was satisfied only when Peter 'was able to grasp, after observing me for a few hours that I certainly was not in mountaineering form, so I knew I would not be bothered with suggestions from him until I was more fit to attend to them'.[5] The guide must have known Freda had been ill after nursing but he had never actually seen her in such a state. A radical change is often incomprehensible to fit outdoor stable people but he was used to 'difficult' females in his work; and as he had faith in her, he probably felt that if he were patient, it would just pass.

But a week of mountain air at Malte Brun Hut, skiing and rest brought a sense of reality back. Nature would always be more comforting than any person. After another week at the Hermitage, with her appetite returning along with her strength and drive, she became aware that some of her trouble was, as she put it, that 'my faith in my climbing prowess was considerabley shaken'.[6] Understanding this, and challenged by less able climbers planning high ascents, when Hugh Chambers and another climber, Frank Wright, guided by Murphy and Clarke set off to attempt Mount Cook, Freda and Peter departed to climb a virgin peak north of the Footstool. Freda was coming back fast but still had to overcome vestiges of self-doubt lurking beneath her now calm exterior.

Once they crossed the ice to the first of three rock buttresses leading to the summit, there was a good warm-up on straight hard rock. Strangely enough, as the climb grew tougher, they did not rope up, on Freda's request. Peter may have thought he'd undermine her if he insisted or he really may have felt she really was better, but it soon proved to be an unwise decision as Freda soon found herself in an immovable position, with 'one passable foothold, one knee against the rocks and both ... hands stuck in snow-filled cracks high above'.[7] Peter's position was not much better. It was a terrible moment for him, unroped as they were, on an exceedingly difficult rock face. He managed to get the rope from his rucksack, using only one hand and his teeth but, by then, the feeling was already going out of Freda's freezing, strained hands. Not really sure one hand would hold her, she removed the other and rubbed it against the serge of her dress, in an attempt to warm it up, then swapped it for the other thinking that, if she was killed, Peter would lose his job, his future and it would be her fault. She had that good reason to hang on, but she was in great agony because of her frozen fingers. Eventually Peter arrived, tied her to him, then held her hands under his coat to warm them until the circulation returned. Finally, reassured she was all right, he edged away up to a safe ledge from where he 'ingloriously hauled' her up beside him. For half an hour they sat recovering: Freda's fingers felt 'as if someone was pulling the nails off with hot pincers'.[8] She did not complain.

On setting off again she found she was much steadier, with a sense of her old boldness. Once again she'd sloughed off dangerous depression with physical daring, although later on a smooth face with no place to wedge the ice axe or secure herself, Peter suddenly warned her 'in a queer quiet voice' to get out of the way. She reacted immediately and with painful fingers clung to the cliff, as a huge boulder he had accidently dislodged, missed her by a couple of feet. From then on they treated rock buttresses with cautious respect until they came out onto a snow arête that took them to the summit.

Cloud stopped them spotting Hugh Chambers and his team on Mount Cook but, for Freda, 'the disappointment of having no view was somewhat alleviated by the joy of achieving such an exciting peak' and the fact the mountain was to take her name. There would always be Du Faur Peak.

The next morning, with no word of the Mount Cook attempt, Freda and Peter tried to climb into the Copland Pass to get another view of the mountain but were forced back to the Hermitage by the weather. That night the Mount Cook climbers returned after a successful climb, although it appeared to Freda that Hugh Chambers was just thankful that the climb was over. It hadn't helped that Wright had suffered, from what Freda called, 'mountain sickness', which had slowed them all down. But she still thought Chambers complained too much when he went on about the route through the Grand Plateau describing it as 'a monotonous grind'.

Freda, feeling very capable herself, wasn't in the least sympathetic. She decided the men hadn't climbed for the love of climbing but just to bag another mountain. She was not the only one to criticise the climb, but she was scathing about it in *The Conquest of Mount Cook* and did not only target Chambers but other New

Zealand men who she considered climbed just for fame and not for sheer enjoyment. The poor New Zealanders barely had time to knock the mud off their work boots before Freda was scolding them, especially those living near the mountains, for not donning hobnails. Such 'want of energy and interest' was 'appalling' but, in reality it was not that, nor their 'lack of imagination or intellect'[9] that prevented New Zealanders from climbing. More often it was a lack of finance. Freda's claim that most of the men who climbed were poor and saved for one short holiday a year was idealistic but not true. Men like Dr Teichelmann, Hugh Chambers and the Dennistouns were not necessarily rich but they were educated and either owned land or had jobs in the public service or were in professions that provided them with reasonable incomes and holidays. The poor or non-scholastic locals like the Graham brothers could rarely climb for the pure pleasure. Guiding was one of the few ways a poor man could spend his life in the mountains. With such comments she played right into the hands of her critics who claimed that she was an arrogant, wealthy young woman who had no conception of what the game was really about.

While waiting for Alex to arrive and Peter to free himself from the tour groups, Freda hired Murphy as her private guide. Hugh Chambers, who obviously hadn't been too offended by her lack of sympathy, asked her to join him and Jack Clarke on a climb. Her opinion of the two men had not changed but she was flattered at being asked, and was keen not to waste her opportunities. To her chagrin, at Hooker Hut, Clarke and Chambers changed their destination without consulting her and selected a virgin peak she and the Grahams had planned to climb. Against her better judgment she did not withdraw but, almost immediately after departure, disagreement arose over the route from the Hooker Glacier to the lower rocks of the mountain. Murphy deferred to the senior guide until fresh arguments erupted over routes and who would lead.

This time Murphy and Freda, as they were on a separate rope from the others, took their own line. They had no trouble but Clarke and Chambers then asked for assistance. Murphy helped them but, in the middle of a difficult traverse, Clarke stopped again. He was having difficulty with his rucksack, which forced them to wait on icy cold, sunless rocks, while he fixed it in a secure position, climbed up, then hauled it up afterwards. Freda pointedly noted later that Murphy managed to deal with the traverse and his rucksack. At that stage, she and Murphy decided to go completely on their own: in the end, too much time had been lost and when they came to an impassable rock tower, there was no time to find another route.

Unlike the others, Freda was cheerful in descent. She felt she had betrayed the Grahams by the attempt, even saying to the others, 'How the Grahams will grin over this failure of ours.'[10] Freda was to be criticised for her attitude to Jack Clarke, who was very much a hero in the area, with some justification as she did realise he was ill that day and may well have been carrying a heavy pack. But even his omission from the index of her book was seen as a deliberate slight of 'an incomparable guide, clever, resourceful and with a wonderful intuition for discovering routes in new country'.[11] She was much kinder towards Clarke when she wrote an article for the *Dupain Quarterly* and described the failed climb as, 'a beautiful day but we unfortunately chose an impossible route up. The choice of a route on a virgin peak is, of course, often a difficult matter.'

What was interesting, apart from the squabbles, was that on the descent, on steep glacial ice, they used crampons that Clarke had 'thoughtfully' brought with him. This was Freda's first attempt with them. They were relatively primitive, at that point, as were techniques, but they would come into common use when publicised by the arrival, in 1927, of two highly experienced men: an Englishman, H.E.L. Porter, and a Swiss, Marcel Kurz, who wanted to 'bag' traverses, particularly Mount Tasman. They managed the traverse with ten-point crampons and no guides. A new era that particularly appealed to the young and poor New Zealanders began: with crampons there could be fast climbs, two-man or two-woman teams and guideless climbs.

Despite their occasional tensions, Freda missed Hugh Chambers when he left as there was no one else of his calibre to climb with. Fortunately, late in February, Peter became free as did a new guide, Charlie Milne. It is unlikely she hired both; probably a climb with the chief guide was a chance for a new guide to gain experience. Bad weather foiled an attempt on The Footstool so the three, accompanied another guide, David (Darby) Thomson, and his group to the top of the Copland Pass.

Darby was a favourite of Peter Graham's. They had been friends in Westland, where he had worked logging in the Hokitika bush, and it was Peter who brought him over as a guide during the 1908–09 season. Darby was always an asset in a team as he was quickwitted, could always see the humorous side of a situation and could cut steps as quickly as his boss.

The clear sunny day afforded Freda and Peter a good view of one of their future destinations, the ultimate, the Grand Traverse of Mount Cook, but there would be no opportunity to attempt it that season as the route was already covered in ice. The traverse of Mount Sefton, a beautiful mountain overhanging the Hermitage with an eastern face of avalanches and curves, was also unlikely so they decided they would leave the traverses for the following season. Instead, they decided on Dampier, a rocky mountain with a sharp snow cone, after which they determined to try Tasman again. It was still an optimistic agenda as so much snow had fallen on the lower slopes.

Freda was feeling marvellous and was confident that there were few situations she couldn't get out of, especially as she'd soon be back climbing with both Grahams. While waiting for Alex to join them, and tired of a week of inaction through wet weather, she and Peter took on their most daring climbs, one which greatly amused those at the Hermitage and particularly Alex. The climb started innocently enough, up the eastern face of Mount Sebastopol. The western side, overlooking the Hermitage, was a pleasant, if steep walk, to the Red Tarn but the opposite flank, for which the mountain was named, was as impregnable as the fortress of Sebastopol which the British Navy had laid siege to during the Crimean War.

The pair got into difficulties almost immediately on smooth rocks devoid of hand or footholds. Peter even took off his boots to get some friction from his woollen socks. Freda only got up with support from a rope. Three times they repeated this manoeuvre only to find themselves caught again with no way up and no way back. They even considered sitting all night and waiting for someone to come up the track, drop a two hundred-foot rope to them and haul them up. It was only the ignominy of this solution that spurred them to try, what Freda described as, an ugly traverse which got them nowhere, again. The area was too steep, it overhung the valley in some places and the only way they could move was by digging in ice axes and inching along.

Finally they finished the 'magnificent climb' of sixteen hundred feet in four hours. Alex, when he arrived that night, shook his head in disbelief and thought it hilarious they had bothered, but it was as hard a climb as they were likely to encounter. They certainly would not have attempted such difficulties on a high climb. Freda always put their safety down to the Graham brothers' ability, but she also realised she was climbing at a highly skilled level. It was a great disappointment to be so sure that she was ready but the peaks she wanted were not.

On 13 March when the weather cleared, Freda and the Grahams tramped up to the Hooker Hut and the next morning set out to attempt the virgin peak that Freda had failed to climb with Chambers, Clarke and Murphy. Freda was sure they would succeed now they were all together, although their path after the Hooker was up the Noeline Glacier, which was cut by huge crevasses up to sixty feet wide. Despite a howling wind, which fortunately was at their backs, after a steep rock climb they reached the summit just after midday. Under such conditions they lingered only long enough for an aneroid reading of 9,850 feet and took photographs.

Freda named this mountain 'Nazomi', a Japanese word for heart's desire. The peak provided a rich view of some of the territory she still wished to cover during the planned traverses – the lowest peak of Mount Cook and Mount Sefton – but a thick bank of yellow cloud across the west coast was a warning to the experienced Grahams. With the wind still strong and chill, they decided to return the way they had come rather than continue on and traverse the peak.

Rain, then snow fell; the season was one of the coldest and snowiest periods anyone could remember. It kept them in the Hermitage until eventually, on 17 March, when the storms had abated, the mountains were white and while Peter was up the Tasman Glacier, Freda, Mary Murray Aynsley and Alex left for the Hooker Hut. Again they were trapped inside by rain and snow. On the 19th, leaving Mary to follow her love of, what Freda called, 'painting and botanizing', Alex and Freda set off to climb a small rock peak, Raureka, south of La Perouse, but there was too much snow and ice so they had to turn back. The season was coming to an end. Daylight hours were shortening and there were rarely two consecutive fine days, yet Freda and the Grahams decided on a last possible attempt on Tasman.

There were plenty of climbers to criticise the decision. Tasman had the reputation as the greatest ice and snow climb in New Zealand and that season there was too much of both. Of course it was extremely cold although, as a concession to having to sleep out at 6,600 feet at the Haast bivouac, they each took a piece of felt to sleep on, as well as a blanket and sleeping bag. Unstated was the decision that the three of them would again share a tent, thus lightening swags and maintaining warmth.

On 22 March they reached the bivouac. At 1.30 the next morning, the cloud was down and snow was drifting over the canvas but by 3.00 a.m. the weather had cleared and an hour and a half later they were on the tediously long slope up to the Grand Plateau – Freda counted 900 steps with still more to go. By the time they were over into the Plateau, the sun had begun to rise, although it wouldn't reach them until they were up the other side where spiral whirlwinds of drift and snow touched by the rising sun curled around them. It was beautiful but freezing and hopeless. During short breaks there was no shelter and snow constantly poured on top of them. The wind grew stronger, too strong, forcing them back to the bivouac. With the knowledge that they faced that long haul again, Freda may have had a little more sympathy for Hugh Chambers' monotonous grind up to Mount Cook.

The next day, armed with foreknowledge and pre-kicked steps, they made better time and by 5.00 a.m. were across the Plateau and reached the top of the Silberhorn at 8.30 a.m., ready for the next leg across the the connecting arête, that thousand feet of treacherous ice ridge to Tasman. This time they could see their destination but the ridge was far more icy and the wind was so strong that, within five minutes, one of Freda's woollen gloves was frozen, her face began to freeze and all feeling went from the side of her nose. She must have been feeling very uncomfortable because she mentioned the problem to Alex. Aware of the danger of frostbite, she refused to give in and latched onto one point of hope, a tiny spot of sun, in shelter, east below the ridge. In that one warm patch, the men dug out a hollow to hold them on the steep slope, then rubbed warmth back into her fingers while they revised tactics. The arête above them was obviously far too exposed to be on continuously so the only alternative was to traverse along the east face with the intention of regaining the ridge near the summit.

Ironically, out of the wind, the going was too hot, the glare blinding, but they found brief respite in an exquisite cave created under the lower lip of the schrund. Freda described the cave as 'about 50 feet long by 20 feet broad, with gleaming icicles hanging from the roof and rounded pillars like marble columns. Stray gleams of sunshine lit the ice to rainbow colours while the deep blue of the shadowed depths made a wonderful contrast to the silvery-white stalactites and columns.'[12]

The schrund had been useful but they still had to get through. As they couldn't find an ice bridge over, they had to settle on climbing up at the shortest point, about eight feet. Peter stood on Alex's shoulders, then Freda handed him two axes which he drove into the snow above the lip; he then pulled himself up. Freda followed, and with the assistance of the rope, half sprang up. But their elation at having got that far was short-lived. The slope above grew steeper and steeper, steps had to be cut, as large as 'soup plates', and even fingerholds had to be created in what was solid ice. One traverse was beneath an overhanging wall and around a steep corner. And once out on the summit ridge they were in the bitter west wind again.

By the time they reached the summit at 1.30 p.m. it had taken them five hours to just climb the last six hundred feet when earlier that day they had climbed four thousand in similar time. Frozen in inadequate clothing and weary, Freda carelessly fell, jarring her arm. It was painful but luckily still mobile. The fierce wind whirled Freda's hat from her head: 'It hovered round for a moment uncertainly then fluttered gracefully off to Pioneer Pass.' Her motoring veil, little more than a piece of gauze, from then on was all she had for protection.[13] They stayed up there only long enough to admire the view and take photos, then began their descent, made easier by the earlier enforced cutting of steps and handholds. Even on the difficult corner, they could jump down the schrund. But it was hard going in the areas sheltered from the westerly where the sun had melted the snow, and again particularly so in the basin of the Grand Plateau where they floundered through waist-deep snow. They reached the bivouac at 7.00 p.m., in sixteen hours, exactly the time of their previous attempt, 'but oh! the difference in our feelings'.

That night Freda, with her 'brothers' on either side, slept huddled in those mountains. It was as she put it 'peace which passeth all understanding which surely is the reward of those who come close to the heart of the mountains'.[14]

Despite the weather, momentum was up. When the New Zealand newspapers, which were following their activities in detail, reported that two other climbers had the unclimbed Mount Dampier in their sights the following season, Peter and Freda could not resist the challenge of taking the third highest mountain in New Zealand first. It did mean that, because of the conditions, the route they preferred up the Hooker was closed because of ice, which would force them to take a more difficult route up the Tasman Glacier, across the Grand Plateau again and up the Linda Glacier. As well the attempt would be without Alex, who was needed back at the Franz Josef Hotel.

Three days of bad weather held them back until, on 29 March, in clear weather which 'set the blood racing and made mere living a matter of delight', and despite a heavy fall of snow, Peter and Freda set off from the Hermitage, with Charlie Milne as third guide. They travelled on horseback as far as Ball Hut, talking mountaineering and the possible climbs 'undefiled by the foot of man, much less by that of a mere woman'. After some time, the path left the tussock plain and followed a stream up into a valley where the track grew rugged and the valley steeper. With the old packhorse ahead and her snow-tanned guides 'swinging along', Freda felt she was in another world, in a scene from the opera *Carmen*; the men were smugglers and she 'longed for some gay Mexican blankets and toreador caps wherewith to drape them'.[15] Such was romance for Freda; it was theatrical and poetic, physical and natural, although not quite accurate with the mix-up over the Spanish *Carmen* and Mexican images.

The next day they progressed to the Haast bivouac and the morning after that, in moonlight, they were on the familiar route through the Grand Plateau. This time, instead of climbing the Silberhorn, they traversed or rather trudged along the base, through powdery deep snow and onto the Linda, a high glacier, immensely unstable. It was still too cold and too early in the day for unsettled slopes to collapse into avalanches, nevertheless Peter quickened their pace. Time was also important as they could rely on only thirteen hours of daylight at that time of the year.

Deep snow became deeper. Silence pervaded as they concentrated on their slow progress across crevasses, frail snow bridges, more broken ice, then steep snow slopes at the head of the glacier. Freda's woollen suit grew clammy and dragged at her body, her limbs felt shaky and her fingers weak; the sheer slog without much sleep the previous night, the alternation of cold then heat, was more debilitating than any straight climbing. Even Peter, who seemed to face anything easily, wrote in his autobiography fifty years later: 'as we climbed up a very slippery pitch, I saw black for a moment and thought that I was going to drop off; this is the only time this has ever happened to me.'[16] He was pushing too hard.

They stopped briefly to fortify themselves with Brand's essence, lime juice and oranges then, before their bodies stiffened up, tackled the steep, jagged ridge ahead. It turned out to be a nightmare of a climb over sharp rocks which cut their hands but, mercifully, any loose stones were still frozen.

A two-hour climb up the one last steep, snow ridge brought them to the sharp, narrow summit. It was Milne's highest climb ever on his second season. Freda found it the most tiring climb she had so far done. After an hour on top, at 1.30, they attempted to follow the ridge to Green's Saddle in the hope it was easier to tackle the snow slope there but the ridge was so jagged and icy they soon changed their minds. Avalanches were coming down the Linda but they made it down safely, and, after a cup a tea to get their energy back, slogged for three more hours through the the Grand Plateau. By 6.30 p.m. the moon had risen, a huge personal lamp that lit their way up the Glacier Dome. They reached the bivouac at 7.30.

Buoyant after one day's rest, they decided to attempt Mount Lendenfeld (10,551 feet). No one else had attempted it since Alex Graham and his friend the Rev. H.E. Newton climbed it in 1907. On 2 April they set out again. It was their fourth day out, four days in which no news had reached the Hermitage. Four days for those going about their daily life to wonder, watch the weather and wait for news, hopefully good news, not bad.

Once again they had to traverse the Grand Plateau, deep with crusty snow, which made the going harder for the heavier guides. Dawn found them in a maze of 'great rocks and pinnacles ... intersected with crevasses' which took them into, what Peter Graham described as, one of the 'most ticklish pieces of ice-work he had encountered'.[17] At one point they found themselves in a crevasse, in which they crossed a snow bridge, then rounded a tight overhanging wall of ice on a very tight rope, too short really for such a manoeuvre.

At the foot of the saddle they were aiming for, between Mount Lendenfeld and Mount Haast, they were confronted by another crevasse which they crossed at a point where the edge dipped sharply down and created a bridge that culminated in a pillar of snow. Then, while Peter was blithely cutting steps to get over the upper lip, there came a sharp crack. He was completely vulnerable, perched high over the crevasse. No one moved but, as soon as he established that the shocking sound wasn't the snow pillar crumbling beneath him, he went back to his work with his usual cheerfulness, hauled himself up to the snow slope to a point where he could anchor himself to get the others up.

Fifty foot higher found them facing another crevasse, the upper face of which was slick ice at a 70 degree angle the traverse of which required half a mile of step cutting, all of which had to be done by the chief guide, as Charlie Milne was not used to such work. Freda realised Peter was under great strain. She offered to turn back but he would do so only if she needed to. It was the kind of quandary they would increasingly find themselves in; getting away with taking more and more risks, positive their skills would always match the challenge but, at the same time, working on each other's weakness: not to lose face. They thrived being out on a limb and trusted each other. So they continued, neither willing to make a decision to stop, always hopeful that they'd reach snow and such painstaking cutting would no longer be necessary. Charlie said nothing.

Freda began cutting handholds to Peter's footholds, but taking as much time about it as he did. Then, to their dismay, when they did reach thick snow they found the ice beneath too hard to cut, so Peter had to stamp down hard on the snow and 'trust to luck' it would hold. If the slope went, there would be nothing to hold any of them. They were lucky and after a tense half-hour reached the saddle between Haast to the north and Lendenfeld to the south.

Freda and Peter had, at one point, planned to climb to Mount Lendenfeld then cross back to Mount Haast, but one look at the rotten, heavily iced rocks of the latter was enough to convince them they were not as invincible as they hoped. Instead, they took the easier seven hundred-foot snow climb to the higher peak of Lendenfeld.

Milne led. Freda clearly liked the guide and congratulated him on his work, but she made the descent sound so easy; as if it was just a merry jaunt over broken ice, down overhanging buttresses, and a stroll through the Grand Plateau. After four days of living in snow and tough, tiring climbing, she was just pleased they were heading home. Even the next day on their way back to the Hermitage the contrast of soft greens, browns and yellows in the valleys actually compared favourably to the 'eternal glitter' above.

On her return to Australia news arrived that, on 12 April, in freezing conditions, Annie Lindon had climbed Mount Cook with Darby Thomson and Peter Graham. Then, despite feeling the cold badly, the older woman had finished her season by climbing Malte Brun. It must have been a strange experience for Freda to have another woman, and another Australian at that, following her up.

But the possibility of a real rival did not concern her as much as it would have earlier, because Freda had begun to make other plans.

12 Vast And Silent Places

> ' … the better, happier and stronger for my days and nights spent
> among them, but a prey to that longing, which all the excitement,
> gaiety and turmoil of city life cannot deaden, for just one glimpse of
> snowclad heights and the peace of the vast silent places'.
>
> Freda Du Faur
> THE CONQUEST OF MOUNT COOK

Freda and Muriel had decided to get away overseas together, as
both knew they could too easily be entangled irrevocably in the
needs of their respective families. Eccleston could well have many
years of life ahead of him, and his nurse, Miss Swain, might not
remain as a permanent member of the household. Guy was consistently more tender with their father than Freda had ever been, but
he might yet marry and not always be on hand.

Muriel was still running the Cadogans but it was her relationship with George Dupain that gave her the most concern. Much as
she liked him and was grateful for the start he had given her, some
of his attitudes were stultifying. She objected to the secondary place
of the female in the Dupain Institute and found the idea that
women's bodies should be saved only for child-bearing was an
insult to her and every woman like her who had no desire to have

children. She was tired too, of doing all the day-to-day work there and not getting real credit. Interesting new ideas were coming into the country from overseas, in particular from Sweden and the Ling Institute, pioneered by Madame Bergman-Osterberg, which fostered women teachers in sport, with a focus on educational and remedial gymnastics. Ling even had a Gymnastic Teachers' Suffrage Society.

Both women were tempted by the adventures mountaineering could provide in Europe and even in the Himalayas, but the first step in any greater plan was to get to England. Freda, in particular, had relatives living there: her father's sisters, Frederica Du Faur, Mary Taylor and Ellen Bryans, and their children. England was the home of the revered Alpine Club and the pivotal point of a strong climbing scene. There was also the opportunity of having a book published in England: at the Hermitage she'd been befriended by the retired English publisher, Mr Stanley Unwin, founder of the prestigious London firm George Allen and Unwin Ltd, who offered to publish a book of her experiences. Heeding his advice that she must strike quickly, Freda had begun to collate her diaries, notes and photographs.

England was also at the forefront in published health magazines and health clubs. As well, both women were following the activities of the British Suffragettes, at the height of their influence and causing great excitement in the newspapers with their militant action. Removed geographically from the scene of this action and politically well read but naïve, they saw the Suffragette actions as the action of heroines. Such times of change in England were not to be missed.

But Freda needed to farewell New Zealand; she needed to 'finish' it off so there was no hankering and regrets. There were still two climbs to 'bag'; the Grand Traverse of Mount Cook, (Peter had already traversed the High Peak) and the traverse of Mount Sefton. In the first week of December 1912, Freda set sail for New Zealand, still suffering from the effects of a bout of influenza. Once again, precious time was needed to get her fit again.

The second problem arose when Alex was unable to come as second guide as there was illness at home. This was a blow to all three as these climbs were to be, or so Freda saw them, the 'crowning-point of their ambitious pupil's career and the triumphant proof that their faith in her powers and years of training had not been wasted'.[1]

Peter and Freda, as usual, warmed up on a number of smaller climbs. The first was an unclimbed peak, south of Nazomi, which she would name Mount Pibrac. Because of the heavy snows of the last season, it was Freda's first big rock climb since Malte Brun. She recalled: '[I] became painfully conscious of my lack of wind and sighed regretfully for the form of 1910 when I could romp gaily up the western ridge of Mount Cook.'[2] Always keen on rock climbing, she realised that at least when guides had to cut steps in snow she was given the opportunity to rest. Freda's fittest year was always 1910 and illness, two years in a row, did not help. She was able to make these more difficult climbs because her skills had increased as had her determination and her patience. But once she gained her second wind on that six and a half hour climb she was fine.

The summit supplied them with a view of the east face of the traverse of Mount Cook, between the second and third peaks. It was not encouraging but Freda was confident and engaged Darby Thomson as the second guide, an asset on any intended climb, especially as Freda was acutely aware of the onus put on Peter when he cut steps on his own on Lendenfeld. Nor would Darby's sense of humour, always timed to relieve a tense situation, go amiss.

On 22 December 1912, Freda and Peter climbed as far as the Raureka Saddle to get another angle on the Cook range. The third and highest peak was still too iced up but Peter envisaged that with warm weather they could make an attempt in a week.

By Christmas the Hermitage was inundated with visitors, including three old friends, un-named male friends (two from Dunedin and one from Timaru) and a Mrs Westmacott and her daughter Erica. The Westmacotts had been in the mountains since the beginning of the season as Erica, an adventurous 22-year-old, was trying to get rid of a chronic cough produced by what they described as 'the gaieties of town life' – primarily a love affair.[3] Erica was less concerned about her health than her mother, for she was very attractive with a beautiful figure and a lively open personality. Freda would later provide Otto Frind with an introduction to the women and commented that, 'I am sure you will find both Mrs and Miss Westmacott very interesting; I think the latter very charming in addition to her great talent.' This talent was their musical ability; both taught music in their home town of Timaru. Mrs Westmacott in particular was a highly trained pianist but Freda believed Erica was brilliant, with a voice 'rivalling Clara Brett'. Freda probably meant Clara Butt, a famous English singer, whose worst critic, Charles Baeyertz, described her performances as 'a concession to the bourgeois'. Despite this opinion, she was immensely popular and, as Freda seemed to have popular tastes in music, she intended her comment as an immense compliment.

Another woman Freda became friendly with was Dorothy Theomin whom she would describe to Otto as 'the little Jewish girl from Dunedin'.[4] Dorothy was a daughter of one of the most wealthy families in the province. Their house, Olveston, remains as it was when Dorothy graced it, because, as the surviving member of the Theomin family, she eventually left it to the city, ensuring her name, which did not endure in the mountains, would do so in her home town. Never a climber of Freda's calibre, Dorothy loved being in the mountains, worked hard to make and keep friends, especially the Graham family, and thrived on the social scene of the Hermitage.

Freda also met a close friend of Mary Murray Aynsley, Eleanor

Joachim, who worked as a journalist on a magazine, *Holiday Roads*. Often unsure of her own intellectual abilities, Freda felt it was a great achievement to write lucidly and excitingly. She admired Eleanor as well for having a paid career and a reason to visit fascinating places. Freda was interested in writing and had been approached by various newspapers in New Zealand, which had successfully published her articles. As well two articles, on the ascents of Dampier and Cook, were printed in the SCEGGS magazine. 'Mountaineering: an ideal sport' was published by Muriel in the *Dupain Quarterly*. Freda reached the ultimate heights when she was eventually accepted for publication by *The Lone Hand,* a magazine edited by the brothers Lionel and Norman Lindsay, who were much admired in Edwardian intellectual and artistic circles in Sydney. The first article, 'Alpine Climbing in New Zealand', was published on 2 March 1914. It included a serene photo of Cook mirrored in Red Lake on Sebastopol, one of Malte Brun Hut and another of the Tasman Glacier and moraine. A month later a second article, 'High Climbs in New Zealand', was published, along with Freda's photographs of Mount Cook, Mount Sefton, various dramatic views of the Hooker River and the Copland Valley.

While waiting for the Christmas tourist rush to finish, Freda amused herself by taking these new friends up the Sealy Range, to Sebastopol and to Ball Hut. She was most impressed by how quickly Erica Westmacott picked up climbing techniques. The young girl began to thrive as a climber, then began going out on the mountains in groups guided by 'the charming Peter Graham'. Her skills increased quickly so Peter urged Freda to assess her, as he thought she had an excellent chance of becoming the first New Zealand woman to climb Mount Cook. Erica handled ice and moraine superbly although it wasn't until she was through, when Freda and

Peter simply 'looked at each other and nodded',[5] that she realised it had been an audition.

Throughout her life Freda would meet young women and go out of her way to help them realise their potential, especially if her aid could be freely given, without demands. She had often benefited from others, such as Edith Badham, Aunt Emmeline and even the Grahams, taking an interest in her. She understood the balance of power in the situation, how to advise in a kindly but not intrusive way, although she particularly liked the fact she could retreat from involvement if she found it too tiresome. But while playing the role of a kind and playful teacher to Erica, another part of Freda was still the skilled mountaineer, waiting and watching. As soon as the rush of Christmas tourists slackened and Peter was available, they set off on 1 January 1913 for Hooker Hut. Darby Thomson accompanied them as second guide. The next morning, with New Zealand friends helping them with equipment, they began their attempt on the Grand Traverse.

By 11.00 a.m. they reached their designated bivouac at 7000 feet, beneath the western arête leading to the third and lowest peak of Mount Cook. There the guides scraped away a clear, flat place and built a retaining wall with the stones they'd removed so there was somewhere to safely pitch a tent. Then, knowing the next thirty-six hours were going to be gruelling, they attempted to sleep. Freda found it impossible; her head, near the rock, was freezing, and her feet, in the sun, were boiling. She only fell asleep when Peter rigged a tent for her. They were wakened by the New Zealanders shouting farewells across the valley; Peter and Darby then went off to cut steps.

Freda remained behind and on that afternoon experienced a heightened sense of her own isolation. In that landscape of great, awful beauty, Freda believed she heard strange sounds, like voices whispering to her. She wrote later that she observed 'a phenomenon

Freda, Peter and Alex Graham. Posing in full climbing regalia after the
Mount Cook ascent 1910, for the photographer Guy Mannering.

Eccleston Du Faur

Blanche Du Faur, Freda's mother

The adventurous Cyprian Du Faur – painted in the Bastille, and his wife, Sarah Du Faur, Freda's great grand parents.

Rev John Woolley

The Woolley Women. Mary Margaret and her daughters (*clockwise*) Blanche, Emmeline, Constance and Catherine.

Chateau Pibrac – the seat of the du Faur family, in the Garonne Valley near Toulouse, France.

The hut built by Freda's father in Mount Wilson. Freda, unable to stay in it as a child, adored her days in similar, although smaller, mountain huts.

The Du Faur family on the steps of Pibrac, Sydney about 1892. Possie Freda's first climbing companion is nestled against her. Guy is nearest to her, Bertie standing behind.

Pibrac – The first major house built for the Du Faur family, in Warrawee, Sydney.

Cowan Creek
in Ku-ring-gai Chase.

The stern musician,
Aunt Emmeline Woolley.

John – Freda's nephew

John, held by Uncle Guy

Bertie Du Faur

Wynifred – Bertie's wife

Miss Edith Badham, first
headmistress of Sydney Church
of England Girls Grammar.

Botanical watercolour painted
by Freda. One of two surviving.

Mosman Bay

Muriel Cadogan the lady expert (*front row on the right*) with some of her healthy ladies at the Dupain Institute.

Professor Baldwin Spencer, without his customary pipe.

MT. COOK FROM COPLAND PASS.   PROTECTED 16

Above: Freda and Peter Graham in the Copland Pass
with Mount Cook in the background. 1910.

Opposite: Sefton Bivouac

Malte Brun Hut

Freda on the rope on her hearts desire, Mt Nazomi.

Christmas Day – after being snowed in, Malte Brun Hut, 1910
(l.to r.) standing – Mary Murray Aynsley, Jack Clarke, Freda,
Jim Dennistoun, Alex Graham, George Bannister, Peter Graham.
Front Barbara Dennistoun, Ada Julius, Hugh Chambers, George Dennistoun.

The Hermitage after the flood.

Above: Sefton and Cook from
Maunga Ma. The men in the
foreground are Conrad Kain
and Otto Frind.

Left: Peter Graham in the moraine
near Ball Hut.

Red Cottage, Freda and Muriel's home in Pinner. Compared to the houses that characterised the historical town, it was modern and roomy with an unusual adornment, a 'witch's hat' roof.

A quiet morning in Pinner, 1913. Elizabethan houses, with shops underneath, line the High Street. The Church of St Johns is at the top. The popular café, The Cocoa Tree, is in the front of the church.

Fishing Fleet at Lizard, Freda and Muriels favourite holiday place.

Doctor Norman and Gertrude Deane

After Marie Byle's conquest of Mount Cook (*from left*) Guide Arne Larsen, Marjorie Jones, Marie Byles, Alf Brustad.

I have met before in the great silent places. Every now and then a voice seemed to rise from nowhere in a faint cry. Again and again I have started up, sure that someone was calling me.'[6] Freda never denied that the source might have been 'the gurgle of an underground stream, or the wind sweeping into a hidden cave and raising an echo from the distant ridges'. For those not placed as she was it is easy to scoff and find pat explanations, that such events were caused by strain, weariness, excitement or bird calls. Whatever the source, in those hours of waiting the sounds made her consider things she had been questioning for some time, in particular her own place in life.

Her favourite work of literature at the time was a long epic poem called *The Light of Asia*, written by Sir Edwin Arnold. Based on the life of Gautama Buddha, the volume had been the subject of many printings, sometimes just by wealthy fans who could indulge in the choice of plates and covers and give them as gifts on special occasions. Freda was searching for that heavenly place, a kind of Nirvana that she felt she could glimpse tantalisingly in the mountains, but couldn't manage to hold on to and recreate elsewhere, let alone inside herself. She professed to be a member of the Church of England but would ultimately believe in a mix of the Christianity of her childhood, fatalism, rebirth and Buddhism. As well, her interest in romantic poetry had always allowed her to understand God, not as a greater being in the form of a man whom she must worship, but as a benevolent spirit of life, a part of the trees, the rocks and the mountains that created beauty and was destroyed by civilisation.

Mr Practical himself, Peter Graham, had a favourite story, rather less esoteric and more humorous than Freda's, but coming from a similar source. He liked to tell the story of 'The Ghost of Hooker Hut'. In 1913, after staying at the Hermitage late in the season, he set off to cross the Copland to visit his mother, before going on his regular winter trip to Wellington. He left at dusk and was carrying a lot of money on him. There had been workmen in the area, tough characters, and perhaps unnerved by the sound of water roaring over the boulders of the Hooker River, he began to feel someone was following him. Eventually, when he arrived at the Hooker Hut, he had the feeling someone was in the hut, 'like someone moving about on the bunk in the inner room'. Taking a candle and ice axe, Peter approached the door, sure someone was going to rush him. There was no one there, yet still aware of a presence, by 3.00 a.m. he'd had enough. When he locked the door, of what was only a two-year-old hut, he was sure he was locking something in, but even then he felt something was following. By the time he got to the top 'his nerves had gone to the pack'.[7]

The following spring others, including three guides, said they'd heard the unexplained 'similar noises'. Mary Murray Aynsley was the last person to claim such an experience. She was painting at the hut door on a calm day, 'and all of a sudden the door between the two compartments opened stealthily. No one was there ... '[8]

On a strikingly chill day at 2.00 a.m. on 3 January 1913, Peter, Freda and Darby were roped up and on their way, following the steps tramped the previous day to the base of their chosen route below the western arête. As the sun rose they reached the end of the steps, put out their now useless candles and soon 'the tuneful ring of ice axes and patter of falling crystals broke the morning stillness' as 'a brilliant crescent moon sailed in a sky of velvet blue'.[11] Behind them was the exquisite view of the plains, below the Cook River twisting through yellow tussock across which 'Mount Cook threw its shadow over the shining waters, a phantom pyramid stretching up the horizon'. Freda's God was truly at work.[9]

By 4.30 a.m., after an hour of step cutting, they reached the rocks of the western arête which were coated with 'a film of green ice' and hung with icicles. Climbing with great caution, they reached the foot of the snow cap of the lowest peak where they stopped for a second breakfast and by 7.00 a.m. they were in sunlight on the first summit, a ridge which was so narrow that they had to straddle it to stay upright, not unlike the cheval ridge on Malte Brun. Below on the other side was their route, a 'jagged saddle of saw like teeth', covered in loose snow, with sheer drops on either side, which rose up to the steep, spectacular ice face of the second peak. Freda even admitted how terrifying it was and had difficulty not letting her imagination take her, with the stones beneath her feet, 'falling, falling, falling into the abyss'.[10] But surprisingly the ridge up to the middle peak was frozen and stable and as they moved up it they began feeling optimistic. With the weather holding, they chipped rapidly, although one bad overhang on the final snow slope necessitated a detour to the south, then two hours of step cutting, on a 60 degree angle in hard ice, under blazing sun. For half an hour they lingered on the middle peak; Freda avidly photographed all she could see of the MacKenzie country, the lakes and great line of gleaming peaks.

Freda had been haunted by the 'knife-edge ridge' they were next to face that would take them to the highest peak, and the reality was no better. It required climbing down one hundred feet of a steep narrow ridge where 'more than once, as we descended it an icy shiver ran down my spine, as the ice-axe sank deeply into the overhanging cornice, and on withdrawal disclosed through the tiny hole the awful gap between us and the glacier far below'.[11] No experience or skill could provide the vital information of how thick those cornices were; even the shock of one cracking off could have been enough to 'startle' them into eternity.

Once ascending again, with a solid face in front, they found the work easier and by 1.30 p.m. they stood on the highest summit, marvelling at their luck. For another hour and a half they remained up there, loath to leave, hardly believing they had only one descent to go. Freda used two cameras, her old 3a Kodak and a new panoramic, photos from which were to grace pictorial magazines. This was one climb she never wanted to forget.

At 3.00 p.m. on descent, they were buoyed by discovering they only needed to kick down soft snow, then cut across to the eastern arête. After two hours of step cutting down snow-covered rocks suddenly 'a great boulder leapt from the ridge' and whistled past Freda and Peter in direct line for Darby. At their shout, he glanced up, shocked. He flung himself out of the way onto a frozen slope but, with nothing to hold him, rocketed down the ice. Freda braced herself and, with Peter behind her, the wild slide that could have taken them all off the mountain was stopped.[12] It was a reminder of Freda's own cautions: 'beware how you tread on her virgin heights except with love and reverence'.

With great care, they finally reached the upper regions of the Linda Glacier by 6.30 from where, in the last moments of daylight, they made it through the crevasses. In the dark they toiled again through the soft snow of the Grand Plateau. After the Dampier and Tasman climbs, Freda must have felt she was haunted by the place, although this time it was only one way and they were sensing home. By 9.00 p.m. they were at the top of the Glacier Dome with a thousand-foot breakneck descent through dark below them.

Like the madmen mountaineers are reputed to be, they did glissades down the lower snow slopes, slid over small crevasses and stopped where they were sure wide ones existed, their confidence based on the fact that Darby had been over that territory a week earlier and knew the position of all of them. As well as flawed information, they were depending on flawed reactions, in near dark, and, after twenty hours on the go, flawed reasoning. Freda called it 'the valour of ignorance' but it also showed a great confidence in each other, as well as skill and endurance.

As soon as they reached the bivouac Freda lay down exhausted on the stones and slept while the men put up the tent. Next
morning, she woke to an aching face; her lips were 'a woeful spec-
tacle, swollen, with the skin stretched tight'.[13] She had smothered
her face with protective greasepaint but must have been licking her
lips and wiped it off. Unable to eat, she could only sip lukewarm
tea. Aware there would be a reception committee and not wishing
to cause any more damage to the reputation of climbing for women,
she covered her face with a handkerchief, in the manner she imagined of a Mexican bandit.

For a brief time, as they rode back on horses brought up to Ball
Hut by Charlie Milne, who had spotted them on the summit, Freda
could forget her appearance but the household who waited out for
them did not; there was usually someone to speculate the worst, in
this case that she wore the handkerchief on her face because she'd
had all her teeth knocked out. It would have been a satisfying out-
come for any armchair critic who loved to prophesy disaster. Freda
fled to her room, applied hot water compresses to her face and by
dinner time could reappear, her smile showing small, even, undamaged teeth.

Peter always felt Freda had no idea what a difficult climb the
Traverse was, that she took it lightly and easily, but she put this ease
down to his training and her apparent nonchalance down to the
fact that she had no knowledge of mountains elsewhere, so had
nothing with which to compare the Southern Alps. She would only
begin to understood later, when she received a letter from a very
experienced member of the English Alpine Club congratulating her
on their achievements. He wrote: 'The ridge of Mount Cook would
be shuddersome at the best of times ... I can confidently say that
there is not such a ridge in Switzerland; mixed rock and ice perhaps

… but nowhere the endless stretch of knife-edge snow, perched far above everything else in the world as it must seem.'[14]

Writers and climbers have been quick to point out that Freda was arrogant, and often have used as an example of this flaw that she had stated, during the after-climb celebrations, that the Grand Traverse was impossible for anyone else. It was actually the enthusiastic Darby, probably in his celebratory 'cups', who prophesied that the climb wouldn't be done in twenty years, if ever. Freda was proud of her achievement and may have secretly hoped it would be a long time before anyone achieved the climb again. However, what she said was that they had been extremely lucky, that few would attempt such a climb and that success would require time, patience and perfect weather. Freda was competitive, certainly, but not unsportsmanlike. She had, after all, the most desirable firsts to her name: the Grand Traverse, Dampier and, as a woman, Tasman, Lendenfeld and Chudleigh. Her names would mark the mountains Pibrac, Du Faur, Cadogan and Nazomi forever. She would later write 'from the other side of the world I shall eagerly watch and wait in the years to come to see who will be the next party to thread their way over that long icy ridge'.[15] Scarcely the words of an ungenerous mountaineer.

She had nothing but praise for Peter and Darby and wrote how the Hermitage could hardly hold their pride and pleasure, and readily gave them credit for their work, saying 'Theirs is the real triumph: they planned and thought out and led the expedition to a triumphant finish; their knowledge and hard-won experience, their courage and endurance made it possible.'

13 THE LAST

'I was ever a fighter, so one fight more,
The best and the last!
I would hate that death bandaged my eyes, and forbore,
And bade me creep past.
No! let me taste the whole of it, fare like my peers
The heroes of old…'

Robert Browning

By the middle of January 1913 the unsinkable *Titanic* and over fifteen hundred of its occupants had become a romantic tragedy that created records of heroism. Captain Robert Falcon Scott had reached the South Pole, but had been beaten to the prize by his great rival, Amundsen. But who were the heroes and who were the losers? Scott and his team died on the return journey but would be remembered for the heroic failure while Amundsen's name must be looked up in history books. 'Home' in Britain there was concerted action by the Suffragettes, who cut slogans into putting greens, sliced through telephone wires, pelted parliamentary speakers with oranges and mud, and placed a bomb that exploded in the uncompleted house belonging to the Chancellor of the Exchequer, Lloyd George. In Europe, as the winter season was drawing to an end, climbers were planning expeditions at the same time as various politicians and the Bishop of Bathurst expressed his relief to the Ladies' Alpine club that a war between England and Germany had not yet broken out.[1]

Freda was only aware of the events on which her life depended. The decision, that this was to be her last season in New Zealand, had seemed sound when discussed with Muriel during a bland Sydney winter and she knew that a deadline on New Zealand climbing would stop her drifting along for years with always another mountain to climb in that country. But away from Sydney and the reassuring Muriel, in that much loved environment of the mountains, such reasoning could easily become suspect. She would write later, 'Some day, if my dreams come true, I hope to tackle some of the giants of the Himalayas and I ask no better fate than to be led up them by one of my New Zealand guides.'[2] However, in those last days of summer, unconsidered emotions and nostalgia began to dominate her thoughts.

Freda began to doubt everything: her inability to create a life for, and within, herself; the silent places glimpsed from the mountain tops; the path she had chosen with Muriel. Surrounded by what felt like the uncomplicated relationships of the climbing fraternity, life with another woman, without yet the complexity of sexuality, seemed unnecessarily final. The distorting, exquisite isolation of the mountains and the idea of leaving her 'brothers' and the camaraderie she had searched for so long, made the thought of leaving the Mount Cook area unbearable. Her relationship with Peter Graham was imbued with great emotional significance. What was love? Was she more alive struggling physically with Peter in the mountains than in a comfortable and civilised society, stimulated intellectually, with Muriel?

Relatively minor events, to outside observers, became important. It was a ' bitter blow' when all the photos she had taken on the

Traverse of Cook with her 'dear old Kodak' were ruined. She believed the camera had become wet at the Hermitage or in the bivouac, resulting in the lens remaining open, but she forgot another, and more likely, source of damage. This was the same camera that had been dragged into the Sealy Tarn by a kea. It had been pronounced fixable but may have been deteriorating from that point on. So distressed was she that Peter agreed to return with her to the middle peak, just to recapture the lost shots. It was unusually indulgent of him, and he may just have agreed to go back in order to calm her, but it is likely Peter was also caught up in the emotional play of events – of Freda and him taking on the climbs that others had barely considered tackling. He was not in love with her, but he was fascinated. Peter was to marry a young woman, Elizabeth Muriel Pringle, later that year. They had been introduced by her father, a photographer for the Tourist Department but his Muriel, although interested in climbing, was in Wellington while Freda was with him in the mountains.

During those volatile days, when it became known that they would now attempt the traverse of Sefton, Peter had been approached by an unnamed friend who advised him that, 'if I were you I don't think I'd like to take a woman up Sefton. I am only going by Zurbriggen, who considered it the worst climb he had ever undertaken and Fitzgerald, who said after the climb that the next party that went up by that route would be killed.'[3] Sefton was steep with wide schrunds, prone to avalanches, and exposed to all weathers, particularly freezing, wet rain from the west but, in reality, much of it was unknown and Peter was, more than anyone, aware of the risks. They decided to go, but straightaway it rained non-stop for sixteen days, 'in solid sheets, each drop seemed to contain a bucketful'.[4]

Freda tried to maintain her fitness but found that the only suitable garment to wear on her daily walk was a bathing dress. Despite the jokes, the atmosphere must have been oppressive, the frustration debilitating. Finally, on the sixteenth day, a shout from Mr McDonald warned them that the Mueller River was coming down Kea Point! A 'yellow flood' was coming straight for them carrying shrubs, uprooted trees, boulders and ice churned about in its raging waters. By chance most of the water was diverted by a rise in the land at the front gate and veered off down the road, but the rest came swirling towards the Hermitage, filled a small lake near the front door and flooded the garden.

Rising water also cut two calves off from the Hermitage. Caught by tether ropes around the throat, they were in danger of drowning until Peter Graham waded out into the torrent. Twice he was almost carried away. On his 'perilous' return Freda was 'dying to cheer' but feared embarrassing him and perhaps also exposing how enraptured she was with him. She kept silent and, with pride, basked in her favourite guide's heroism and the admiring comments from others.

That evening the rain appeared to ease. Freda crept gratefully off to her usual room in the old section of the building while those in the front rooms, in the new annexe of twenty rooms built the previous year, had to attempt to sleep with the unusual sound of water lapping the foundations. It was hopeless. Kept in a half awake state by an immense thunderstorm, they were jolted completely awake by a crash that shook the entire building. In the dark, it sounded as if the entire face of Sefton had landed in the valley.

Grabbing her coat, Freda ran into the hall to find that the wavering lamplight exposed 'a shivering, whitefaced crowd and their most cherished possessions'[5] trying to get to the safety of the old part, as water flowed under the front door and into their bedrooms. Dawn and vivid lightning did not make anyone feel more secure. Water was swirling under the windows of the annexe and, even more alarming, a great mass of debris had been piled up against the slight rise in the grounds. A few more inches of free water and it would have hit the hotel. With at least the annexe, and probably the entire Hermitage damaged, it was not auspicious for a government trying to assure the world at large that the Tourist Department had high quality accommodation and that there was civilisation in New Zealand.

These were all exciting times for Freda and she wasn't missing any of it. When, by morning, it was discovered that Duncan McDonald had been trapped overnight by the water while out milking the cows, her 'Sir Peter' went to the rescue and bridged the torrent with a rafter. Freda, keen to take photos, hurried after him, but was spotted by the men on their return with the milk pails and was 'hustled' back across before the bank collapsed. But there was no more keeping her inside and, as usual, it was not hard to persuade Peter to accompany her.

How could Freda not wonder whether they were soul mates as, on her suggestion, they went off to investigate what actually had caused the flood to reach the Hermitage? Who else would wade waist deep through unpredictable water with her or battle through the rain and mud? Peter did have to carry her twice over streams, not out of chivalry, but because the current was so strong he needed her weight to hold him down. Once they reached the Mueller Glacier they discovered the cause of the disaster: the moraine bank of the Mueller Glacier that separated the lake from the valley had been washed over and water was even pouring out of cracks in the ice. Across the remaining mud lake was the rare sight of sheer, clean ice at the glacier's terminal. They followed the shore for a while but it was so unstable that the shingle slid away under Peter's feet and he ended up in the ice-fed lake. Freda took great care not to fall in herself. What they did discover was that the continued flow of water, the instability of the moraine, even the possibility of chunks of ice coming away, meant that more flood water and rock could wash down and the slight rise in the land in front of the hotel could not be relied on as a defence. They needed to build their own flood bank to protect the Hermitage.

Perhaps the tourists, settling in for morning tea, did not believe their garbled story, or they had the attitude that the hired hands could do the work for, at first, just Peter and Charlie Milne slogged through the mud and water to build a levee. Then Freda, Erica Westmacott and another young woman 'divested as many garments as was compatible with decency' and came to their aid. In two hours of the hardest morning's work Freda had ever done, in icy water sometimes waist deep, they managed to drag together as many trunks and boulders as were available. When the freezing water got too much, they ran up the valley, to gather more drift wood, to return 'glowing and ready for the fight once more'. Freda was well aware that the onlookers, who she couldn't comprehend not helping, 'thought we were qualifying for an lunatic asylum if not already fit to be inmates'.[6] They all appeared even more crazy when the water retreated, leaving behind a mass of slime and boulders. The disdainful tourists, appalled by the mess, took the opportunity to flee to less dangerous lodgings, leaving the poor old building and real climbers behind.

As soon as the weather settled the Hermitage became busy with departing expeditions. On the following Wednesday, 22 January, with the intention of getting a good a view of their proposed desination, Peter and Freda left the Hermitage and climbed, in seven hours to Tuckett Col, an area only a thousand feet below Sefton's summit. With them, was the young, relatively inexperienced guide, Jock Richmond, who was a possible third on the traverse of Sefton. So close were they that they actually considered attempting the traverse there and then. The scheme was to descend into the west, reach the camp of the men who were building a new track below the Copland Valley, and obtain essential food and warm clothing from them. But a sudden change of weather brought in a suffocating warm mist and cut visibility, forcing them to dismiss their reckless plan and retreat.

The trip had been useful, apart from sounding a timely warning. They had made a route through the broken ice of the Huddleston Glacier and had a good idea of conditions facing them, or so they thought. Once again snow began falling; a well-planned climb in the Mount Cook region never seemed to begin without a few days of rain but snow to low levels was not entirely expected at that time of year.

Freda briefly considered cutting her losses and going home, especially as there'd be a ten-day wait, but she had learned an important lesson. Instead of hanging around getting depressed, she joined a party of women that Peter was guiding over the Copland. It was to be a short trip as, once on the other side, he was to hand them over to another guide coming up to meet them from the Franz. At first Freda climbed at the tail end of the rope but, on reaching a big schrund that cut them off from the snow slope up to the pass, she took the lead, climbed on Peter's shoulders, pulled herself up on her ice axe, then cut for the other women as they came up. Freda was very impressed with their prowess, and her own. Finally the swag and Peter were 'dragged up and a heavy load he proved'. The women would have teased him mercilessly for being in their power, but his thanks for Freda's work left her feeling she'd just been 'decorated with a D.S.O'.[7] She could take the lead, cut steps! She could be relied upon! She was finally climbing as a man might!

Because of the changeable weather, the group had to stay for two nights in the new Copland Hut at Welcome Flat until the new guide arrived. As the hut wasn't entirely finished they had to sleep on the floor but, once their charges had been collected, there was still no escape. The Copland River was in flood. Hunger made the extra day's stay seem even longer, until they were supplied with fresh flour from some road men and made damper in a cast-iron pot. Then she and Peter lay on the floor, watched the embers, smelled the baking bread and talked. They had known each other for six years, had shared situations where nerves had been stretched to breaking and had managed to retain tolerance and respect. He was in many ways the closest male to her but this was the first time they had been completely alone, with no purpose other than to pass time. And now they were making commitments to entirely different futures. Freda would have talked about her plans, of perhaps Peter or Alex joining her in Europe. Peter must have had some longing to extend his horizons, especially as he'd soaked up so much from outsiders.

There has always been speculation about their relationship: that he was in love with her, she with him, that they even had a love child. It would have been easy for them, even in those days, to have taken things further as Freda was vulnerable, nostalgic and uncertain of her predilection for women. Peter was attractive, daring, her hero, her closest male friend. She was leaving, no one would know what happened between them but, despite the rumours, it is most unlikely anything occurred – although nothing can ever be proved either way.

When they were finally able to cross the river, they were by then very hungry. Fortunately, they were supplied with boiled potatoes by men cutting back the track. They reached the Hermitage in time to meet Professor Spencer, who had arrived, on his own once again. His wife had won again and taken his daughters to Britain. Freda, along with the Westmacott women, became welcome female company for what was a lonely man with the beginnings of an alcohol problem.

Also at the Hermitage was the expatriate English climber from Wellington, Samuel Turner, who commandeered Peter Graham and

Darby Thomson in an attempt on Tasman and the traverse of Lendenfeld. Turner will probably go down in the history of the Southern Alps as the most disliked climber ever. A superb amateur, he was to make a solo climb of Mount Cook in the 1918–19 season, perhaps because he felt to climb with others retarded his progress. He was a braggart and even angered the mild-tempered guides when Peter overheard him complaining to a young female newcomer to the mountains. Peter wrote how Turner had said: 'how tiring long periods of step-cutting had been, more so for him than the guides, because he had to back up two men, one in front and one behind and had to watch carefully in case they slipped'.[8] What enemies he didn't make on the mountains, he made on the publication of his book, *The Conquest of the New Zealand Alps*, which was full of complaints about others and how they hindered him.

On this trip, Turner was even more disgruntled than usual and found a target in Freda. He was convinced that Peter Graham had been going to meet him at the Haast Bivouac to climb Mount Tasman, but instead the guide had climbed it with Freda. Then, when he'd booked Peter to climb Sefton, he discovered he had just gone out to check the possibility of climbing it with her as well. To add insult to his usual list of injuries, Peter had refused to take Turner up until Freda and he had completed the climb. So 'the powers that be decided I was to stand down … ', Turner wrote bitterly, ' … until the Australian lady climbed Mount Sefton'.[9] Turner often criticised women climbers, implying that several of them had reached the summit because of their 'childlike' faith in the guides. On crossing Freda's cheval ridge on Malte Brun, he would boast, 'my mind was made up to show the great Australian lady climber the most lady-like way'.[10] But Freda was relaxed with this difficult man as she was with others like him, was never unhappy being with him and never criticised him herself. However she was, despite Peter's promise to 'keep' Sefton for her, a little nervous that, if Turner's climbs went well, he might persuade the guides to go with him up Sefton first. Her lack of faith was not justified. On the men's return, after succeeding on Tasman but failing the traverse of Lendenfeld, the plan was made to attempt Sefton the next day. Freda, Peter and Darby Thomson would make the attempt by climbing the east ridge and descend into the west, to Douglas Rock.

Freda was no longer the young woman who had fallen in love with snow, ice and mountain peaks in 1906. She was 30 years old and the cool winds that made a climber feel shaky on a mountain blew around the Hermitage. That night, quietly in her room, she wrote letters and fixed up her affairs 'just in case the arête might live up to its reputation and the party come to grief'.[11] She was right to feel this way, despite her skills. She had to consider the possibility of death, and hoped that if it should come, she could face it bravely. It fulfilled all her fanciful notions of the life of an adventurer. Noble and mad, brave and ridiculous.

At 11a.m., on Sunday, 9 February 1913 Freda, Peter and Darby Thomson left for their attempt on the traverse of Mount Sefton. Accompanying them, to the foot of the Stocking Glacier, was the Professor, Erica Westmacott and, amazingly, Mr Turner. In perfect, hot weather the climbing team bivouacked an easy three-hour climb from the Hermitage, which was enough to give them the start they needed; then Peter and Darby set off to kick steps through the ice of the Huddleston Glacier. Freda found it impossible to sleep; her mind was too full of mountaineering, both future and past. Instead, she searched out the tiny cave the climbers FitzGerald and Zurbriggen had slept in eighteen years earlier. As she crouched to look inside, considering the numerous attempts those strong experienced climbers had made to climb Sefton, and how Fitzgerald had been nearly killed on the east ridge, she was thrown back into the present by the roar of a huge avalanche that had broken off above the glacier and was hurtling down, smothering everything in front of it. The men were somewhere in the area. 'Sick at heart' she scanned the slopes but it wasn't for another hour that she heard them shout. They had been lucky as the avalanche had missed them and the proposed route.

Sunrise found them threading their way through a maze of 'great blocks and pinnacles of ice'[12] blocking out any view of the glacier. Progress was slow but was made even more so by a sheer wall of ice, twenty feet high. Peter, roped and belayed by Darby, had to stand on a snow bridge across a schrund that dropped into darkness, then cut a huge step up, balance in it, then cut ever higher over a bulge in the slippery, ice wall. Freda followed with difficulty as there was no support in the ice wall and the steps were steep with big gaps between each one. The bulge was even more difficult especially because of Freda's size, but she refused Peter's offer to haul her up. Once she was secure Darby followed, his brown face encouraging. The more difficult a situation, the more he grinned, the more he joked.

They then made good time until 6.30 a.m. When they reached the east ridge and were toiling up the steep slopes of Tuckett's Col, which they'd once reached so easily, the weather began to turn. A north-westerly was rolling in and by the time they were facing the worst of the climb on the rotten ridge leading to the north-east arête, huge gusts of wind were blasting up the Copland Valley. Each step required painstaking care. Fortunately, their rope was long enough to ensure each climber could find a safe position before another moved, essential when the ridge was, at the most, two feet wide, with a sheer drop on one side to the Copland Valley and the other to the valley of the Mueller Glacier.

Three hundred feet of climbing like this brought them 'numb and stiff' with cold into the Sefton rocks, where they sheltered and desperately tried to bring back circulation into numb flesh. Slightly warmer, they gingerly scaled the north-east arête, across rotten shale that fell away beneath them to be whirled down into the gullies by the wild wind. Again, only one climber moved at a time, always testing footholds and handholds for the weight-bearing rock. After another hundred feet they reached another wall and decided to detour around it by climbing slightly east, down off the ridge where the rocks were solid, but vertical and slick with snow and ice. They climbed another wall which hung out over the Mueller Glacier, in clear view of the Hermitage below in the valley. If one of them fell it would have been impossible not to drag the others down as well. When they reached the top of the ridge again they waved a towel hoping they could be seen. There was no going back.

Spurred on by cloud closing round all but the peaks of the mountains to the north, they made fifty more feet of difficult climbing, until easier work brought them to one hundred and fifty feet below the summit. They traversed to the west, intending to follow Zurbriggen's route, but there the rocks were overhung by icicles, in an unbroken fringe, exposed to the wind. The choice was to go back and give up, or traverse the snowslope beneath the rocks. What followed was 'an exciting game of hide and seek with our lives for the forfeit', Freda wrote.[13] Darby relieved Peter and, true to his reputation, rapidly cut steps until the end of the rope, then sought shelter as Freda, then Peter ran across trying to gather and coil up the snow-stiffened rope as they went. Any slack could trip them, while those icicles swaying above threatened to break off and bowl them down the mountain.

Half an hour later, they were out of this traverse and ascending the snow slope to the saddle between the two peaks of Sefton but, as they reached the steep arête to the highest peak, they came back into a wind so strong that Freda was forced to crawl on hands and knees.

There was no celebration when they finally reached the summit. Wind and the ever present threat of exposure allowed them only four quick photos. Dense cloud swirled around them and only occasionally cleared long enough to 'disclose great banks of white cloud racing before the gale'.[14] Freda did not hanker for a view this time; she had glimpsed death and it was ugly and cruel, without heroism. Nor did they consider diverting, to climb the lower virgin peak, as they originally intended. Instead, for half an hour, they retraced their steps, then climbed down into a steep snow slope to reach the large crevasse that cut across their destination, the western face. Darby was leading and had been there the previous year but, under such conditions, his knowledge was of meagre help in finding a crossing point. Eventually they jumped the schrund then followed the lower lip where it shelved back into an overhanging cave, almost a copy of the one they had sheltered in on Mount Tasman.

From there, through shifting clouds, they hoped to gain some kind of perspective on the route they were aiming for, an arête that overhung the Copland Valley, down which they intended to climb, avoiding precipitous cliffs everywhere else. They hoped to then reach a pass that led into a large snow basin, and from there reach a grassy slope down to the bush and the Copland River. There was one major problem: an unexpected rift in the arête which required them to skirt south, then find another route back up to rejoin it.

An hour later, with weather worsening and the drifting fog hiding more and more terrain, they were working through broken ice, barely able to see a body length ahead. Then, when they expected to rejoin the other side of the arête, it wasn't there. Instead, a peak rose up in front of them. Darby was puzzled. There were no peaks on the ridge they'd been aiming for, he was sure of it.

Perhaps, they decided, if they climbed up this peak it would lead back to the arête or at least close by it. Perhaps they'd climbed down lower than they realised. But, after crossing a flat area, there was still no sign of the ridge and another peak loomed up, higher than the previous one. The misty rain turned to snow. There was a puzzled silence. Uncertain, the guides decided they should climb down but instead of the lost ridge that could take them to safety, they found an unexpected and uncrossable crevasse.

Around 4.30 p.m., they took a break, hoping to have a fresh look at their predicament, but resting only made them aware of the snow falling in large flakes, covering their bodies and settling on their hats. Needing every ounce of energy, they forced themselves to eat, with the growing awareness that if they didn't find the ridge down, they would have to sleep out overnight. There would be no rescuers, no sheltering rocks or ice caves. If they survived the night, the next day's conditions were unlikely to be better. Was this to be their 'last'? Refusing to consider that fleeting thought, they retraced their steps to the flat area after the first peak. Illogically, as it sloped down towards the Copland Valley, it seemed their only hope. The climb down was not difficult and they realised they were actually on the rocks below the ridge they'd been after. Then a sound reached them, as mysterious and disconnected as Freda's voices. Stopping, they attempted to locate it, afraid that the sound, so like trickling water, was in their imagination. It wasn't. And if it wasn't, it had to be Scott's Creek and if that was so, they weren't as far off track as they'd feared. Then Darby spotted something; an empty pineapple tin on a small stone cairn. He had placed it there when climbing with Samuel Turner. Sure now of their exact position they pushed on down through broken ice, on as direct a route as possible; the sound of the river grew louder. As snow turned to rain they recognised the snowfield of their plan. It was 6.00 p.m.

With thousands of feet still to go, they moved along the ridge onto steep grass slopes, slick with rain and snow, tumbling in their haste, with only the rope saving them from injury. They traversed into scrub and pushed through bushes, creepers and thorns. They stumbled over steep creek beds, through rapids, fell into pools and were soaked, scratched and covered in mud. By the time they came out of that creek into a tributary that flowed into the Copland River, it was 8.00 p.m., nightfall. With only lantern light, they made a 'weird and wonderful progress'. Freda called it 'the most extraordinary in our eventful day'.[15] Lighter than the men, who were barging ahead, she was often slapped in the face by wet undergrowth, or left struggling on her own for long critical moments when the lanterns went out or when she found herself in terrifying situations: on one occasion she found herself out on some branches that overhung a river of boulders and dangerous, white water.

Finally, they reached the Copland River, which was familiar enough territory for them to find the track and get to the road workers' camp. At 10.00 p.m., they burst in on the workmen, who stoked up the fire and produced warm food. One confessed to having tried to climb Scott's Creek in daylight and had given it up as too tough a job. After eating they tramped the last long quarter-mile to the Douglas Rock bivouac where they were forced to stay for two nights because of the flooded river.

Eventually, knowing that Alex would be waiting for word at the Franz Josef and that the people at the Hermitage who had seen the storm on the summit might already have a search party out, at the first sign of clearing, they fought their way over the Copland Pass through a near blizzard to find the weather improved on the eastern slopes. By the time they reached the Hooker Hut, it was not unpleasant. After a quick meal, they finally arrived at the Hermitage at 8.00 p.m. Outside the smoking room Freda 'collided' with the Professor who did a 'war dance' of relief. They were just in time to stop disaster telegrams going out.[16]

Waiting for them also was Tryggve Gran, who was keen to know what the climb had been like and to compare notes with Freda over conditions on Mount Cook. The Norwegian skier had just returned from Captain Scott's fatal South Pole expedition and had been in the search party that found the explorers. His description of the bodies of 'those heroes of old' and the conditions the men had undergone and their bravery at the end was pitiful and disturbing. Freda was haunted by the images of the snow-covered tent and the last words of the Captain and felt unable to celebrate her own feat. In comparison to the explorers' deaths, the traverse of Sefton was a meagre event. She wrote clearly of her feelings about her own efforts which left her in a kind of post-traumatic depression, 'flat, stale and unprofitable'.[17]

She knew she was a 'victim of her own success' but, nevertheless, everything that had once motivated her seemed dull and prosaic. She wondered about Robert Browning's words: 'A man's reach should exceed his grasp or what's a heaven for?'. Did that mean that excess was the only way to satisfaction, that surviving Sefton was not enough and that the lasting 'heaven' she sought through climbing could never, ever be found on earth? This dissatisfaction was an emotional pattern of enormous elation derived from physical achievement, which was invariably followed by great negative questioning that would leave her depressed. Freda preferred her illusions of heroism rather than reality, yet her climbs were, in fact, more daunting and demanding than her 'dreams of thrilling moments to be spent scaling ... in imagination'.

Gradually the haunting feeling of loss evaporated, not by her own efforts, but through time. The mountain, briefly a traitorous beloved, reasserted itself in her life as she became aware how 'the great mountain dominated the valley, unaltered and unalterable, no matter how many defiling feet might touch its snows'.[18] But the mass of contradictions that had formed Freda was pushing her emotions in other directions too. She felt that she had lost her other hero, Peter Graham, to his success. By 'allowing' him, that is hiring him, to tackle Sefton from the east, she had provided the opportu-

nity for the guides to finally slough off the reproach that New
Zealand guides didn't dare tackle that face, and now other climbers
were 'clamouring' for his and Darby Thomson's services. But she
had to let them go, she couldn't afford to hold them anyway, and
they had been more than considerate in putting all their time into
her climbs. Emotionally, Freda could still not let go of the Southern
Alps. She was, for this last month in New Zealand, stuck as surely
as someone taken fright on a mountain face, unable to take the
desired steps upward and out to the top. Her humour, though, over
the next three weeks was, as usual, directed at herself as she had to
cope with the 'unusual and quite unappreciated pleasure of sitting
still and watching other people climb'.[19]

Two ascents of Mount Cook were attempted. One by Tryggve
Gran, Peter Graham and Charlie Milne was successful, while the
other by George and Lucy Mannering, stalwarts of the New Zealand
climbing scene, did not succeed. They were defeated by weather.

Into March Freda waited until the other climbers were gone
and she could get her guides back – and to do what? It was all finishing off; to pick up belongings at the Cook bivouac and to go
back up the middle peak of Cook to photograph the Traverse again,
so that her six years in the Alps could be 'finished' to her satisfaction. With the intention of photographing a past success, their
descent route of Sefton, she and Peter ('we' as she now referred to
them in her book) climbed an unnamed peak north of The
Footstool. It was too cloudy for successful photographs but Freda
named the peak 'Cadogan' in honour of Muriel.

By Easter, too late for good climbs, Freda was still there, unable
to commit herself to leaving. It rained, and if it was not raining,
then there was wind and snow. She should have been looking forward to overseas, but she clung to any 'fitful gleam of sunlight' as
an excuse not to leave.

In those last days, Peter had been trying to arrange a Mount

Cook attempt for Erica Westmacott but she decided not to try the climb, for reasons Freda would only discover later. Freda's Professor, while out walking with Mrs Westmacott, had pointed out that when he had met Freda she had been 'a soft rounded girl' like Erica. Was that what a mother wanted for her daughter? Erica did admit that her idol was 'a bit stringy ... but of course she was trained down to the last hair'. Erica liked being athletic but there were still doubts about the effect on women of such exercise. The Westmacotts were also, as Erica put it, 'in one of our stages of Hard-Upness'[20] and the £14 required to pay for the climb, guides and equipment, on top of the cost of staying at the Hermitage for almost four months, were beyond their means. Obviously there was money in the family for them to be staying at the Hermitage for so long and so often; but it does seem as if the family were used to times of feast then famine. During their stay, Mr Westmacott and the son, Spen, had gone to the North Island to deal in some property, so perhaps a sale had failed to come through.

Finally, there was no choice for Freda. She had to go. The place would close down around her. As a farewell, Freda and Peter went up to Malte Brun and while there made an attempt on the Aiguille Rouge, which had first been ascended by Mr Earle and Peter Graham in 1909, and never attempted since. After a slow start, due to fog and a 'toilsome march up the glacier' they followed the route up the north-east buttress. Mostly it was fine rock climbing on solid red blocks but, near the top, Freda found it difficult to keep up with Peter. He may have been inconsiderate out of weariness himself or because he was used to her keeping up with him, but he could well have been irritated with her. Freda had stayed too long, demanded too much, was going over old ground and expecting attention while he was probably keen to clear up for the season and get away to Wellington. Whatever the reason, Freda attempted a short cut to catch up with him and when some unexpectedly rotten rock came away she fell, cut her knee badly and toppled backwards. Her shout alerted Peter and although she managed to stop the fall herself, from then on he 'eyed every hand and foot-hold wrathfully'.[21]

He patched her up as well, and despite Freda's stiff and sore knee, the climb improved, but with bad weather on the summit and worsening conditions, they had to struggle through snow and mist on the descent with only their rapidly disappearing footsteps to guide them. Next morning, it was snowing too hard to set out but the following day, 23 March, despite the snow that smothered the hut, they decided to try for Elie de Beaumont. It was too cold, so they tried the Hochstetter Dome, which dozens of tourists climbed every season but that was impossible too.

Even if she hadn't been secure enough to leave, the weather ultimately decided everything. Rain fell 24 inches in 24 hours. The annexe was completely undermined by floods and it was obvious that the next big rain could take the entire building away.

Already a new Hermitage was being built, a mile down the valley. It would be opened in 1914, burn down in 1957, then be rebuilt the following year. The new hotel was going to be, according to Freda, a despised 'fashionable place with tennis courts and golf links etc where you will have to dress for dinner and play about in pretty clothes'. Freda preferred to hold on to 'the happy carefree home-like days in the ugly, rambling cottage' than stay at 'a fashionable tourist resort'.[22]

It snowed again. It was time to go. Sure she would never see the 'star-lit heights and winding valleys' again; she strained back for a last look at Peter Graham, Darby Thomson, the McDonalds and the Westmacotts, who all waved her on from 'the dear home of hopes and dreams' as the car 'rushed away across the plains, and a mist for a moment blotted out the towering mountains, the blue sky and the brown faces of my comrade-guides'.[23] The mountains were turning into memories.

II

OUT OF THE EARTH

'There we sat, alone on a few square feet of rock,
with a precipice on either side,
while the mists blotted out the world.'

Freda Du Faur
THE CONQUEST OF MOUNT COOK

14 GROUNDWORK

'We are the pilgrims, master; we shall go
Always a little further; it may be
Beyond that last Blue Mountain barred with snow.'

James Elroy Flecker

For a short time, on her return to Australia, Freda kept up her regular correspondence with Otto Frind and wrote full, chatty letters
about her exploits to her aunts and cousins in England, and to Enid
and Aunt Constance. By winter, however, letters received, even
from other climbers, went unanswered. Freda was trying to write
her book which would become *The Conquest of Mount Cook and
other climbs: An Account of Four Seasons Mountaineering in the
Southern Alps of New Zealand*, and was not ready to admit it was the
hardest thing she had yet tackled.

Initially, she had been optimistic. The articles she had already
written had been a joy not a chore; she'd sent some to Arthur
Wheeler, Director of the Alpine Club of Canada, via Otto Frind,
and on 13 January 1913 he had written back, impressed with
Freda's writing, the photographs enclosed and in particular her
'occasional flashes of humour'.[1] He was more than happy to make
space for any article written by her, but took pains to point out that

an article was, of course, gratuitous. There was also the promised contract from Stanley Unwin to urge her on, but the process of writing was so long and frustrating that she felt she could barely pick up a pen. It was only the knowledge that she needed it substantially finished before she could consider going overseas that pushed her on. It would not only add kudos to her name in the climbing world, but the journalistic world as well, and perhaps even in the literary world. Why shouldn't she follow in her father's footsteps in this aspect? It would also help her bring her experiences of climbing in New Zealand to a fitting conclusion.

Then, just as she felt she was finally making progress and could consider recontacting her correspondents, Freda contracted severe influenza again. By September, when she had recovered enough to consider attending the marriage of Ruth Gerard and Stanley Abbott, and had begun to make headway with her manuscript, she received a letter from Otto Frind from his home in Vancouver. He was on his way to New Zealand again and wanted her to join him there. She refused, joking in her return letter that she was 'not the young millionaire that you appear to be',[2] but the refusal was not without reluctance. How easy it would be to just go back to what she knew and loved. Nor did she want to offend Otto as he was acting as her backer and sponsor to join the Alpine Club of Canada, a membership she wanted as she'd decided to go over to Canada from England in May 1914. It seems entirely illogical to have only just arrived in England and not aim for the European Alps. She certainly intended to climb there, in fact in all the main climbing theatres. During one of her supremely confident moments, after climbing Mount Cook, it was reported in *The Weekly Press* 'that she would like to attempt some of the Himalayas which she considers would be "really worthwhile" '.[3]

But this was now an underconfident Freda, almost nine months after her last climb, rather rundown from writing and her illness, and not always logical. She may have felt that the Canadian Alps would provide less demanding climbs, and be an easier progression, although even the Rockies loomed in her mind as vast and unfriendly, as she'd asked Frind, in the same letter, for a 'personally conducted tour' to save her from feeling a 'forlorn foreigner'. But at least she had Frind in Canada; the members of the English Alpine Club she knew, such as Mr Earle, may have been more intimidating than she was prepared to admit.

Frind arrived in Sydney early in December and went out to Flowton to see Freda and attempt, as he loved to do, to sort out her plans. As this was the first time Freda's world of mountaineering would impinge on her family world, Freda was anxious about this visit, but Otto was the perfect person to 'break the ice'. On 15 April 1914, an article in the *Christchurch Press* commented: 'He impresses one with the idea of purposefulness and determination; he has the restrained manner of those accustomed to danger and the evident physical fitness of those accustomed to finding their own pleasure in "roughing" it.' As a Fellow of the Royal Geographical Society and one fascinated by surveys, maps and theories, he also had much in common with Freda's father. Unfortunately, he brought with him, as his guide from Canada, someone Freda considered an outsider, a small, lean-faced, weathered man, Conrad Kain. About Freda's age, the Swiss-born Austrian had left school at the age of fourteen to become a goat-herd then, for a while, worked in a quarry until, at the age of seventeen, he became enamoured of mountaineering and forged a career in guiding, which took him eventually to Canada and Otto Frind. Nevertheless, proud of where she lived, she showed them both around Ku-ring-gai.

Frind delivered a letter from her old climbing companion, Mr Earle, containing advice on possible guides and climbing routes in Canada – again not about Europe – but he raised as many problems as he settled. Freda wanted information about costs, but it was useless to ask Otto as money was not one of his concerns. Worse, he suddenly wasn't sure if he'd even be in Canada when Freda intended visiting, and suggested instead that she climb with friends of his, the experienced mountaineers Captain MacCarthy and Elizabeth MacCarthy. They would have been ideal as MacCarthy had been on the first ascent of Mount Robson (at 13,080 feet, the highest mountain in the Canadian Rockies) and about Mrs MacCarthy, Otto, always the expert, wrote later, 'I should not hesitate to place Mrs MacCarthy alongside Freda Du Faur any day.'[4]

Freda was briefly interested in the idea of another woman climber in her group, but she didn't know her and decided she'd managed without the support of other women so far and would be better off with just a guide. Otto immediately recommended Conrad Kain. She found it difficult to explain why she wasn't keen on the idea of hiring the man, but attempted to in an emotional letter to Frind while he was still in Sydney. On 4 December she wrote that she felt Conrad Kain, with his strong accent and swagger, would never comprehend her. Her concerns may have been more than prejudice, as there were always mixed opinions about Kain. Competent judges would say that he was the finest mountaineer ever in New Zealand, and wrote glowingly of his ability, his gentleness and his entertaining stories. Others felt he was wrong to take a relatively inexperienced, middle-aged woman, without a second guide, when he and Mrs Thomson did the Grand Traverse of Mount Cook in 1916. Mrs Thomson, in turn, described Kain as 'a splendid guide' with an 'inborn instinct for finding new routes'.[5]

None of these recommendations would have helped Freda anyway as she saw herself as an unconventional, emotional climber and argued that she would only take on Frind's suggestions for guides 'as long as they are the kind of men I approve'. By this she meant the Grahams, who understood her idiosyncrasies and recognised her abilities. It would be her party and she wanted it to suit her. Peter, newly married, was an impossible choice and, in hindsight, she may have felt he was too headstrong. It was her caution, she felt, that took them off Elie de Beaumont when she'd 'counselled' a retreat, and 'after some discussion we began the descent'.[6] She informed Otto that Alex was 'a man on whom I know I can thoroughly trust under any circumstances ... Kain knows Mount Robson and Canada generally but he doesn't know me ... while fulfilling all qualifications as a guide he might fall short in other respects.'[7] Alex was looking after his mother and the Franz Josef Hotel but a trip to Canada during the New Zealand winter, when the hotel was quiet, might have interested him. With Alex as a buffer, Freda could risk having Kain as a second guide. Despite Otto again remonstrating that Kain was all she needed, Freda would not be moved. Emotional security was too important, especially as she was changing everything in her life.

Things became tense. Otto had brought the guide with him because he felt New Zealand guides were not as experienced, or very good on ice and rope, whereas Freda disagreed, considering that it was a slight and that it was inappropriate for outsiders to push into the New Zealand guides' domain. As well, there was an essential difference between Freda's and Otto's approach to mountaineering. For Freda, it was all or nothing, as her whole being rested on success or failure, conquer or be conquered. Otto Frind liked to get 'acquainted with mountains'. His diary records lengthy concerns with names and heights; he was the explorer rather than a conquistador.[8] Freda complained of New Zealanders not bothering to climb, Frind complained of their reluctance to take on exploratory work with big swags. His descriptions of climbs, on which he took wonderful photos, were detailed technical descriptions. There were no colours, rainbows or poetry in the man's writing: he liked to dissect and improve.

Freda wrote again to Otto and it seems there were meetings as well. She was confused and unable to decide what to do. At first she thought she wouldn't go to Canada at all if Alex could not be with her, then she thought she would give up the idea of strenuous climbing and 'just go over for the club picnic so as to get an idea of how things are and return for climbing in 1915 or never!'[9] The 'never' was a plea for Otto to bully her into not being so silly, to encourage her, by reassuring her she was a marvellous climber. He naturally didn't hesitate to give more advice, little of which was taken up.

Then, with only a few weeks to go, Freda suddenly pushed though her fears as she began to shelter under Muriel's broad and firm ideas of how women should live. Freda's feminist attitudes were not actually far removed from Muriel's but she had never been particularly intense about them. Now, taking herself seriously made her feel she was finally facing up to who she really was and, in those last few weeks before leaving Australia, she began to harden her opinions and was rewarded by a sense of power, a power that was one of the main qualities she admired in Muriel.

She pushed Otto over her stalled membership of the Canadian Alpine Club. The executive board had initially invited her to join as a special member but hadn't got back to her. Apart from the recognition, she wanted to take up their offer to be an active member, as the entry fee would be only $7.50, with annual dues of $5. If she'd just gone in as an associate the annual subscription would have been $25. Uncertain about why she hadn't heard, but confident of acceptance, she joked: 'Have they thrown me out, what do you think?'[10] Whether Otto followed the membership up for her or not, Freda's name would be added in 1913 and she continued, until at least 1917, as an active member: being designated by the Canadian Club as having 'made an ascent of a truly alpine glacier—climbing a peak rising at least 2,500 feet above the timber line of its region'. She could also have joined at that level by being 'distinguished in literature, art or science relating to mountains'.

The English Alpine Club was another matter. Unlike New Zealand, Canada and Australia, women were not allowed to join although there was the Ladies Alpine Club but Freda wanted to be accepted by the only true club and was quite prepared, or at least spoke as if she was, to be the one to break down those barriers too. After all, in her eyes, the conservative hold of the male was going to topple any day under the frequent attacks of the militant Suffragettes. Freda had some reason, although misplaced, to be optimistic. A letter from Claud MacDonald, of the *English Alpine Journal*, had requested a reprint of her article 'The Complete Traverse of Mount Cook' for the February issue. It would be perfect, an article and her membership. It was a perfect time also to make a foray into the climbing society in England; in another year or two any number of climbers could steal her thunder. She hoped, from the security and comparative egalitarianism of Flowton, that once over there, she would meet the 'Editor and all such members as I want to meet'. She would have no trouble being accepted and soon she would be in the 'thick of the crowd ... it ought to be great sport'.[11]

She had teased Frind saying, 'I have high hopes of some of the Englishmen I have met – they seem to be the best going' but the acceptance of Mr Earle and Mr Unwin, older men, who had learned some tolerance and admired youthful ideals, deluded her. Freda had not experienced the full force of the English class system. She was naively amused that the members of the Alpine Club might be 'scandalised by her claim to equality'.[12] In readiness for an 'assault' on this bastion of the English male, if not the mountains they were tackling, Freda worked on her theories, disparaging the famous war correspondent Henry Stephenson for a leaflet he wrote attacking women's rights with 'pure undiluted sarcasm'. She threatened to send Otto all her suffrage papers 'as a grounding for your future education', and would have sent him a copy of her 'Suffrage Bible',

The Subjection of Women. But she was taking her copy with her and was unable to get one for him as it was unobtainable in Sydney, something she was sure her Canadian friend would consider a blessing. She was becoming increasingly firm in her attitudes but was well aware of the change and hadn't entirely lost her sense of humour. 'Aren't enthusiasts a bore?' she suggested to him. 'And you never would have dreamt it of me except as a mountaineer.' But there were moments when she took her opinions rather too seriously and expected others to as well. 'My friends these days have to come into line because as soon as mutual interest and ideals cease, friendships die for want of sustenance …' She continued, '… and I don't like losing my friends if a little probing will wake them up and make them more interesting than before'.[13] She was so sure she was right, she needed this confidence. She was so sure others were wrong, especially as Muriel approved of the new Freda.

Freda was tidying up other loose ends. She had been in correspondence with Johannes Andersen of the Lands and Surveys Department of New Zealand concerning the naming of summits in the Southern Alps and had sent him a photo he'd requested to go into a book he was writing, *The Jubilee History of South Canterbury.* The photo itself is remarkable as it shows a much plumper Freda than has ever been seen in photos from the mountains or even ones from her school years. Her hair is swept back into a kind of rolled coiffure. She is dressed in a scoop-necked, dark dress with a heavy lace collar that reveals a full neck and shoulders very similar to her mother's. It is signed, 'Yours sincerely, Freda Du Faur'. If this was a current photo, Freda had put on a lot of weight during that last year in Sydney and the sedentary lifestyle of writing would not have helped. If so, it would not have been easy for her to get really fit again.

Very aware of Freda's pending departure, Andersen had written back on 29 December 1913 to ask for information on the virgin

mountains she had climbed and named, plus geological information on the Alps. There was a particular problem over Du Faur Peak
as it may have previously been called Madonna. Freda, not liking
the possibility of her name being dumped, interrupted her busy,
last minute schedule and wrote to Andersen, to inform him of what
she knew and prompted Otto to chase up the matter as well. Otto
was happy to do so. Before he left for New Zealand he gave her a
copy of his ice axe tie-pin which she had always admired, although
she may not have been quite so delighted if she'd known that, over
summer, he would give one to each of the women he met. It was
typical of Otto, who saw himself as an old-fashioned gallant and
happily and successfully played that role. It would be the last real
contact he would ever have with her, although both would have
thought they'd always be friends.

At least, the dark tease of 'never' going to Canada was no longer
necessary and her logical and illogical fears were gone. There was a
finality in Freda's actions. The establishment auctioneers Little and
Lawson sold her beloved piano which had once been her mother's,
and the room, empty of it, was now 'horrid'. The piano was not all
that went as an inventory of contents of Flowton, approximately
two years later, proved. It is possible some furnishings went to Guy
or Bertie as Eccleston, like many elderly people, may have been getting rid of his belongings but there was nothing of Freda's in that
later list. Selling all her belongings committed her to going and
raised as much money as possible, although leaving Eccleston,
whose vision and hard work had given him renown and respect but
who now was a rather lonely 81-year-old, was a terrible prospect.
It was unlikely she would ever see him again, especially as she
intended to be 'the proud possessor of a flat there [London] for the
next five or six years'.[14] Muriel was going through the same thing
with her family.

Finally parents were organised, farewells had been made to the

Dupains, the Badhams and even to friends who no longer had 'mutual interests and ideals'. Their large boxes sent care of Eccleston's unmarried older sister, Miss Frederica Eliza Du Faur of Leinster Gardens, Paddington, London, had already gone down to the ship, although there was no permanency in the arrangement as Freda gave her postal address as the Bank of Australasia, 4 Threadneedle St, London. Last minute shopping had been done and final instructions made, but on 9 January, one day before they were to leave, Freda lost her bag containing all her documentation, bank books, passport and even her tickets. She was distraught. The house was searched, the grounds, every possible place. All Freda's poise disappeared.

That evening Freda's bag was returned by one of their neighbours, Mrs Nagle, whose daughter, Velma, had found the bag when playing on nearby Josh's Flat. Freda took the bag gratefully and promised to buy the child a beautiful doll for her efforts. The next morning, on 10 January, the little girl watched Freda depart in the four-wheeled buggy, laden with luggage. There was no doll, there never would be.

Freda had forgotten. She didn't look back at Flowton, didn't look back down that dusty road through the eucalypts into the Chase. She was looking ahead, to a new 'home of hopes and dreams'.

15 ELYSIAN FIELDS

'If anything goes wrong it will be a fight to the end. If your training is good enough, survival is there; if not nature claims its forfeit.'

Dougal Haston

England was waiting. It was art and literature and mountaineering, royalty, grace and opportunity. It was family: Queen Anne Street, Cavendish Square, Sloane Street, Harrow, Norwich, Lyndhurst and Flowton Hall. Freda could savour the opportunities that the publication of her book and her climbing reputation might bring to her. Muriel had her contacts in the health clubs and the magazines that she and George Dupain had written articles for over the previous few years. The two women had read everything they could about their destination and were well aware intellectually of the political situation they were going into. Of course there was 'Votes for Women' but there was also the rising relevance of socialist doctrine, particularly that of Karl Marx, who saw that revolution was the only hope for the struggling poor sinking 'below the level of consciousness that can respond to any hope of change'. Neither situation was ameliorated by the Liberals who, under Asquith, had been in power ineffectually in Britain since 1908. The party could not deal effectively with the situation in Ireland, in fact the offer of Home Rule to Ulster in 1912, which was rejected by the House of Lords in 1913, had aggravated a situation in which civil war seemed likely in Ireland. War in the Balkans was also a possibility, but to Freda that was remote and did not in any way affect her feeling that her future in England would gleam brighter than any of her parents' stories and their hopes.

So that was why they were so surprised when they came off the boat mid-February and felt like the forlorn foreigners Freda had joked about to Otto Frind. A winter of bare trees and stubbled grass did not help. Nor did Freda's physical state. The voyage had taken seven weeks, considerably more that the five days to New Zealand and even that short trip had always been excruciating. Now, in the English wind flecked with sleet, the memory of those plain, blunt, sunny places in Sydney seemed both dreamlike and comforting, a subtle warning that she and Muriel might not find England quite as congenial as they'd imagined.

London helped a little, with familiar landmarks viewed from the narrow-hipped horse that pulled their cab and dodged through the thousands of other black cabs and omnibuses. It was the London of childhood stories and poems, of tall, grey stone build-ings and crumpled, black and white, half-timbered Elizabethan inns, narrow streets, haphazard terraces, street markets and bar-rows pulled by small, pale children in tight pants and flat caps. It was lines of black-suited men walking with umbrellas furled, then unfurled, as the rain came down again. Through the draping green-ery of Hyde Park, their cab carried them out through the Lancaster Gates, then past the tall terraces of Paddington, rows of them, cream upon cream, black railing upon black railing, as the cab turned into Leinster Gardens. There the terraces were more uni-form and bigger: five floors plus attic and basement kitchen, with large, neat porticos confined by exactly the same, overly impressive colonnades that reached from the pavement to the second floor. Frilled balconies ribboned from one terrace house to the next. In the centre were the gardens themselves, well tended, with neat lines of perennials waiting to bloom in heavy, weedless soil. Above spread large trees – elm and silver birch, interspersed with lilac.

The house belonging to Freda's aunt was halfway down the block. There Freda would not be seen as a successful, exciting mountaineer, nor even as the original Freda Du Faur. Aunt Frederica was Miss F. Du Faur and called herself Freda. She was a feminine version of her brother, with spare, small features, pale-lidded, unreadable eyes, a scraping of white hair and a fine skin that had rarely been exposed to the sun. Freda was the colonial niece, a namesake, the daughter of a loved brother. The new arrivals were just two more spinsters to join the household that included Amy Haydon, the housekeeper, and her aunt's long-time companion, Catherine Kemplay.

It must have occurred to Freda – and if not it was the sort of thing Muriel liked to observe being a people's person and fascinated by human behaviour – that there was a pattern in Freda's family. Eccleston, Bertie, Emmeline and now this Frederica were all hidden people, with a wife or companion that humanised them. Catherine Kemplay was more endearing than Frederica, and Freda knew that it was easier for most people to be with Muriel than it was to be with her.

Aware that this kind of formal England was not for them, they were determined to find their ever so slightly bohemian flat, close to 'everything', as soon as they had recovered from the journey. But, before such plans could restore Freda's dented and always fragile confidence, devastating news arrived.

In 1912 the Ladies' Alpine Club, from its comfortable rooms in the centre of London, had analysed accidents in the European Alps. In all, 114 travellers, including ten ladies and eight guides, had died due to a number of reasons: climbing alone, novices climbing without a guide, want of nerve or skill, getting into dangerous places, insufficient equipment, bad weather or a false step on the rock. The four main natural causes were the breakage of a snow bridge or cornice, storms, mist or nightfall. Curiously avalanches were not mentioned. Freda, with Peter Graham and Charlie Milne, had had anxious moments on the descent of Dampier. Freda wrote of the relief of crossing the Linda Glacier and avoiding avalanches 'which were now coming down pretty frequently after the hot midday sun'.[1] On 24 February 1914, her friend and guide Darby Thomson, the guide Jock Richmond, and their client, Sydney L. King of the English Alpine Club, had not been so fortunate.

After completing the ascent of Cook via the Linda, the three climbers had waited for a number of hours on the summit for Otto Frind, Conrad Kain and a new guide, William Brass, to reach them from Earle's route. As they'd been held up on ice and would not make the summit until 5.15 p.m., Thomson, King and Richmond gave up waiting, descended via the Linda Glacier but were swept away by an avalanche. Only Jock Richmond's body was retrieved, despite heroic and desperate efforts by the search parties. Conrad Kain said in an interview later in the *Christchurch Press*: 'You can imagine how it is to search for dead who have been colleagues and mountain friends, with whom one has proposed a meeting on the highest peak of the country.'[2]

For Peter Graham, it was much worse. Richmond and particularly Thomson had been close friends for years, men he had encouraged to become guides. As well as their chief, he was responsible for their welfare and was determined to do well by them. Before long arguments started over the accident and in particular how the climbers would be commemorated. Freda heard both Otto Frind's and Peter Graham's versions. Perhaps Peter was unusually dogmatic because he was tired of the guides' non-existent status:

even New Zealand newspapers made much of the death of the client, King, while the guides were mentioned as an afterthought. Peter wanted a memorial of some kind but many of the traditionalists in New Zealand and Frind, the self-imposed spokesman for the reorganisation of the New Zealand climbing scene, believed it was not a good idea. The basis for opposition was purely traditional: that if there were no memorials in the Swiss Alps, there should be none in New Zealand. Peter would not budge and was supported by what Frind scathingly called, Peter's 'Ladies Admiration Club' who 'have taken the stand that we are acting against Peter's wishes and against all reason'. The main offender was Dorothy Theomin who, only months earlier, had been a recipient of one of Otto's pins. He complained: 'It is annoying to find yourself up against a feminine stone wall.'[3] It would not have been a good time for Freda's suffrage papers to have reached him.

The stress of the deaths and the push by Peter Graham for the erection of a memorial cairn, although successful, were exhausting. Later in the year he became ill for three months with pleurisy, an illness that undermined his climbing the following year as well.

The deaths hit Freda more severely than they might have, had she still been in close contact with those involved and had been able to mourn with people who understood. The news harshly forced her to move from her blind belief that accidents could not happen, to recall, with some horror, the way she and Peter had approached the Sefton traverse and the easy way they had decided 'nothing short of an accident' would stop them. Peter had been right; her lack of awareness was appalling. Darby's face, 'unaccustomedly grave', when they lost their way on that descent would have been haunting. Whenever she'd been uncertain in the past, she could always reassure herself on the rocks in the Chase or in the Southern Alps where the power of her body could beat debilitating sentiments. But now it was all too clear that if accidents could happen on mountains she knew extremely well, what could happen on mountains she was not familiar with, like the Rockies or the European Alps? Once again 'her faith in her climbing prowess was shaken' and the streets of London could give no respite. It was not just death she was afraid of, but the helplessness of mourning at such a distance.

Help was close by if Freda had not been too defensive to look for it, from the close-knit group of high climbers whose experiences ensured they understood, who felt that 'distance is no barrier to the brotherhood of the mountains or the comradeship of those who love the hills'.[4] Freda already knew Mr Earle, and others, 'some of the best men' she had teased Otto Frind with, who had wanted to use her articles or had written congratulatory letters. Freda could also have contacted Malcolm Ross, the New Zealand climber, whom she knew personally and who was in England. On 13 February he had given a talk to the Alpine Club during which he spoke of a climb he had made and how he had faced the reality that death was always possible at any moment. 'I lost contact with the rocks and hung suspended, like Mahomet's coffin, between heaven and earth', he told that select club of gentlemen who no doubt had faced such situations and had feared they would not survive.

There were women she could have met as well but, tenacious in belief, fresh and full of zeal from her fight to climb as a woman in New Zealand, Freda was not interested in associating with them. Nothing in her years of climbing, apart from her friendship with Mrs Lindon, had encouraged her to believe there were advantages in climbing with women. To join the Ladies' Alpine Club, formed in 1907, was to betray all she had fought for. It would give the men's club, with over six hundred members, including the King of Belgium and a member of the British Cabinet, an excuse not to let her in. Not to push for the Alpine Club would be an admission of failure. If she couldn't join it, she wouldn't join any club at all. But she had underestimated the long history of exclusive men's clubs entrenched in British society. Even in 1929, Frind's friend, Captain MacCarthy, when interviewed at Mount Cook, was quoted as saying, 'The Alpine Club, London is a very exclusive organisation and does not admit women to membership, which some ladies find difficult to understand.'[5] Even more importantly, Freda underestimated the high standard of the women in the Ladies' Club, something Annie Lindon always appreciated. At that time pictures had just arrived at the club from her showing a panorama taken from Mount Annette. The members were educated women, of high social standing, artists, writers and linguists. They worked hard to maintain the club, and probably felt as put out as Freda that they'd had to form one of their own. But they'd more than made the best out of the situation. Perhaps, if Freda's struggle to climb, to be accepted and be an equal with men in the mountains of New Zealand had not been so recent – had been a struggle of fifty years earlier, as it had been for the women in Britain and Europe – Freda might have been content and, as most did, wisely prefer the Ladies' Alpine Club. At least, by giving them a chance, Freda would have realised there was much more to them than was suggested by the social gathering at their headquarters at the Great Central Hotel in Marylebone. True, there were monthly lectures and 'At Homes' that cost ninepence for tea, bread and butter, cake and a coal fire, but such gatherings brought climbers from different nationalities together, where they could be a support and inspiration to each other and the younger climbers following. All this would have secured Freda in the mountaineering world of the Northern Hemisphere and helped her to work through her feelings, and get the kind of support the Graham brothers would have given her.

In those early days, everything the members of the Ladies' Club did was a record for women and helped them attain a dynamic public image. One of the earliest members was Lucy Walker, whose daring had opened up climbing for women. After twenty years of climbing she was forced to give up in 1879, under doctor's orders. When Freda arrived in England she was active in other ways and, at the age of 78, was President of the Club. Her speeches at the annual club dinners were 'witty and racy; members looked eagerly for her broad smiling face and her straight smooth hair, neatly coiled in a bun at the back'.[6] Other members were Fanny Bullock Workman and the famous, elegant and bold Mrs Aubrey (Lissie) Le Blond, who moved in the best society, and had been the first President of the Club. She was one of the first women to lead a party and on the ascent of Piz Palu, climbed with only one other woman, Lady Evelyn McDonnel.

Women Freda's age were also members. There was an Irish climber, Margaret Osborne, about whom it was said that the guides 'never reckoned her among women climbers but counted her among the men',[7] who climbed with her brother and by 1913 had completed all of the great traverses in the Alps. One of the stalwarts of the club, Beatrice McAndrew, first climbed in 1906 in Switzerland, about the time Freda was dreaming about the possibilities of becoming a mountaineer, and would continue both before and after the coming war. Interested in painting watercolours as well as climbing, she was also known for her 'unfailing kindness, the warm welcome she gave to everyone and the care she took over each new member'.[8] Freda would have been welcomed, even feted by such company.

Freda lived to climb, but she refused to do so if it meant compromising her ideals. Tenacious to the end, holding onto her ideals and principles, as well as her failures and successes, even more so when depressed, she put the Alpine Club, and the Ladies' Club out of her mind. Freda, too proud to look for sympathetic connections, had lost contact with the rocks but, instead of being hauled up by a fellow climber, she did what she was best at: avoiding confronting how she was feeling. Thus, she proudly went on as if nothing could ever undermine her. The tame cloistering darkness of London life was suffocating, but neither she nor her closest friend, Muriel, were aware of her needs. They were together, in the Home Country: was that not enough? Only that real spring, an English spring, helped clear Freda's mood with the sheer pleasure of its classic beauty. Springtime in England was reminiscent of those rare days up at Mount Wilson, with its faux English environment. It reminded Freda of Guy's beloved garden of exotic plants, her mother's joy in ordered nature and Muriel's idea of classical perfection.

Relatives began to arrive. Frederica's younger sister, by then a widow, Ellen Bryans, came with her married daughter Mary Louisa Wolfe, up from Lyndhurst in the New Forest. There were four sons in the Bryans family as well: Alfred, Reginald, Harold and Maxwell. Joining them, also, was another of Eccleston's sisters, Mary Sarah Taylor, who had five children: Sybilla, Amy, Hugh, Helen and Arthur. As these Du Faur sisters had married at a young age and Eccleston had his children relatively late in life, Freda was actually closer in age to her second cousins, in particular Arthur Taylor's children, Cyprian and Reggie. Cyprian Taylor, a regular visitor, a favourite of both Frederica and Catherine Kemplay, was content, for a few months, to take Freda and Muriel about.

For a time, the two Australian women were satisfied with the novelty of their existence and the shops, operas and restaurants. Encouraged to visit, they caught the train to spend weekends in Hampshire and Sussex, at the homes of the Taylors and Mary Wolfe. They also travelled to Norwich, to wander through the Upper Close and view the house that was Blanche's last home in England, and then to walk into the main street, past the school and onward to the Cathedral that Emmeline had insisted Freda must some day visit. In that refined environment they listened to the music and choir that had so inspired her aunt. As much as they were enjoying it, Freda was not entirely swayed by all this 'gadding about'. She knew it was short-lived, to be enjoyed until they returned to their real purpose but, for a time, frivolity allowed her to suppress her anguish over the accident on the Linda Glacier and ensure her non-climbing didn't depress her.

They were beginning to change their minds about the Suffragettes. Militant attacks by the Women's Social and Political Union (WSPU) that had enthralled them in the papers in Sydney were much less appealing at close quarters. In February alone, the month they arrived, almost £65,000 damage had been done through arson, the vandalising of golf courses and country houses, stone throwing and broken windows. A month later, a large impromptu rally held in Hyde Park had ended in violence. On 21 May two hundred women, some carrying clubs and eggshells filled with red and yellow paint, rioted, resulting in the arrest of 66 women and two men. Lurid photos in the papers of the day of women fighting with police dissipated the sympathy engendered by past years of gaoling and force-feeding. As the US Suffragist Anna Shaw commented: 'Women never show up their real weakness so much as when they attempt force.'[9] Because of the militancy, many women began leaving the Suffragettes and joined one of the groups that had banded together in 1907 under the banner of the National Union for Women's Suffrage with Lady Frances Balfour as president and the renowned Mrs Millicent Fawcett chairman. Among the groups in the union was the National Society of Women's Suffrage which had its beginnings in 1865 when John Stuart Mill, then a member of Parliament, agreed that if suffragists could get one hundred signatures he would help them. Fifteen hundred signatures were collected in the first petition and a women's advice bureau began to help women expand their abilities. Soon the leaders discovered that 'superficial education of girls was not enough and the political disabilities of women were matters very relevant to their main economic problem'.[10] Constitutional societies were then set up, through which they could lobby municipal councillors and government ministers from centralised headquarters at 58 Victoria street, Westminster, London. After only a few months in England, Freda and Muriel had no doubt that this branch, the London Society, was the way of the future. They became two of the nearly two thousand new supporters to join in the first six months of 1914. (Freda's name appears as 'Du Fane' – a clerical error.) This brought the number of supporters in the society to 27,700.

Muriel began to cross London by underground to the head-quarters. She was a useful addition to such an organisation as she had, long ago, learned to satisfy her own needs by organising others, taking part in discussions and training women in fitness. She was also skilled in writing articles and producing magazines, which was especially useful to a group that engendered its own publicity.

It was much harder for Freda to fit in. Muriel had trained her teams of women athletes while Freda had trained to climb as a solitary woman and had rarely been committed to enhancing women's theoretical rights except as a consequence of her own career. So, while Muriel was busy at the London Society, Freda followed up her initial, fortuitous meeting at the Hermitage with Mr Stanley Unwin. She presented herself at the publishers, George Allen and Unwin, of Ruskin House, 40 Museum Street and an agreement was made to publish her book. But if she had thought she would just hand over her manuscript and that was that, she was mistaken. There would be no rushing off to Canada while rewriting had to be done, titles chosen and photographs organised, some of her own, some donated by Dr Teichelmann and one of the flood at the Hermitage by a Mr Severn Storr. There was now an official reason why Freda and Muriel could not go mountaineering that summer.

There had been no rushing back to Canada for Otto Frind either. The end of the season in New Zealand found him in

Auckland, minding the climbing scene there. On 24 April he sent Freda a parcel containing, what he described as, an 'art production' given to him by an uncle. As he prided himself on being a irredeemable Philistine, knowing it irritated Freda, he asked her 'as you are well up in the ways of these un-understandables, you might be able to suggest some reason why he fired a missile at me?' It was also an excuse to give Freda a present she would enjoy more than he would. Believing Freda was still intending to get to Canada, if not that year, the year after, he reported that Samuel Turner, who had been up in the North Island with him for a month, was 'rather keen on climbing the Rockies in a year or so'. As Freda was 'hell bent on invading the same ground', he suggested she should consider climbing with them at the same time. Harking back to their teasing relationship and her attempts to indoctrinate him in the rights of women, he teased her to stay out of Holloway, where the Suffragettes were being force-fed.[11]

Otto Frind never received a response to his letter nor acknowledgment of the painting. He did not try to contact Freda himself again, although he had Aunt Frederica Du Faur's address at Leinster Gardens until 1925, and Freda's own address in England until 1918 through the Alpine Club of Canada. Despite this, he would write in 1915 to Johannes Andersen (concerning the naming of Mount Pibrac) and confessed he could not ask Freda about the peak as he hadn't heard from her again. As late as 1928 the abrupt loss of contact concerned Frind. Older and cooler, perhaps recalling the change from teasing to seriousness in Freda's letter to him from Flowton, he wondered if it was his attitude that had alienated her. He noted at the bottom of his papers concerning the letter to her, 'I do not know whether Miss Du Faur saw more than mere banter in these remarks of mine. They can be listened to but not stand reading.'[12]

Freda had been hardening her attitude to women's roles and

rights, and nothing the two experienced in England weakened that stance; but for all her sensitivities, she had not suddenly turned into a serious, ill-humoured creature. It is likely that Freda deliberately lost contact with Otto because she had made a significant change to her lifestyle and she had no desire for her old friend to come blundering into a situation he would never understand. In England, away from familial expectations, in a society that saw them as outsiders, yet tolerated greater differences, in a London in which the avant-garde ways of the Bloomsbury Set were at least regarded as an element of the creative society,[13] Freda and Muriel were presented with an opportunity to recreate the way in which they wished to live. Spending so much time together, their emotional dependence and, no doubt meeting up with women like themselves, the sexual side of their friendship flourished. Although, as in most relationships, such personal details of their life together were never recorded in detail, Freda would later describe their friendship in the psychological terminology of the time as an 'hedonistic inversion'.[14] However they lived, it was as lesbians in 'a mode of life in which a woman's political, intellectual, emotional, social and sexual energies are focussed on other women'.[15]

16 LANDLOCKED

'Over the hills and over the meadows
Gay is my way till day be done
Blue as the heaven are all the shadows
And every light is gold in the sun.'

Metroland Poster: 'PINNER via Bakerloo'

Everything had finally fallen into place. Freda could understand now why she had never wanted to marry, how the repression of her real instincts had led to depression and why she had been so adamant about appearing feminine. She understood Emmeline and Ethel now, and so many of their friends. The world suddenly looked vastly different, a new and thrilling place open to her and Muriel. There were no brothers to say this or that was wrong, no school friends to be shocked, not even Enid, too far away to worry about. They could live utterly as they wished. The first essential was a private place, a safe base in which to build their relationship and from which to go out and conquer whatever they wanted. This new development was their next great adventure; then they would go to Canada, go to Europe, go anywhere as soon, of course, as Freda finished the book.

For Muriel, it was simple; she was determined for it to be so.

Determination could overcome anything and worries were to be dealt with by willpower, but she was conscious that Freda's money and connections were providing her with the kind of lifestyle to which she had not been accustomed. She was used to the autonomy of her own career and financial freedom for all its haphazard nature, so she set to work to justify her existence by organising, as she had done with her own family, their life together. She found a house, Red Cottage, away from their 'straight' family connections, in Pinner, a quintessential English village on the outskirts of London.

The town appeared to combine the best of both worlds. It was not too small but there was a certain amount of anonymity in seven thousand inhabitants, it was cheap, with fresher air and countryside and only two and half miles from a favourite place, the famous old town and school of Harrow, where Freda's father had been a student and with which he still communicated.[1] Established five centuries earlier, on the banks of the River Pinn, the historical charm of Pinner was also appealing for two women from a country where there was scarcely a house more than a century old. Pinner had bloomed during Elizabethan times so the High Street was lined with two haphazard rows of half-timbered shops, with tiny diamond-paned windows of that period, tethering posts and water troughs. Dominating the steep street, at the top was the Church of St John. Dedicated in the thirteenth century, its floors and door steps were worn from daily worshippers.

Even in 1914 many of the quaint old ways were still practised. Horses were taken through the front door of houses to be stabled at the back and, as a local put it, 'cows had to be taught carefully to pick their devious way through the shop to reach the milking place at the rear'.[2] But some change was beginning to encroach on Pinner's sedate past. It had become the main trading centre for the district and over the weekends of summer four local hotels did roaring business. Farmers and their workers had been gradually making way for an educated middle class of intelligentsia. Lawyers, accountants and businessmen who prided themselves on some kind of soul had moved out with the industrial prosperity of the Victorian age and the arrival of a railway line without which Freda and Muriel could not have considered moving out of London.

Muriel may well have made a connection with Pinner through women at the London Society as the town had been associated with women's help groups for years. A Pinner Townswoman Guild had been established to encourage education for women, and there was a determined suffrage group at 77 Paines Lane, just behind Freda and Muriel's new home, where Jamie Terrero, local secretary of the WSPU gave garden parties, raised money and organised rallies.

Red Cottage was only a few minutes from the station, in the first group of new houses on the long, narrow Elm Park Road, or Rotten Row as it was originally called. Red Cottage was, and still is, an unusual looking house, but pleasingly spacious. In some ways it is a small version of Pibrac, with long eaves, a shingled roof and multi-paned, bay windows. What Pibrac did not have was a kind of turret that encompassed the hall and the landing on the first floor, and which had a chisel-edged witch's hat topped by a weather vane. It was entirely appropriate as Pinner, over the centuries, had had its time of persecuting primarily single women, women who did not conform, women like Freda and Muriel, who were self-sufficient, rather secretive, corsetless, often hatless, given to strange causes and therefore strange ways. Women who could easily be regarded as 'the sort that went out with the ducking stool'.[3]

There were still forces in Pinner keen to repress uppity women, although opposition was primarily that of the naughty schoolboy type. As one man reported gleefully about his childhood:

I used to get paid 3d a week to go to Gurneys, the grocer, who

used to save the bad eggs and to Peters, the baker, for flour and
... across the fields to the United Services Club near Paines Lane
we used to give it to them ... But they never gave in and you
could never beat them ... And the police used to ignore them
because I suppose anything that a woman did at that time of day,
well they didn't used to worry about.'[4]

But militancy aggravated this attitude and anything that smacked of
violence was immediately ascribed to any woman who supported
suffrage. When the St John's church organ was dismantled for
repair, the resulting temporary mess was blamed on a Suffragette
bomb. Angry crowds actually attacked suffragists in High Street and
they had to seek refuge in a few sympathetic households.

Largely immune to this as newcomers, Freda and Muriel were
determined to settle properly into their new home. They dug a veg-
etable garden in the backyard, fixed up the old hen house and
bought hens; and from their central position soon became
acquainted with the area. On the town side of the Red Cottage was
the entrance to Little Common and on the other side was North
End Cottage. Across the unsealed and uncurbed road was a most
distinctive house, The Lodge, a Georgian building with a curved
driveway lined by beautiful standard roses. It was all so charming.

Tucked into nearby lanes, overgrown with native cherry,
hawthorn, elder and lime, were tiny, storybook houses with shingle
roofs and walls made of uneven planks. Along Westend Lane, wildflowers grew in profusion on the grass verges, and up the path from
Pinner Green, opposite the Belle Vue Cottages, was an historic
bridge and a rather boggy field where they could find marigolds
and little wild orchids. Pinner Park was also a popular recreation
spot, beyond which could be seen the tall chimneys of the Kodak
building where a hooter announced the start of the work day for
young, single women. And beyond Pinner were the farms and big

houses that marked the boundaries of once great woods and lakes, properties that had been in the same families for generations, most of which had benefited from the enclosure of common land in the early nineteenth century to the detriment of their poorer neighbours.

They travelled regularly into London through the emerald green hills and bright green willows, past suburbs of narrow, brown and white speckled houses decorated with a hodgepodge of windows and drainpipes and angled roofs, where washing was strung so close to the embankment that the draught from the train at once dried, then dirtied it again. They attended suffrage meetings in Harrow and in Pinner. Freda worked on her book. So busy, so interesting was their new life that they did not realise that Pinner was not so very different, although in different clothing, from Croydon and later Turramurra, even the new Hermitage.

It was civilisation in its most cloying yet comfortable form, a middle-class suburban life of bungalows, pretty gardens and trimmed hedges, sandwiched between the big houses like Pinner Place and Mayfield and the 'rabbit hutch houses of the poor who looked at another life through their railings'.[5] It was a town where everything revolved round the parish hall and the church, where everyone knew their place and lived within it. It stuck hard to the very rules Freda railed against but, as an outsider, found useful to gain acceptance. She was comfortable with the social graces of the calling cards on the table in the hall. It was a society, despite all the newcomers, resistant to change and the inhabitants liked it that way. In 1910 they protested against the introduction of public lights. Traders later rejected buses as spoiling the old-world village. Even the Lawn Tennis Club, which Freda and Muriel joined, was proud of the 'spacious old world character of its pavilion as of its six hard courts'.[6] Until the changes wrought by the war and by an increasingly mobile population came into effect, Pinner remained the true home of Mrs Beeton, arbiter of British household manners, defined in her classic work, *Mrs Beeton's Book of Household Management*.

War was not entirely unexpected but it was certainly something Freda had preferred not to consider when planning a life in London. She had only been in England five months and now distant squabbles over territory between Serbia and Austria, a series of treaties between the major powers of Europe and Britain's promise to defend Belgium if invaded lead Britain into declaring war on Germany and her allies on 4 August 1914. Soon Belgian refugees would be billeted in Pinner as the German forces moved through Belgium into France.

Freda and Muriel felt pride when the Australian Prime Minister, Joseph Cook, declared, 'If the Old Country is at War, so are we!' – as early as 1 November a volunteer force and a fleet of 36 troopships and three cruisers left Australian shores – but it turned to indignation when *The Annual Register* condescendingly stated: 'The declaration of war against Germany was not taken quite so calmly by the Australian people as by the people of the United Kingdom. The Australians, as a youthful community, naturally exercise less restraint in time of Imperial stress than the experienced veterans of the Mother Country.' It was more than irksome. It epitomised the petty discriminations concerning their colonial ways they had been feeling since they arrived.

High Street was rife with the gossip caused by the uncertainty of information. Secret prewar preparation by the British government became obvious when posters were put up in the shop windows, which advised the populace that 'In case of invasion stay at home unless advised otherwise.' If invaded, directions were to 'Proceed over the Downs, a Special Constable at the crossroads will direct you. Obey their instructions. Take to fields when necessary.' There was an air of unreality about the war, despite the presence of refugees, and a pervasive feeling that it would all be over by Christmas. Freda was confident that her book would be finished and they would be over in Canada for the first of the climbing in 1915.

Instead, the demands of war began to encroach upon their lives. No one would ever need take to the Downs but, if it had been necessary, the only way would have been on foot. Buses, trucks and new cars disappeared from the streets. Horses were led away down the lanes. Pinner had 'get fits' in the hall, volunteer parties were set up to take over the roles of men who had left and the Parish Hall was turned into a recruiting centre, from where the first of 654 young men were signed up and cheered off in carriages supplied by the big local houses. Young men leaving was a scene to be found in most other towns in Britain and soon to be emulated, not only in Sydney, but in New Zealand, in the farming towns like Manakau and at the Hermitage itself.

Soon, not only refugees, but the wounded brought an undesired reality to the war. Signs had appeared in windows saying, 'This house has sent a man to fight for King and Country', but it would not be long before these would be replaced by plaques and flowers for the men who had died. Accounts of ferocious battles and the Roll of Honour dominated the newspapers. Military funerals, led by the rotund, white-bearded local undertaker, Mr Ellement, began to make regular trips along Moss Lane to the cemetery.

The push for 'Votes for Women' was suspended despite the feeling by many that the war was a male choice. 'Let us show ourselves worthy of citizenship, whether our claim to it be recognised or not!' proclaimed Muriel's heroine, Mrs Fawcett, in the journal of the London Society, *The Common Cause*. Within a fortnight of war being declared Muriel's precious society had evolved, with government support, into the Women's Service Bureau. There were four departments responsible for registration of paid and voluntary workers, hospitals, munitions, and information and training. The first workers employed needed to be experienced, ideally without dependents, be healthy, of good character and have qualifications. Already a member, Muriel was a perfect candidate for the war work the bureau had to offer as it immediately supplied helpers to 293 organisations. Over the period of the war the bureau would interview over forty thousand women, many who had never worked in cooperation with each other. Training centres were set up which not only taught new skills, but also suffrage ideals to women who had never been in direct contact with such concepts before.

The Service Bureau was regarded as part of the operations of the army and subject, in theory at least, to its rules. A letter arrived for the successful applicant which reminded her of the 'severe penalties for breach of confidence'. Punishments ranged from admonishment to imprisonment. No one could be shot. The bureau was run in a paternalistic fashion and agreed with the government that, 'If the women are comfortable, happy and well cared for they will be far easier to control as well as remaining healthier.'[7]

Despite their 'need' for such guidance, the women did eventually 'manage' to provide war emergency work, social services, Belgium relief hostels, clubs for women, maternity centres and women street patrols. It had its own vehicle maintenance school and welding schools to provide skilled workers for the factories. Women had not received the vote but, in the absence of men, they were allowed to report the business of the House of Commons and work in dangerous industries like munitions. In one explosion alone 24 women were killed as they worked. Initial reluctance for them to be near the battlefields was overcome. Members of the bureau were active organisers of the Red Cross and established field hospitals and medical units, such as that under the auspices of the

Scottish Women's Hospital. Initially the British government resisted, so they helped the allies, the French and particularly the Serbians.

Almost a million and a half more women would be employed during the war, but the urgency of the situation did not permit the keeping of good records. Many thousands of women, like Muriel, were pleased to get paid work, although they would not be paid the same as a man would for the same job. There was a form of justification, put out by the War Office in 1916 that, although women had 'shown themselves capable of replacing the stronger sex in practically every calling', rates of pay took 'into consideration that an equal number of women cannot replace an equal number of men'.

Muriel was in her element. Freda was not. Initially her time was very much taken with the final work on her book, which came out at 246 pages, with 49 photographs but, even when she had the time, she was chary about making commitment to anything outside her own interests. Having financial freedom, coming to England had meant that at last she was not beholden to anyone. She would not give that up for anything. In the past, when she'd given herself to another's needs, she had ended up an emotional mess. She could not face that again and could not be like the old girls from SCEGGS who went to war, women like Olive Kelso King who took her own ambulance to Serbia, and Joan Twynam who would be one of the first nurses into Gallipoli. Nor could she, even for such a calamity as war, lose herself in group activities. She had to defend her individuality and not be like members of the Ladies' Alpine Club, who made the necessary changes with their usual good spirits, as 'ice axes were converted to knitting needles and ropes into bandages'.[8] Climbing went into abeyance but those fervent members of the club firmly believed that one day the war would end but mountaineering would go on forever.

Nor could Freda, as many financially independent women did, spend the duration of the war, 'riding, reading the papers, altering the flags on the war maps, knitting' and saying, 'I pity the people who wear my woollies.'[9] That would be too pathetic. She had to do something, if only out of shame and, it appears, volunteered her services to the devil she knew, nursing. Hospital trains were bringing up to five hundred men a time from the front to rest stations at convenient towns such as Abbeville. There the wounded were sorted into two groups: those to be treated where they were and those able to travel by ship across the English Channel and then by train again to the various hospitals. As a volunteer, Freda would foot her own bill for her uniform but could work as and where she wished. There was plenty of choice in the Pinner area which had a VAD Hospital Fund, a War Hospital Supply Department and the St John Auxiliary Military Hospital. Also, one of the big local houses, Pinner Place, had been converted to a wartime hospital and was run by the upper class women of the district. It was perfect for Freda.

When the war that should have finished in December was clearly continuing, Muriel and Freda encountered their first real winter. Elms lost their leaves which lay rusting in the heavy mud alongside the roads, their bare branches harsh against the shortening daylight hours. There was little joy in the snow-laden villages and little cheer in those elegant London shopping streets. In front of the fire, with ice crystals patterning the windows, it was hard to believe summer was beginning in the Southern Hemisphere and that only two years earlier Freda had been setting out for New Zealand. Letters arrived, months late through shipping restrictions, some from family and some from New Zealand.

Life and climbing of a kind were continuing at the Hermitage. Dorothy Theomin and Eleanor Joachim were still going there from

Dunedin, the latter, in particular, 'was up with everything '(according to Frind) with whom she was very friendly, and was dealing with him over his photos for *Holiday Road*.[10] In September 1914, Eleanor was staying in Christchurch with Mary Murray Aynsley and reported to Frind that Jim Dennistoun was going to the Rockies and she would take up his offer and go the following year. She, Dorothy and Mary intended going to Mount Cook over summer. The Southern Hemisphere for once, through terrible circumstances, was one of the few places left to climb. There was a frustrating irony in this, given Freda's decision to go to London.

But she had great hopes of her life opening up with the publication of her book. Under the circumstances, it was not surprising that its launch did not attract much publicity, but it received its necessary mention in *The Times*, which, despite the war, still published its smart and informative 'Literary Supplement'. The announcement of its pending release appeared on Thursday, 18 March 1915 and the book was briefly described as, 'A handsome volume which will be of much interest both to the mountaineers and to New Zealanders.'

The full review in *The Times* on 8 April would not be so brief or so kind. It had been reviewed by a man, probably Edward FitzGerald, whose ego was more on display than the book he was reviewing. He wrote from the point of view of an 'expert' (his designation) on late nineteenth-century mountaineering in New Zealand. Freda, in his eyes, was a snippet who had overreached herself. The first half of the review was a scolding and even the title was attacked as 'an overly ambitious title for Miss Du Faur's account'. He took her to task for not realising 'how much the success of the present day in the district was due to the laborious and unrewarded work of her predecessors'. Otto Frind would also criticise her for her first chapter, on the history of climbing in the Southern Alps, as 'misinformed and unsound'. In some ways they were right; Freda did not go into the past as much as she might have but the book was, after all, a history of her climbs, not a history of New Zealand mountaineering.

The second half of the review did give Freda some credit. Contradicting his own self-proclaimed and unclear theory on the development of a climber – that it takes many years of hard work – the reviewer called her 'a natural mountaineer' and said that 'few people of any sex can regard four years of achievement more noteworthy than that described'.

In the last paragraph, the reviewer finally talked about the book itself, and summed it up as a 'splendid and crowded tale' but despite being so described, he then wrote that it was 'without any great distinction of style but it is simply and pleasurably told'. Then he expressed relief that Freda had managed to write in a way that was not 'hyperbolic nor facetious nor more monotonous than is inevitable'.

Finally he pronounced magnanimously, 'She loves the mountains and is worthy to climb among them.' Freda did not need such a blessing and was far more coherent in her writing than he was.

In Canada, *The Conquest of Mount Cook* arrived via the New York publishers, Chas. Scribner and Sons. The Canadian *Alpine Journal* contained a short review in 1915. With no personal interest in the book and not a great deal of time to review it, the reviewer felt that, 'While it is the work of a young climber, it has the inspiration of high hopes founded on assured successes in the past.' There was 'value' in what she wrote about women climbing and the closest to a criticism was the comment: 'the illustrations are illuminating but a map would have added greatly to the pleasure of the reader'. It was a fair enough comment.

Frind bought a copy and wrote on 8 June to Johannes Andersen: 'The lack of maps and the careless manner of collecting the data in the introductory chapter detracts from the value of the book, but her style is generally rather breezy and interesting. The suffragette ideas are rather amusing. I shall be glad to learn how it is received in New Zealand.'[11]

Frind and Andersen would have to wait until the book was reviewed in the *Alpine Journal* of that country as late as March 1921. The review, or rather the defence of New Zealand mountaineers, was presumably written by the editor, Thomas Fletcher, who was sensitive, as no doubt were Freda's New Zealand readers, to her criticism of climbers of that country. Fletcher was extremely put out by her comment that she had 'never met anyone, apart from my own guides, who were as keen as myself'. He noted that enthusiasts did exist and Freda was unlucky, by which he meant that she was undeserving of meeting them. He noted that New Zealanders were still roughing it in order to climb, which 'is more that Miss Du Faur has done' – a cry that continues through the decades that Freda had it easy and was lucky. Fletcher reminded Freda, as if she'd ever forgotten, that her guides, 'on whom she owed her success', were New Zealanders, 'and it is doubtful if any country has produced such excellent guides'. Freda only criticised Tom, the porter/chaperon, and Jack Clarke, in one small section of the book, but the reviewer took great issue with the fact she blamed Clarke for the failure on Nazomi, that she omitted to attribute the second ascent of Sefton to him, and that she had not included him in the index. Fletcher then included a potted history of Jack Clarke, deserved but misplaced in the review, and proved, in doing so, that other climbers could be as one-eyed as Freda. Fletcher did admit, after complaining that *The Conquest of Mount Cook* was 'tainted with egoism', that it was beautifully illustrated, and contained few mistakes and 'is one of the most attractive books yet published on the Southern Alps'.

Records of sales of *The Conquest of Mount Cook*, which sold at fifteen shillings a copy, no longer exist so there is no telling the impact it made. At 33 Freda was not sure her money would last her all her life and was definitely looking for a career. However, she realised that she had been anointed as a climber only, not as a writer of a fine book. There were no offers forthcoming of more writing work; developing writers was not a priority as numbers on the Roll of Honour in *The Times* increased daily. There were already plenty of journalists, experienced ones. No one was interested in news stories from the top of mountains. As always, Muriel's love and sympathy supported Freda through the disappointment.

17 DARKENED LANES

> *'Set your eyes on the forgotten peaks of Honour, Duty, Patriotism*
> *and clad in glittering white, the great Pinnacle of Sacrifice pointing*
> *like a rugged finger to heaven.'*
>
> Lloyd George

Those years in England during the Great War were a strange time for women such as Freda and Muriel. On one level, their lives were easier than they could have ever imagined. No one was interested in their activities as long as wartime rules were abided by. Hair was bobbed, the hindering corsets discarded and Freda's abbreviated 'frill' of a mountaineering skirt was becoming common; and under the circumstances there were too many women providing emotional support to each other and sharing homes for them to stand out. The single woman was, briefly, acceptable. Nevertheless Freda began to mull over the life she had left behind and the one she was now living. The Romantic verse she had admired before the war no longer stood up. There was no 'beauty through blood' and the poetry of the battlefield that succeeded in touching her soul was too painful to recall, yet too often inescapable. Blood was mud and the rumbling of the guns on the battlefields in France and Belgium was a sound that eventually rattled the windows of English villages like Pinner.

On 1 February 1915, Zeppelin raids began on London. Rumours ran through Pinner when attacks might begin. There were thought to be spies everywhere. Blackouts were enforced and, every night, wardens walked those already dark lanes, looking for the giveaway chink of light from a careless household. Full moon meant an air raid, not brightly lit lanes and walks. Londoners were billeted in Pinner. Strangers came to live at Red Cottage for a few days, then left again, still strangers. Freda tried to get Aunt Frederica out to stay but neither she nor Catherine Kemplay wished to leave the home that they felt had survived far more difficulties than the present one.

A gun emplacement sat on the hill above the village although no one had any idea what kind of defence it would really be. They found out when the Zeppelins came over, 'silver maggots' which crept through the clouds and were exposed by the huge spotlights trained on them. Guns were next to useless although the overhead threat was largely ineffectual as a destructive measure but succeeded in adding to the already existing sense of oppression. It would not be until 3 September 1916, when a dozen Zeppelins came over Pinner, that one was brought down. Then there was enormous excitement. Few watching the burning frame of the airship as it drifted to the ground considered that people were being burned alive in it. Thousands went to the site, wreckage claimed to be part of the craft was sold and the newspapers chortled 'well played England!' It was a man's game this war and feminists could not cheer.[1]

The war escalated thoughout 1915 and Asquith's Liberals were forced into a coalition with the Tories. The country was now on a war footing. Fleeing from an invasion over the Downs was no longer a joke. Nor was fleeing back to Australia, at least until the war was over, as shipping was often in danger and neither woman would leave when most of Freda's male cousins were at the front

(Cyprian Taylor had already been made captain) and while so many young Australians and New Zealand men were already sailing through the Dardanelles. Spen Westmacott, Erica's older brother, was in Gallipoli; the first reports described the landing as 'almost bloodless' but in reality almost a thousand Australians and New Zealanders (ANZACS) were killed in the first three days. Also killed was the Mount Cook guide, Will Brass. The Head of the Department of Health and Resorts in New Zealand, Mr Wilson, wrote to the man who was everywhere, Otto Frind, in May 1915: 'Very sorry to see your boys got such a mauling at the front in Flanders ... We got the list of casualties from the Dardanelles and very sad reading it was.'[2] Some of the reports from the battles came from Malcolm Ross, who went to the Dardanelles in June as a special war correspondent.

During that year there was more to mourn. A telegram arrived at Red Cottage. It heralded the death of, not a young soldier, but an old man. On 24 April Eccleston had died at the age of eighty-two. He was buried beside Blanche, in the grave at the St John's church-yard, Gordon. Freda's father had pared his life down in the years after the death of his wife. There was no dinner set, nor silver left. He had only one personal item listed, a Waltham gold watch, worth ten pound. But each room had remained furnished, as always, in walnut and cedar, there were still 230 miscellaneous volumes in the library, along with paintings and the photographs of relatives and family places.

On 5 May 1915, probate was granted to Windeyer and Williams, the faithful family connection going back to Rev. Professor John Woolley and his friendship with Sir Charles Windeyer, a supporter of Sydney University. Some months later, Freda was sent a breakdown of her father's estate. Guy, as executor, had paid outstanding bills, there were minor bequests to old friends and to a niece of Blanche's, Agnes Gray, and £400 to Guy. What remained of the estate of £1,440 and whatever was realised from

Flowton, was shared equally between Guy, Bertie and Freda.

Gradually life at Flowton wound down. Over the next year, household furniture to the value of £262 7s 6d would be sold by Lawson and Little. Neighbours gathered at regular on-site auctions as farm equipment, the four-in-hand, the buggy and horses were sold. Flowton was empty. Guy began to consider what to do with the house itself.

Ku-ring-gai and Flowton of Freda's childhood were gone. An era was over. Adulthood was there, responsibilities, a household of her own, no chance to find herself again in the mountains for months if not years and worse, an unhappy Muriel.

Freda's companion, Muriel the extrovert, could not 'let the side down' as Freda sometimes did and become ill when things weren't going well. She liked to be able to put into words what was happening in her life but had no explanation for the mild, depressive nervousness she began to suffer. She put it down to the war or homesickness or weariness, and cast around to find something to renew her strength. She found it, or so she hoped, in an old interest, parapsychology. It was a subject she had been introduced to by her disgraced, half-uncle, Alfred Shaw, who had made a hobby of hypnotism and spiritualism, then had developed a following in Sydney before his fraudulent tendencies had overwhelmed him and others. Muriel had attended a number of dynamic lectures and demonstrations he had given with the support of his son, Cyril. Also, she and George Dupain had often discussed all aspects of the power of the mind and the supernatural. Muriel bought books in the hope of mastering self-hypnosis as a way of settling herself down.

When this did not work, she looked for something more powerful and found it in the booming spiritualist movement. Muriel, along with many others, became fascinated with some of the incidents that were reported from the war. One, popular at the time, was the legendary 'Angel of Mons'. In August 1914 a vision of angels reportedly halted the German advance during the Battle of Mons and saved the British troops from sure defeat. It provided a sense of hope over the war, and life in general. It was proof that the huge losses had some value, that the British would win as God and Right were on their side against the Heathen Hun, and more, that there were possibilities of powers beyond human experience that were guiding their lives. Large organised gatherings took place over the following year, where witnesses, or those who had heard accounts from men in khaki, attested to the visions of the angels. Muriel attended meetings in Harrow and became both expert and dependent on such events.

Freda, the searcher on the mountain top, was somewhat sceptical of Muriel's new passion, but she began following her own: painting. Some evidence exists that she dabbled before living in England – there is a rather muddy painting of a New Zealand lake scene – but considering her background and her need to express her inner passions and her adoration of nature, it is not surprising that Freda turned her thwarted ambitions to such an outlet. There was talk in her family that she exhibited in the Royal Academy and two, much finer, botanical watercolours which she gave to Guy Du Faur do exist, but it is unlikely she was more than a talented and keen amateur.

Carrying an easel also allowed Freda to leave Muriel without hurting her increasing sensitivity to slights and it gave her licence to be out and about on her own and not seem bizarre. A child searching for flowers was adventurous and sweet, an artist searching for flowers was creative, but a woman wandering on her own was crazy, was trouble, was a witch.

Some things did not change during the war years. The main thoroughfares of Pinner were still busy, even during the week, the local policeman, P.C. Killinback, rode past on his white horse; on the rare occasions he wasn't about, he was at harvest and was out in the orchards ensuring that no one pinched any apples. Rarely did crimes in Pinner amount to more. The old blind man continued to weave baskets in the front garden of his semi-detached by the railway bridge and the train from Marylebone, with its glossy green engine, billowed steam over those caught on the overhead bridge in Marsh Road. A penny was needed every Wednesday when the organ grinder filled the Pinner streets with his jaunty music. The annual Pinner Fair continued on Wednesday after Whitsun, as it had existed for nearly seven hundred years, with tents, like circus big tops of bright red and white stripes curving down High Street. Sometimes on the rare afternoon when Muriel wasn't working, for she worked extremely hard, there was afternoon tea at The Cocoa Tree. The little cafe, by then bereft of suffragists, was 'the ideal pleasure resort for homemade cakes and strawberry teas' – its sign, depicting a cup of cocoa was a symbol of the teetotal nature of the establishment.

Guests began arriving at Red Cottage, but invited guests not desperate billets. Erica Westmacott, by then in her mid-twenties, had come to England to look after her brother who had been seriously wounded at Gallipoli. She did have relatives in the country, as her father had emigrated fom Worcestershire to New Zealand in 1860, and her mother's sister, Kate, lived in London, but Erica stayed with Muriel and Freda for a time. Erica was a free-spirited woman who accounted for the fact that she never married by saying that it was not due to 'any distaste of male company. Nor from lack of offers. Just from a tendency to drift along.' Erica was curious rather than shocked to discover Freda and Muriel lived in a 'very close relationship, like a married couple'.[3]

She was more amazed that Freda kept house, without even a regular maid, while Muriel went out to work. Freda was Erica's heroine; this was not how she expected the famous mountaineer, her idol, to be living. But Erica was welcome company for Freda and for the first time, in what felt like years, there was mountaineering talk. She learned, on this visit, why Erica had not made her attempt on Mount Cook but her amusement at the Professor's unflattering descriptions of the changes climbing had wrought on her body was usurped by disappointment with herself that she had not been more aware, had not given Erica moral back-up and perhaps even more vital, financial help.

Homesickness receded with such visits. Jim Dennistoun arrived, his dark hair dashingly trimmed, dressed in the drab khaki riding breeches, long-belted jacket and slouch hat of the North Irish Horse Regiment. He was such a dynamic character, always active and competently daring enough to have been to Antarctica. Over the summer of 1911–12, he'd gone on the *Terra Nova* as support for Captain Scott. A year younger than Freda, he would be in France by mid-November.

When the Kaiser threatened to starve the British people until 'they who have refused peace, will kneel and plead for it', the convoy system managed to bring in enough food, despite mammoth losses from U-boat attacks, but rationing could no longer be put off. Beginning with white bread, food began to be more and more limited. Sometimes things ran out, alarming for many, especially in winter. Angry housewives picketed the Food Control Office even for the ghastly margarine. The comfortable afternoon teas, so favoured, almost disappeared.

Freda, who could remember when a billy of boiled potatoes had been a luxury, thrived on finding her own way of getting by. She was intensely grateful they had never opted for that flat in London. In Pinner, the garden was growing beautifully, although subject to occasional raids from local children. Both women took renewed joy in it, as a tiny, orderly act of personal empowerment. Neither was afraid of wielding a spade, they worked together and, in such times, the fresh growth of potatoes and spinach, Brussell sprouts and cabbage renewed their spirits. Ingenuity was sometimes required to make the luxuries of carrot and rhubarb jam, but they could barter with neighbours for food they were short of. Coal was rationed but they scavenged the countryside for scraps of wood and hauled in fallen branches; so the days became as hard and as pleasurable as when she and her climbing friends had built the flood bank at the Hermitage. But winter itself was unbearable; no amount of exercise could warm the cold away.

In Pinner, the Belgian refugees were now regarded as too common and a problem, and were criticised for failing to assimilate. Wounded soldiers from the local hospitals, on the other hand, were accorded encouraging greetings as they sat in their blue clothing on the low wall at the bottom of High Street.

A letter arrived for Muriel from Australia, written by her brother, Hilton. A letter from him was always business, or bad news. This time it was both. On 26 July 1916, her father, William Cadogan, had died at the age of 57, leaving a note that was tantamount to an apology to his wife and to his family, but no money. He had lived too well, there had been expenses and, as always, there was the embezzlement by Alfred Shaw. Mrs Cadogan, with no possibility of earning an income and with ten-year-old Max, had let their old home go. Hilton, Tiss and Sylvia were in boarding houses, Queen was living in at Crown Street Hospital as a trainee nurse and Nell had gone into the country to housekeep. Mrs Cadogan and Max had moved north to the industrial city of Newcastle and were staying with an old friend, Nan Hughes, who ran a successful pottery up there.

Muriel was devastated by the news and the break-up of the family. She could not get it out of her head that Alfred Shaw's widow, from what she had heard through cousins, was living very well in Canada, no doubt on the spoils – that is living on what rightly belonged to Mrs Cadogan. Muriel also believed that the son, Cyril Shaw, as a lawyer, was no doubt making good money as well. She may have been right; his friends' nickname for him was 'King'. Muriel's bitterness was intense and disturbing and, despite knowing that 'Mick' (Hilton), as an accountant and a partner in the old firm of their father's, W.H. Cadogan and R.A Stewart, would make sure no harm came to Muriel's mother, Muriel felt her brother did not understand the importance of the family staying together. She was convinced only she could save them. She had to get back to Australia and could not rest until she did.

Freda, too, was desperate to get back. She wanted to support the one woman she regarded as her sister, the new widow, Enid Bacchus. Aunt Constance had lost her sons, Harry Bacchus and Lance Bacchus, on the same day, 15 September 1916, during the battle of Flers Courcellette. Reports of the battle in *The Times* were as gung-ho as any describing a football match: 'a chaotic struggle of bomb and bayonet fighting' created 'a thrilling narrative in eulogy of the New Zealanders'.[4] The battle ended with the taking of the town of Flers, west of Paris. On that day, there had been such heavy bombardment and casualty rates that some of the infantry were being used as stretcher-bearers. The brothers had gone out to pick up their last wounded man for the day, had barely placed him on the stretcher when they were hit by a shell and all three were killed instantly.

The year 1916 had brought relief to the Australians with the evacuation of Gallipoli, but it brought the worst of the trench warfare and infamy to places like Verdun, Ypres and the Somme. Four hundred and twenty thousand were killed at the Battle of Somme, between 1 July and 13 November 1916. An urgent push for conscription began, emotive posters were tacked up down High Street, on the windows of the hotels and outside the church hall, warning what would happen to the volunteers if no help ensued.

It was the dark moments of the mountain, the crevasse, the avalanche, the cracking cornice as poetry for Freda, this time the work of Siegfried Sassoon, again conveyed the emotions she was feeling.

> The thundering line of battle stands
> And in the air death moans and sings.

This time it wasn't about achievement or beauty. Intensified by the death of her cousins, the cruelty and ugliness of the Great War overwhelmed everything.

It brought more tears. On 26 June 1916, Jim Dennistoun was severely injured. He had transferred to the Royal Flying Corp and while serving as an observer on a bombing expedition his plane was attacked by a Fokker, caught fire and crashed behind enemy lines. Jim died later in a German hospital on 9 August.

Sir Baldwin Spencer, Freda's Professor, visited London during late 1916 and early 1917 to set up war artists for the Australian government. He was at a low ebb in his life. His wife was more 'nervy' than ever as the war and her concern for their daughters had caused some kind of breakdown. Added to that, he'd had a wild trip over on the convoy as it had been attacked by both U-boats and planes, an event he used to explain his own tensions and need for a drink. When Freda expressed the opinion that it was a shame that Erica Westmacott had not taken the opportunity in 1913–14 to become the first New Zealand woman to climb Mount Cook, the Professor would have none of it. She could have ended up like Freda, 'sexless', that is, lost her real purpose of being a women. It was clear to him the kind of woman Freda had opted to be.

The Professor was 'full of art talk' which Freda loved. He was having his portrait painted by the Australian artist George Lambert in London throughout January 1917. They attended an art exhibition of Australian work at the Guildhall before he was off again, hunched into his overcoat, in a trail of pipe smoke, for Glasgow where his daughters were living.

Gradually the stories came out of the activities of the Southern Alps guides. Alex Graham, who enlisted in 1916, reached the battlefields in 1917, fought in the battle at Passchendaele. He was awarded a Military Medal on 23 October. On 2 December 1917, he was severely wounded, then again on 5 November 1918, six days before the end of the war.

Frank Milne, Charlie's younger brother, was wounded in May 1917 then gassed. Although he would eventually take over from Peter Graham as chief guide in 1922, his expertise as a climber only just staved off the damage to his nervous system and lungs. His constant struggle ended in his premature death in 1933 from tuberculosis.

Distressing also was the war going on inside Britain between the workers and the employers, the rich and the poor. After the First Russian Revolution, March 1917, thousands in Britain donned red ties, shirts and scarfs, and came out in rallies to support the cause, while, as *The Times* wrote, 'those of our ruling classes who most bitterly detest freedom are already pale with anxiety lest Russia should become too free'. But that was not all; many men who had been excused war service on the basis that they were part of the essential services, were striking for better conditions and wages at home.

The situation for the Allies in Europe – apart from the entry of the United States – continued to deteriorate. Russia looked like pulling out of the war because of revolution. U-boat attacks increased and the Zeppelins were superseded by the much more efficient Gotha bi-planes. These attacked London with increasingly larger bombs at any hour; in one raid 24 bombers killed over a hundred citizens of whom a quarter were children. On one cheeky midday raid more than one hundred and fifty were killed. Londoners, including those in Pinner, began to live under greater stress.

The Kodak factory hooter blasted through the night when raids began. Angry, depressed people and wounded, shell-shocked men milled in the streets, as Pinner House and nearby hospitals overflowed. Rain filled the River Pinn, flooded Marsh Road and the cottages just under the railway bridge and filled the ditches with gushing water. Mist smothered the countryside. Strangers were still being billeted at Red Cottage and the house was no longer a haven or even a symbol of the strength of Freda and Muriel's life together. At Christmas 1917, the Salvation Army played, as always, in the High Street, Fred Johnstone played hymns on the bells of St John's, which he had done and would continue to do for fifty years. The sound could be heard all over the village. There were New Year carols outside the church and the singing of 'Auld Lang Syne' at midnight as usual. But, standing there in the great ring of people holding hands and broken hearts together, Freda and Muriel, closer in their losses than in their joys, were reminded of their homesickness and that they were full of 'deadening disillusion'.

The New Year did not help. Despite his cheerful veneer on becoming Prime Minister, Lloyd George had privately been in 'black annihilating despair'. By February–March 1918 talk in the street was of the Allies retreating, with the German army less than one hundred miles from Paris. In England, the populace were exhorted by the Prime Minister to remember the 'forgotten peaks' of honour, duty, patriotism and sacrifice but, as soon as the German attack was finally rebuffed, 'pride' overwhelmed Lloyd George's lofty statements and, as soon as the Germans were in retreat, the internal war began again in the mines and essential industries. Bus conductresses stopped work, refuse workers let the rubbish pile up, even in Pinner, where everyone was identifiable and the finger could be pointed, the police force struck primarily over pay and union recognition. The poet Siegfried Sassoon protested in *The Times* at 'the callous complacency with which the majority of those at home regard the continuance of agonies which they have not sufficient imagination to realise'. Australia became even more idealised, although the 'pleasure-as-usual-brigade' was rife there as well.[5]

There was one high point in those long war years. During 1916, the tide turned for suffrage. The coalition government, led by Lloyd George, had a number of other 'suffragists' as cabinet ministers, and it was impossible to ignore the way women had mobilised and how the country had relied on their patriotism. Nor would women, such as Mrs Fawcett, allow them to. As well, no one wished to return to militancy. Discussions took place in Parliament, and a majority were in favour of extending the suffrage to women with an age qualification they set so that they wouldn't immediately dominate the elections. There was an easy passage of the bill through the Commons on 19 June 1917. Royal Assent was granted on 6 February 1918. Women over 30 who were householders, wives of householders, occupiers of property of £5 or more annual value, or university graduates had the franchise. It wasn't until 1928 with the commonly called Flapper Vote that the vote granted to all women.

18 THE BEACON SOUTH

'... at times I wondered if I had not come a long way only to
find that what I really sought was something I had left behind.'

Thomas F. Hornbein

EVEREST: THE WEST RIDGE

At eleven o'clock on 11 November 1918, the raucous sirens at the
Kodak factory verified Armistice. The inhabitants of Pinner, at least
those not still in shock from the latest telegrams, gathered for a car-
nival, sports and a 'bunfight', but those celebrating in the streets
were inviting as ruthless a death in joy as the bullets and mud had
supplied in Europe. Hugging a stranger was a direct way to catch
Spanish influenza. It struck the country for the first time in spring
and returned with renewed force in winter. It killed quickly, blood-
lessly and indiscriminately.

There was no cure. The only prevention was practised avoid-
ance. Having made up their minds to return to Australia, Freda
and Muriel were as rigorous as any in the useless defences promulgated by the British Health Department: 'Wash inside the nose
with soap and water each night and morning; force yourself to
sneeze night and morning, then breathe deeply; do not wear a
muffler; take sharp walks regularly and walk home from work; eat

plenty of porridge.' Doctors and chemists were crowded as were the undertakers. Public facilities, schools, picture theatres and hotels were closed. The streets were sprayed with chemicals and anti-germ masks were common – a poor welcome for soldiers returning to the land they had fought, for so long, to save. Inhalation chambers were set up in which the populace could inhale zinc sulphate and more germs, then be put out of the heat into the cold air. Leaving England did not mean an escape from a disease that could kill in 24 hours. Twenty million were to die in three waves around the world. In Christchurch, New Zealand, that comfortable, distant town, 'the city's hotels were like hospitals, full of the sick and dying'.[1] Australia, with its strict quarantine laws, was by the New Year of 1919 still free of the ravages but every day counted. If they did not get out of Britain soon, or if their ship carried the disease, the quarantine laws protecting Australia might stop them getting in at all.

Their future plans, as well as their emotional needs, depended on them getting to Sydney. Muriel had decided she wanted to be a doctor and that sense of purpose dispelled her lingering depression, as did the thought of being back with her family. In Australia, as it was cheaper and there was less competition for places in the university, she had a better chance of obtaining training. Freda, at 36, saw the opportunity to get back into climbing in a country she knew, with people who knew her. Then, in a few years, with both their skills honed, they'd both be ready to go back to the Northern Hemisphere.

With great optimism, Freda and Muriel left Red Cottage and England to join the great exodus of soldiers, nurses, doctors and journalists who intended to arrive in Australia early in 1919. Poor food, cold winds, pale skins and watery-eyed children, the ingrained social system, the hopelessness of a country where some of its people fought for their country overseas, while at home others fought for greater comforts, was a place of memory; five years contracted into a brief moment.

The return to Australia seemed to be all Freda could have hoped for, although there was the initial difficulties of life there without Eccleston or Flowton. Guy was still on his own, in his early forties and an even more shadowy and gentle figure. He had believed his great loss was Blanche's death but had discovered, on the death of his father, that Eccleston's irritating interference was not a deliberate put-down but the only way the old man could show he cared. To Guy, Freda was worldly and successful, impatient with his dithering and his lack of drive. He could not see that the very qualities that he now saw as love in his father were being exhibited by his only sister.

There were practicalities to take care of: Freda had decided to fund Muriel in her medical studies and placed £2,000, most of which came from her father, with Mick Cadogan in trust for Muriel. On 16 January 1919, Muriel made a will leaving everything she had to Freda with Mick as executor. Now, permanently away from Pinner, she put her address as that of Mick's business at 12 Castlereagh Street. Freda would later maintain that she was the only beneficiary because she had lent Muriel the money and it was to ensure she received it back, but this was ingenuous. Freda and Muriel's lives were completely bound up together and the money for Muriel, a hard worker never in a position to acquire a nest egg, was a commitment of faith in their relationship and their future.

With finances settled, Muriel went straight into reorganising the Cadogans. Mrs Cadogan and Max were back in Sydney but had moved at least three times in two years and were again in Mosman. Muriel considered the broken family as destructive and entirely impractical: it was ridiculous for the older girls and Mick to be paying good money for various boarding rooms when, with a bit of organisation, a pleasant, permanent house for them all could be afforded.

With Muriel occupied, Freda relaxed and began visiting old friends, among them the Edward sisters, her cousin, Agnes Gray, and Ruth Abbott, who had moved to Quirindi, north-west of Sydney and beyond the Great Dividing Range. Ruth and Stanley had started a stock and station agency and had a family of two girls and a boy. Freda also visited Bertie, Wynifred and John, still at Mount Morgan, and was eager to get to know her nephew, already four years old, whom she only knew through photographs. He was a round-faced, serious little boy, with flat, fair hair brushed to one side. Bertie had gone grey early, like his father, and was craggy and lined with none of Eccleston's clear-eyed, upright elegance.

Wynifred was still teaching elocution. Peering over wire-rimmed glasses, hair slightly straggling, she would question Freda about life in England. Wynifred did not necessarily want to go there as, irritatingly, she believed travelling in the mind was enough. Freda found herself in disagreement with Bertie as well. She could not resist taking him to task over, what she saw as, his lack of interest in John. Bertie felt his job as a father was to ensure there would be enough money for John. He felt that Eccleston had squandered the opportunity to become really wealthy and in doing so had not given his children the future they deserved.

Freda openly showed that she considered Bertie to be cold and narrow and that she was irritated by his laxity as a father. She compared him, unfairly, to the now idealised Eccleston, and the even more idealised Grandfather Woolley, the beloved Papa. After all, both of them had worked for the good of society, whereas she felt little pride in her brothers. They were now judged with the same eye that had dismissed New Zealand men for their want of energy and interest. Even she, 'a mere woman', had done more in life than both her brothers. She saw them as two half-men: two parts of Eccleston split into the poetic dreamer tending flowers and plants, and into an explorer and practical man of the land.

Because of John, Freda stayed longer than she intended and during walks tried to impart her own love of nature and her sense of the Du Faur heritage to him – something she feared Wynifred, and knew Bertie, would never do. Later John barely remembered the stories about the family and their adventures but remembered his aunt's attention and the feeling of admiration he had for her. Finally Freda left with the promise to return as soon as she and Muriel were themselves settled. She was positive that would be so. Instead she disappeared out of his life until he was a teenager, when their natures were such that it was too late to start again.

Freda was right about the way John was being brought up. The emotional neglect was to leave its mark in his adult life. He did well in his work and reached a high level as a mechanical engineer in the elite Department of Supply in the New South Wales public service but he was most unpopular at work: his secretary of many years described him as 'not only the most secretive but the meanest man' she had ever met.[2] In 1940 he married a young woman, Marjorie De Courcy, who already suffered from erratic and, at times, aggressive behaviour which, exacerbated by John's nature and the death of a baby son in 1946, became full-blown schizophrenia. John's main interest was stocks and shares – buying, not selling – and he kept meticulous charts and graphs which he checked each morning. Their house was run-down, there was little furniture and dangerous wiring was patched up because John refused to spend money on it. On the suggestion that he might set up a Du Faur Prize at Sydney University, he was shocked at the idea of such a waste. His nights were spent on a ham radio calling people he would never meet around the world, with a bottle of whisky beside him to keep him company. When John died of an heart attack in

1982, the millions squeezed out of cheap living provided night and day nursing for an increasingly incoherent wife. When she died in 1992, the last person to bear the name Du Faur, all the money went to charity.

Returning to Sydney had wiped away the gloss that homesickness had placed on it. Despite a beautiful harbour, it was a city made plain by winter, without the invigoration that really cold air could bring. The lack of planning and the ineffectual attempt to mimic the institutions of England made Woolley's ideals and the possibilities he entertained of a Greek state almost farcical. Bushfires and severe strikes did little to improve this opinion. Sunshine, good food, fresh air could only slightly lessen the impact of influenza which was now rife. It would kill a small number compared to other countries, mainly because of the quarantine laws rather than an inherently more healthy population or a more able medical profession.

Freda began to realise that civilisation, of the type Britain valued, appealed more to her than, what she was beginning to regard as, a narrow and reactionary environment. Freedom of intellectual and artistic discussion could yet be a fair enough exchange for the country of her birth. In Sydney, anyone attempting something new seemed to be immediately scorned. Modern art, particularly post-impressionism, in which Freda was most interested, was being openly attacked by such luminaries as Julian Ashton, whom she had never quite forgiven for dismissing her father's tenure as president of the Art Gallery. Now, he and his champions nibbled at the next generation of artists and 'the air was heavy with the arrogance and respectability of old men, tired in spirit and the handling of paint, if not yet quite old in years'.[3]

The Dupain Institute did not settle Freda's uneasiness. There were the elegant, old iron lifts with the intricate brass buttons and levers, the well-fed bodies and the familiar smell of massage oil, particularly eucalyptus, enhanced by the steam and the supple fingers of a masseur. The business had expanded but finances were just as difficult. George borrowed £80 from Muriel but there was no work for her there. He had other associates, all men. She had been usurped by the trained scientific mind of Professor Leo Cotton, from the University of Sydney, and an associate, Edgar Herbert. Without Muriel's input, the magazine no longer existed. The institute still provided the basics but had become essentially a coaching centre for anatomy, biochemistry and physiology for the University of Sydney. George Dupain was still far ahead of his time and would produce publications with titles such as *Exercise and Physical Fitness*, *Baffling Obesity* and *Curing Constipation,* but he was also becoming more and more the rationalist anti-Christian. Discipline was everything, all could be controlled. Freda, with her flights of fancy and impractical ways, did not impress him, nor did her fickle approach to climbing and exercise. Women were unreliable. Despite his struggles to develop their masculine sides – that is rationality, strength, athletic grace – both Muriel and Jeannie Dupain had deserted him. His sister had married a dentist and become a Christian Scientist. And Muriel, of all things, a lesbian.

Dupain's lack of time for Muriel was difficult. He intended his son, Max, to be a doctor but he gave her little encouragement to enter the same field. Max Dupain became, not a doctor, but one of the most famous photographers in Australia. His father, unwittingly, provided the grounding for such a career as the young man honed his photographic skills in the Dupain gymnasium. Max would become renowned for the precise bodies, some almost naked, which he imbued with a sense of not only 'the moment' but with classical, sculpted beauty.

Dupain, in his negativity, was just reflecting common consensus. Studying, and presumably practising, were both easier in

Australia and at the same time harder. Australia was still well behind Britain in opportunities for women. The sister of Emmeline's friend, Louisa MacDonald, had been a practising doctor in Britain in 1870; in Australia in 1920 women were still regarded as a 'somewhat disturbing element' in a medical school and, although the first two Australian women had graduated in medicine in 1893, diverse and bigoted attitudes were held against the female doctor. Prejudice itself nourished further prejudice. There was still a general belief that women, unlike men, were subject to moods and nervous tensions, lacked strength and needed protection, and worse there was a great fear that their natural instincts would be cut away, undermining the designated roles of men and women which were the basis of their society. There was little doubt Muriel had the drive and intelligence to become a doctor. Although lacking a basic education, she had taught herself well and probably knew more about the functioning of the body in her first few years with George Dupain, than most medical students ever did.

Freda and Muriel had been through the struggle for the vote in Australia. They had been through the same in England and been present at the great (and somewhat temporary) growth in the autonomy of women. But what the variety of work in wartime had provided for women in Britain had never been offered to Australian women, who were too far away from the direct action. To remain living in such an environment would be like stepping back in years. They wanted to enjoy the changes, not start again.

All this would have been frustrating but bearable, if it had been possible to live in Australia, if not openly in their marriage, at least comfortably with the people they knew. In England, Freda and Muriel did not flaunt their sexual status but there was a niche for them even if a rather stereotyped one. There, excuses could be made for obviously single but attached women: that they had lost their true loves during the Great War and were in fact just making do with each other. These working types of women might be looked at askance, derogatory comments might be made about their cropped hair and tweed suits, but the sexual side had not been fully acknowledged so lesbian friendships were not yet regarded as a threat to heterosexual society. Such a group did not appear to exist in Australia and if it did, it was so hidden as to be non-existent to the casual observer. Freda and Muriel missed the companionship of other women like themselves and could now appreciate Britain for the haven it had granted them. There was no point waiting on, so they decided to return to England, putting Muriel's prospective career on hold until they were settled again. A planned trip to New Zealand, to see Enid, became the first part of the voyage back.

Freda, with such a decision made, felt she had finally left the remnants of her childhood behind. The homesick woman who had longed to leave England now seemed extraordinarily indulgent. When old friends like Heinrich Von Haast asked about her climbing she could say there had been the war, she had been back to see family and now they were returning home to Britain and would go from there to the European Alps. Why she left £1,500 with him to manage before she left Wellington for Manakau is unfathomable. It may have been nostalgia, or they saw New Zealand as a possible living place if England did not work out. Or the intention of keeping it in Wellington may have been to back up Enid if necessary, or even Aunt Constance. Whatever, the money which Von Haast put out in three separate mortgages at an interest rate of between 6 and 7 per cent, would never be used during Freda's lifetime. As well, before boarding the train to Manakau, Freda deposited almost £200 in a savings account at the main Wellington Post Office.

There was some apprehension about going to Manakau. Freda already knew from Enid how hard it had been keeping the properties maintained, hard enough when the men were still alive. Even years later, the writer George Bernard Shaw, on a visit to New

Zealand, would complain: 'But I don't like your stumped paddocks. They look like old battlefields on the Western Front, with the tree trunks all battered and smashed and burned by the shells.' But the three Bacchus women had dealt with the deaths of the men, in some ways, better than Freda had. To keep the farms going they'd had to deal with their losses quickly and work extremely hard, but had been aided by the decimation of agriculture in Europe during the war, which had meant countries in the Southern Hemisphere could find markets for their produce. What the three women had not dealt with was their own relationships without the buffer of Lance and Ralph.

Constance was well into her seventies but wasn't prepared to hand her power to anyone, not even to the mother of her much loved grandchildren, Barbara and George, then in their mid-teens. Sabrie had no children to give her status and had to deal with Enid who, unable to dominate her mother-in-law, ensured that Sabrie was at least on a level below her. Enid, according to her step-daughter, 'never suffered fools gladly' – a fool was anyone not as quick-witted and adventurous as she was.[4]

Freda, always to thrive on the powerful role of benefactor, offered the money in Wellington to Enid if she wanted to start a new life. But she misjudged the situation as Enid was not yet ready to leave a farming community in which she had been making her rather eccentric mark. She loved to shock her neighbours with her high-handed ways, wicked stories and her habit of smashing through local mores as efficiently as she and Freda had crashed the tram when they were young. She had her own group of local people, her supporters, who met at the golf club or came over to play croquet or for tea. Among them was a neighbouring widower, John Ellis, whose wife had died only two years earlier after the birth of a daughter, another Barbara. There was also a son, Brian, aged four. The Ellis family were perfect marks for Enid's energies, not to sew for or provide with baking, but to organise and make decisions on how they were to live. Enid was not sure that the city would find her quite interesting enough. Freda, her mind settled, departed for England with Muriel.

19 SEA ROAD

'It was a city of detached mansions; a Mediterranean lounging place on the English Channel; and as seen by night it seemed even more imposing than it was. It was heaven.'

Thomas Hardy
TESS OF THE D'URBERVILLES

By late 1920 Freda and Muriel were back in England, briefly at 48 Leinster Square with Aunt Freda whose companion Catherine Kemplay had died. She was not keen on Freda and Muriel leaving her too quickly, but the difficulties of living in a house with a much older and determined woman had not improved over time. They had to decide where to set up their own home and were determined to live courageously in all aspects of their life.

Neither woman was under the illusion that life back in England was going to be easy. The war, the debts and high unemployment levels, especially devastating for women sent back into the home, would not see the country flourish for a long time. In fact, a chronic depression continued right through the 1920s, into the worldwide Great Depression of the 1930s. Freda believed that the buffer of a private income would protect them from the adverse financial effects but only if they were careful. She was profoundly

aware that her income was a finite sum, although she did have at
least £4,000 in ready cash, the money in New Zealand, as well as
the money from the sale of Red Cottage. She regarded London as
too expensive a place to live while waiting for Muriel to take up
medical studies. The City also reminded her of the Ladies' Alpine
Club and her stubbornness, in not joining, would always haunt her.
She was aware, from newspaper reports, that mountaineering was
beginning again. Women of her own age, such as Beatrice
McAndrew, were tackling a number of European mountains including the Matterhorn. Eager to get climbing going again, the famous
Winthrop Youngs, Geoffrey and Eleanor, assisted Mrs Emily (Pat)
Kelly to found the Pinnacle Club. Eleanor Winthrop Young wrote,
an echo of Freda:

> Even then, after all the madness and death, climbing was regard-
> ed as a strange activity. One had really done something drastic
> by becoming a climber … And it wasn't smiled upon either …
> In those days, even up in the Lakes, a girl couldn't walk about a
> village in climbing clothes without hard stares from
> the women and sniggers from the youths.[1]

They wanted to negate this attitude by sheer numbers so the
Pinnacle became the first rock-climbing club founded by women
for women. The one qualification was 'the ability to lead an ordinary, difficult climb'. It would have been the perfect place for Freda
to begin again.

Instead, she and Muriel looked for a stable base from where
they could reorganise themselves and ensure their money was not
frittered away before they could take up their plans. Landlocked
towns, ancient charm and neat countrysides felt regressive. They
wanted a bolder life, unfettered by social pressures and far enough
away from Aunt Freda to avoid daily demands, but close enough to

visit her if needed. The wanted the wide beaches and the safe, warm sea they had enjoyed back in Sydney, so Freda purchased a house, The Pines, at 28 Sea Road, Boscombe, a suburb of Bournemouth, one of a number of seaside resorts on the south coast of England. Both women were familiar with the area as they had visited the nearby New Forest frequently and had, once or twice, joined the migrations of holiday-makers from London and the surrounding cities to this 'English Riviera'. The town was only 108 miles out of London, a two-hour journey through the pretty countryside of Hampshire, on the Waterloo to Bournemouth line. There was a regular tram system along the coast that joined the ancient port of Poole, five miles to the west of Boscombe, and Christchurch, five and a half miles to the east. As well, good roads meant coaches could cover such places of interest as Dorchester, Stonehenge and Bath, or even travel directly across into Wales.

Bournemouth was a town full of romantic and literary connections that would have appealed immediately. The bays and chines (valleys) that cut between limestone cliffs, had been infamous for the smugglers who, for centuries, had dominated the coast, although by the middle of the nineteenth century, smuggling had made way for another source of wealth. The area claimed to have the warmest sea in Britain plus dry soils, warm winters and cool summers, pure water and long stretches of beaches and gardens, so it was perfect as a spa and holiday centre for the English upper classes. It became the seaside town of 'Sandbourne', where Thomas Hardy's Tess went to live with her seducer, Alex D'Urberville, and in the 1920s it had little changed from Hardy's description:

> This fashionable watering place, with its eastern and western stations, its piers, its groves of pines, its promenades and its covered gardens was to Angel Clare like a fairy place suddenly created by the stroke of a wand ... By the midnight lamps he

went up and down the winding ways ... and could discern between the trees and against the stars, the lofty roofs, chimneys, gazebos and towers of the numerous fanciful residences which the place was composed.

Boscombe itself was dominated by the 74 acre Shelley Estate. Originally owned by Mary Wollstonecraft, who wrote *The Vindication of the Rights of Woman*, and the writer and novelist, William Godwin, the estate was passed on to their daughter Mary, the author of *Frankenstein*. She was married to the poet Percy Bysshe Shelley.[2]

The big plain beaches and the fine houses, often empty over winter, were perfect for improvident writers with wealthy benefactors. John Galsworthy, D.H. Lawrence and Henry James worked there; and Robert Louis Stevenson wrote *The Strange Case of Dr Jekyll and Mr Hyde* and *Kidnapped*. Beatrice Webb, the Fabian writer, spent three winters there and while she initially found the view over the bay depressing and the sound of the waves mournful, she derived great joy and inspiration from being there.

It would be the reverse for Freda and Muriel. They believed their life on the southern coast was going to be, finally, the way they wanted it to be, and in their first years they had no reason to suspect they were wrong.

Boscombe was a middle-class suburb of red brick and cream render, of three-storeyed houses, of slate roofs and turrets that provided a neat but not unattractive uniformity. The Pines was one of four similar, freestanding houses with a wide, dark oak-panelled hall, a spacious drawing room with a big bay window, four bedrooms on the first floor and a maid's room and box room in the attic.

The Pines had none of the character of their old home, Red Cottage, but from the rear there were views to the ocean. At night they could hear the soft lap of water, the distant sound of steamers crossing the bay and the dry rustle of the wind through the pines, from which their home took its name.

When Freda and Muriel arrived there was a lively feeling in the tree-lined streets, in the well-stocked and imaginative shop windows and the delight of the time, Sainsburys, at 639 Christchurch Road, Boscombe. From the walnut-framed windows of the store, they could choose New Zealand lamb, white milk-fed capons or little boxes of Bourdeaux pigeons, cheeses and vegetables from all over the country. The focal point of Boscombe was an impressive L-shaped arcade 'The Grand Continental', which was covered by a glass and metal roof that stretched like an elliptic spider web over an orchestra that entertained the shoppers and those sipping tea in the various cafes.

Next to the arcade, created in the same dainty brickwork and elaborate, delicate plaster facade, was the Pavilion Theatre. When built in 1895, there had been enormous opposition from the local clergy, temperance workers and land owners who feared the spiritual demise of the populace who might view such infamous characters as Lillie Langtry, the lover of Edward, Prince of Wales. But, if anything, the theatres and cafes in the early decades of the century provided succour to the already spiritually bereft.

The warm waters and dry soils welcomed the sick as well as the hedonistic. Wicker chairs lined the verges of the parks and the waterfronts and the place was as rife with nursing homes as hotels. It was, as Osbert Sitwell, brother of the writer, Edith Sitwell, observed, 'a camping ground of godly invalids, everywhere breathing heavily in red tiled shelters ... under pine trees, or reclining in beds and sofas under turrets and pepperpots of red brick ... behind luxuriant hedges of arbutus and fuchsia'.[3] White-capped nurses pushed their frail charges in ever greater numbers into the sunshine but, in deference to the sensibilities of the healthy, the

name of the famous path through the park and pines of
Bournemouth Square, 'Invalid's Walk', was changed to the more
suitable 'Pine Walk'.

Compared to sedate Pinner and graceless Sydney, Bournemouth's
indulgences and hedonism appeared confident and exciting. The
populace, superficially, were rebels who had learned during the war
'tomorrow we may die' and they would die, this time, with a smile
on their lips and their feet tapping.[4] Amusement was the catchcry,
gardens were 'pleasure gardens, music was everywhere. People
indulged themselves after the repressed war years and dressed for
every occasion. Appearance was everything. Freda always loved
clothes and the style of the 1920s suited her small-boned body.
Despite the warnings that she would lose her complexion through
snow and windburn, her skin was smooth and ideally pale. Her
hair, like her mother's and unlike her father's, showed little sign of
grey. Her favourite item was a shimmery grey, panne velvet shawl.
It was more difficult for Muriel to look as stylish, especially as she
was not exercising as much. She suited a tailored style, the plain
military cuts of the war, not dropped filmy waists. Her face, always
fleshy, had began to lose its shape particularly around the chin.

Nor did Freda stint on jewellery, although none was elaborate.
Her preference was for small neat rings and brooches with interesting stones. She already had pieces from Aunt Emmeline and her
mother which included a stamped gold locket, a pearl and ruby
ring, a topaz brooch, a gold ring and two superb opal ones. She
wore, with pride, a gold brooch from her father that featured the
native New South Wales waratah which they had tried to protect
from its predator, the Sydney flower seller. She adored turquoise,
which was popular in art deco styles, and owned a matrix ring piled
with it, as well as a gold ring inset with five of the gemstones. She

still had her ice axe tie-pin from Otto Frind and a gold Mount Cook badge.

Most mornings in summer Freda and Muriel walked down the hill to the crowded beach. Mixed bathing was allowed, although, for those of more demure character, which did not include them, covered swimming pools were 'available for ladies on certain days'. Blue and white striped deckchairs and parasols, and yellow, mauve, blue and red beach huts lining the beach created a gaudy link with the flowers in the well-tended flowerbeds. On the promenades, graceful white dresses or neatly smart skirts drifted around delicate silk-covered legs, black coats cut sharp figures down the lawns from the big hotels or thronged the Undercliff Road, vying for space with black-topped cars and observation vehicles, filled with ladies festooned with motoring veils that wafted in the breeze, as Freda's had once done after her hat had gone over a mountain onto a glacier.

There were marvellous walks along the cliff tops, views down either coast for miles, wildflowers and seabirds. Freda, inspired by her observations and the 'Exhibition of Australian Paintings' she had gone up to view in London in December 1923, began to paint with renewed energy. If a mountain could be conquered by scrutinising its smallest part – the rock face where the hand and the eye became aware of every crevice, wrinkle and colour – she felt she could do the same with nature in the landscapes she attempted. By painting a tree as a leaf, a rose as a petal, shadow and light began to appear and she found some success. As obsessively as she had begun mountaineering, Freda began painting. Painstakingly, with great eye for detail and concern for shape, she created a perfect representation but with an abstract cast, so that, on a canvas, the flower became, at a distance, a series of delicate green and creamy-white curves. Freda's pleasure and ability grew. She liked the contained colours and the neatness required and the exploration of the depths of flowers. She liked the quietness of it all, being alone, once again with a purpose. The continual process of improving her art took on all the long-repressed passion that mountaineering had once held, as she searched once again for that exquisite moment of freedom, when she painted without thought, when instinct and skill by-passed the questioning, interfering mind. This was a new 'nazomi'. This time, she was mature enough to find her achievements within herself, and it scarcely mattered that she might never be acclaimed. As she painted she could forget her past failures, her uneven abilities and the headlong stumble towards a loathed middle age, where all opportunity was rumoured to be extinct, when a barren woman was said to dry out to a rattling shell.

Freda could now look back at Mary Murray Aynsley with comprehension perhaps tinged with envy. If she had painted, as Mary had done, and as other mountaineers liked to do, during those days when bad weather closed in on the mountains, she might have set herself up as a real painter. As Freda retreated more and more into such ponderings, she outwardly projected her concentration as a cool indifference.

Surprisingly Muriel, who had not been keen on living in Bournemouth initially, had settled in well. Her determination to do so may have come out of thwarted ambition, but Muriel also had a nature that genuinely enjoyed being involved with people and although frustrated at not getting straight into her studies, she felt she had a purpose as long as she was understanding more about that most fascinating of all subjects, the body. She had become interested in a new organisation in Bournemouth, The Swedish Institute. The couple who founded it, the Odbergs, were part of the wider movement of Ling, the group Muriel had always admired. Although Madame Bergman-Osterberg had died in 1915, she had revolutionised physical education by disproving the notion that exercise destroyed both womenhood and society by creating 'neurasthenic women, incapable of marrying and of bearing children'. Many practitioners, among them Arthur Odberg and his wife, had trained with Ling in Paris then moved to Britain to practise, when the Education Department rubber-stamped the Swedish methods.

From their premises at 31 Meyrick Park Crescent, the Odbergs promulgated, what they called, 'The Swedish Manual Medical Treatment', which was a similar program to that offered by the Dupain Institute, but without the obsessive theory. Arthur Odberg also provided a 'Ladies Swedish Educational Gym' class and trained women to teach them. It was just the place for Muriel, although it is not clear whether she taught with the Odbergs, went there to learn new techniques or to just brush up her old skills.

Muriel was busy, feverishly so. Her low moods seemed to have gone and it was easy to believe they would never return. There was so much to catch up on, especially as the girls, the masseuses and trainers were so much younger. She inspired Freda to become fitter as well and to go for even longer walks, along the cliffs towards Swanage where the sea was tumultuous and the landscapes wilder than the bland bays near their home.

Feeling confident, Muriel began to see more of an old friend, an Australian woman, Gertrude Deane, nee Allnut, who lived with her doctor husband in nearby Christchurch. Orphaned at a young age, Gertrude had been brought up by older married sisters on various sheep stations throughout Victoria. Muriel and Freda befriended the younger woman on the boat to England in 1914, on her way to stay with another sister in Liverpool. While in that city, she met her future husband, Dr Norman Deane, an Irishman, born in Limerick in 1890, who had trained as a doctor at the Royal College of Surgeons and Adelaide Hospital, Dublin, before taking up a job as house surgeon at Bootal Hospital, Liverpool. They were engaged at the end of 1914 when Dr Deane joined the army and became part of the West African Medical Service based in Sierra Leone. After he and Gertrude married in 1916, they spent one tour of duty out there, a brief one in a country that was too hard for whites and particularly for a pregnant one. Gertrude was to have an anxious time after returning to England as, soon after this, the ship Dr Deane was travelling on was torpedoed by the Germans. He was captured but fortunately repatriated via the (then) neutral America. After the war, the Deanes with six-week-old William moved to Christchurch. A year later a daughter, Claire, was born. Both the Deanes were gardening fanatics, were popular in the area where Norman ran his one-man practice, and often held tennis parties to which Muriel and Freda were invited.

Muriel also had a number of friends interested in spiritualism, although it may have been harder to find a friend who didn't have that interest in Bournemouth. The town was 'mad' for it. Its popularity had been fuelled generally by the famous, such as Lady Arthur Conan Doyle who wrote: 'If I were offered all the wealth of New York in exchange for the knowledge which Spiritualism has brought me, I would rather live in a two-roomed shack than part with the intense comfort, the glorious vision of that wonderful future world I know of, which lies ahead of me.'[5]

Adding to the general excitement in Bournemouth was the murder in 1921 of a young woman, Irene Wilkins, which brought spiritualists, particularly 'The Boscombe Circle' to prominence. The 'spirit of Irene' spoke to 'The Circle' through the resident clairvoyant, Mrs C. Starkey; it was through their seances that the murderer was found. He lived in Windsor Road, only a hundred yards up the road from The Pines.

So great was the fascination with the topic that a book on it went into three printings, shops opened selling everything from fairy stars to ouija boards and crystal balls, columns in the papers advertised the services of tarot readers and palm readers and a spiritualist church at 16 Bath Road promised prayers and 'clairvoyant descriptions, spirit control and inaugural service'.[6] The Theosophical Society thrived, with such programs as 'The Psychology of Prayer' by Mrs Daisy Grove, who lectured on the belief that 'the most powerful prayer was the expansion of consciousness which brought realisation of spiritual being'.[7]

Freda did not have the same interest as Muriel; she questioned less and expected more. God was just a part of life as was breathing and needed about as much attention. There were less esoteric matters to take her attention. Enid's daughter, Barbara Bacchus, then aged nineteen, had been hired by a New Zealand couple to mind their young children on the trip over to England. She continued to work for them for a while in London but spent her weekends off in Bournemouth. Barbara, as tall as her father, with the dark Woolley hair, brought a welcome vivacity to The Pines, as well as news of Enid, who had moved into Seatoun, Wellington and had married her old Manakau neighbour, John Ellis.

The Ellis family now shouldered the burden of Enid's intensity. Two unwitting Ellis children and quiet John had a busy life ahead of them. Enid had expanded her interests and, through Heinrich Von Haast, had put on a farewell party at the Wellington Art Gallery in January 1923. She then moved to Auckland, to the Ellis house at Takapuna, on the north side of the harbour.

Midway through Barbara's three-year stay in England, Constance Bacchus arrived. Barbara left work to stay with her Granny and was relieved when they eventually got to Freda's as she'd been dragged around elderly relatives and old acquaintances. Then, all too soon, the Bacchus women were gone again, on to Belgium and France, to the graves of Lance and Harry, then to Cologne where they had friends. Barbara eventually returned to Wellington and took up nursing in 1926.

When her relatives left Bournemouth, Freda departed with
Muriel for a favourite holiday spot, a tiny fishing village, Lizard, in
Cornwall, the most southerly point of mainland Britain. Although
they stopped off at various towns such as Plymouth and Torquay on
the way, most of the six weeks was spent living in a stone cottage
with a slate grey roof, at the top of the narrow, winding cobbled
Bailey's Lane. At the bottom of the lane was the harbour, walled by
a high stone quay, where an old-fashioned fishing fleet was moored.
Freda was fascinated by its quaintness, for there was 'nothing like it
in the colonies', and mourned that the fragile vessels, which were
not much bigger than the row boats they had used in Cowan
Creek, were 'doomed ... as all the boats were beginning to use
motor engines'. Things had changed in other ways. Freda and
Muriel had wandered the Hooker Valley in the rain, now Freda
wrote to tell Enid that they hated 'sightseeing when the sea is all
grey and everything else too'. On the rare fine day during those
weeks, they visited some of the nearby beaches and wandered
around the coast, past lovely, old thatched villages smothered in ivy
geraniums, making 'a mass of colour ... nearly to the top of the cottages'. From there they went on to the villages of Mullion, on the
coast, north-west of Lizard. As much as they were charmed by the
whitewashed cottages and an ancient little church at the fork of the
road that divided the village, it was a nearby rocky cove that really
took their fancy. It was 'about the finest beach in England'.[8] There,
no one came near them, they could relax out of the wind and talk.
The distance between them and the stresses of the past had, at last,
been overcome. Or so it seemed.

Muriel was 40, Freda 42 and there were questions pressing on
them. Was it too late to take up careers? Was mountaineering, was
medicine only for younger women? Freda in photos at the
Hermitage sometimes looked like any young woman of today, and
she aspired to things a young woman at the turn of this century

aspires to, but the era she was born in made her vulnerable to great self-doubts, despite her beliefs and desire for strength. As well, she was, for the first time, relatively content and for someone who had never been content, there was relief in that condition. Added to this indecision was the matter of Muriel, who was focused and appeared happy at long last. Wouldn't it be mad to start putting pressure on her again, on them both? These things had to be considered, balanced, they shouldn't rush. Happiness was not something to be destroyed lightly in the name of ambition.

But the life that Freda was living, if she could have recognised it, was what she had always avoided on the verandahs of the Hermitage, those afternoon tea parties she had missed because she had been on a mountain face taking tea from a thermos. Jane Thomson had completed the Grand Traverse at 57 and Annie Lindon was older than Freda when she climbed Mount Cook. Freda was too young for Bournemouth, for that kind of retirement.

20 CRACKS

'From depth to height, from height to loftier height
The climber sets his foot and sets his face,
Tracks bringing sunbeams to their resting place,
Which counts the last pulsations of their light.'

Geoffrey Winthrop Young

Bournemouth was the front line of the 'bold and noisy face England kept to the world' but the apparent joyous disregard for convention, as with real contentment, was an illusion. When a bold face slips as it did during the 1920s, nostalgia began to rise for the old ways, before unemployment was so high, and before women ran their own homes and had jobs. Popular writing began to place women back where they used to be and one of the targets for change were women who lived without men: the lesbian came to be regarded as a sexual deviant and an outcast. 'Lesbian!' gradually became the insult that was thrown at any woman who stood up for women's (or just her own) rights. Lesbians were 'inverts', either born with a problem or, in the popular Freudian theory of the time, damaged by a childhood trauma. Even women such as the renowned writer Radclyffe Hall, who could be held up as an example of a radical lesbian by both supporters and detractors, judged the sexuality of 'her kind' in this new and destructive way. In her famous novel, *The Well of Loneliness*, she wrote passionately of 'the terrible nerves of the invert, those nerves that are always lying in wait ... like live wires through her body causing a constant and ruthless torment'.[1]

Well intentioned, but doing her part to alarm heterosexual men, the emancipist Marie Stopes wrote in her *Marriage Manual* in 1920, lesbian love 'is so much more practical these days, particularly by the "independent" type of woman ... If a married woman does this unnatural thing she may find a growing disappointment in her husband and he may lose all natural power to play his proper part.'[2]

By 1921 there was an attempt to outlaw lesbianism in Britain, which failed primarily through a technicality. The popular opinion in Parliament afterwards was that 'To adopt a Clause of this kind would harm by introducing into the minds of perfectly innocent people the most revolting thoughts.'[3] Books including the infamous *Well of Loneliness* were banned, jobs were lost and women began to hide their relationships. For those who had committed themselves to this subgroup of society and who had no use for the restrictions of a life dominated by men, these changes would effectively marginalise them into a kind of ghetto, a threat to the heterosexual society through their sexuality and greater economic and social freedoms; in effect, the witches of the twentieth century. As Muriel's youngest brother Max explained, 'They sustained each other',[4] but such dependency also pushed the relationship of two women, of very different personalities, to breaking point.

Freda's response to this growing and alarming prejudice was to mantain a discreet determination to get on with life, but it undermined Muriel. If she had been less sensitive and more sure of her own directions it may not have mattered, but work of any value was difficult to find in a place like Bournemouth. Muriel found that her increasing financial reliance on Freda, and the way Freda always dominated the choices in their life, made her both grateful and resentful.

It was part of the arrogance of Freda's upbringing that she could not see why Muriel should concern herself over such things, yet Muriel had cause to feel uncomfortable. Freda always watched her money and invested carefully and was also inclined to oversee the money that her friend used. Every year that Muriel did not commit herself to training as a doctor, the longer that £2,000 lay unused, the harder it became for Muriel to use it and the more distressing it was to her.

A visit by Heinrich Von Haast, who was not well and therefore not in a mood to make anyone feel better, did not help. Over in London as a member of a fine arts committee to look at the British Empire Exhibition of 1924, he had news of Freda's finances which were not performing as well as he had promised. Two of the mortgage holders were slipping behind in payments. Freda found this upsetting. She hated not being able to resolve the problem and the loss of money made her feel vulnerable to outside forces, especially as the inflation rate had reduced the value of her income from investments.

Von Haast also brought back old names which gave her both pleasure and nostalgic awareness of times past. Alex Graham was still at the Franz Hotel. Peter, after retiring from the Hermitage in 1922, had joined him and their sister-in-law, Rose, by then widowed, in partnership at the hotel. There were children. Peter had three, two boys and a girl. Alex and his wife, Louisa (a Londoner he met during the war) also had three. Frank Milne was head guide at the Hermitage; his assistants were a new breed of unfamiliar names. The Lindons had retired from teaching, and the couple were devoting themselves to the outdoor life from their new base in Tasmania. Annie was a loyal supporter of the Ladies' Alpine Club and would become a vice president in 1925. In a letter to the Alpine Club she wrote that, in 1920, they had travelled 2,399 miles just to get to the Hermitage. She had also been climbing Mount Field in Tasmania.[5]

Freda did as she always did when confronted by unpalatable doubts – that she had betrayed her abilities, that it had never been too late to begin climbing again – and escaped on a trip to France. She and Muriel first travelled to Normandy to the flat, farmland of Caterpillar Field to find the graves of the Bacchus brothers; by train they went through Paris, then south to the city of Toulouse and the Chateau De Pibrac. Because of heating costs and the high cost of repairs the chateau was used primarily as a summer place but the building and grounds were still impressive and both women were made welcome.

The return, from an ancestral chateau to a small house with neighbours on either side, from beautiful countryside to a backyard – albeit with a view of the sea – had other consequences. Freda became aware of another important change: she did have enough money for both her and Muriel to live on, but not at the level she had been born to. It may never have concerned her in Australia but such matters were a part of life in England. Their home was pleasant and roomy, with the added advantage that it could be divided into two flats but, on long walks along the cliff tops, it was noticeable that the houses she was passing, those large mansions belonging to successful businessmen or minor peers with plenty of money and enough good taste, were the kind of homes she had been welcomed to in Sydney.

The owners of the Bournemouth mansions were the English equivalents of the Wynnes, the Abbotts, the Edwards. Freda was, in modern terms, downwardly mobile. Emphasising this was the increase in housing estates around them, rows and rows of dull brick houses that smothered the farmland beyond the chines. They foreshadowed a lifestyle they could slip into: of cheerless streets, too narrow and cheaply created to provide trees, parks and flowers.

Money again became an issue when, on 11 May 1925, Frederica Du Faur died. Her will, made in 1919, appointed her nephews Gerald Bryans and G.B. Wolfe as trustees. Her estate was not substantial but had been boosted by £6,000 left to her by Catherine Kemplay, although with the stipulation that, on the death of Frederica, Captain Cyprian Taylor should inherit. Frederica left £100 to Amy Haydon, her maid, divided up her estate between various (English) nieces and nephews and left a third to Bertie. He received in the vicinity of £1,500 but had spent too many solitary days mulling over the unfairness of life for this bonus to smooth his resentments. There was nothing for Guy and Freda as 'they are already well provided for'. Freda was genuinely saddened by her aunt's death but felt – not just felt but knew – that neither she nor Guy were as well off as had been assumed.

To make matters worse Muriel broke with the Swedish Institute. Always geared towards analysing the state of women, she knew Freda was worried but, for a while, assumed it was Frederica's death that had upset her. After a time she took Freda's remoteness personally and felt her friend was now not confiding in her because she judged her as inadequate. Muriel became aware of how much she talked and how rarely people, especially Freda, listened to her. She listened to herself and criticised herself as she was sure others did. She felt that her once sparkling ideas had become dull, little more than a bland reiteration of past observations, while about her floated the cheeky avant-garde conversation of the flappers who flocked to the institute. Physical education was the domain of bright young things who did not care about the sacrifices women such as Muriel had made to break the ground that they, corsetless and short-haired, trod on so carelessly.

In the bright, dancing shallows of Bournemouth, Muriel saw herself as one of those faceless grey women she had vowed she would never be. The past, Sydney, the Dupain Institute now glowed with lost opportunities masking her memories of the long tiring days, her irritation with the demands Dupain put on her and her lack of recognition. The thrills of the war years now seemed selfish, her lesbianism distressed her, yet her relationship with Freda was essential. They sustained each other – or they once had.

By the middle of the decade Muriel began to feel there was no place for her in this new harsh society and she became subject to a variety of minor illnesses, difficult for someone whose entire self-image revolved around her robust good health and pride in her ability to maintain herself in 'tiptop' condition. News from home should have reassured her but in fact made her feel even more redundant. The Cadogan household was managing very well with-out her, especially as the youngest, Max, had won a scholarship to Scots College, one of the best private high schools in Sydney. He would go on to become a lawyer in 1931. Muriel, unconvinced, continued to send off advice, long out of date, after weeks at sea. In return, Mick wrote precise letters about everyone, including exact costs, but Muriel was sure he was hiding the real situation, what-ever that was, from her.

For a time, confused and trying to find a solution to her dis-tress, Muriel turned back to the darkened rooms and velvet table-cloth, the ouija board and the mysterious voices and rappings. The calling of the spirits provided excitement, warmth and sharing, fre-quently absent from Sea Road. As well, she began to spend more time with Gertrude Deane in the acceptable world of the hetero-sexual family, the kind of family life Muriel adored and missed. Norman Deane had in fact been treating Muriel. She could take one of the convenient trams along Christchurch Road through Southbourne to Avenue Road, Christchurch where there was a sym-pathetic ear.

Freda did not think to seriously take into account Muriel's dis-like of being dependent and saw her concerns as resentment. She

swung between anger and sympathy depending on her level of concern with Muriel's sickness and her own fears that in time she could
be entirely responsible for her friend. Underlining this possibility
was the plight of their elderly neighbour at 30 Sea Road, Miss Erin
Canton, whose sister, with whom she shared a house, was failing
probably from senile dementia. The old women struggled to maintain themselves on dwindling resources, in a society that had no
sympathy for them. Newspapers, full of the continuing financial
crisis in the country – there were exhortations to buy British, pressure to send more emigrants out to the colonies, an insidious
increase in costs and taxes and a rise again in the unemployed. All
this exacerbated Freda's financial fears and she became openly tight
with her money. This, in turn, fed Muriel's anxieties – the money
Freda had lent Muriel now festered in both their minds.

Freda decided to sublet Sea Road in the hope it would take some
pressure off what she perceived as the excessive demands of her
mortgage of £1,000. It seems a peculiar business practice to borrow
so much in England, when she had money on mortgage in New
Zealand and as much in trust in Australia.

By early 1927, three flats were created in The Pines. She and
Muriel shared one. The 'Top Flat' was let to a Mrs Fabins and the
'Small Flat' to a Miss M.F. Hutchinson. The change would provide
just over a pound extra a week and seems hardly worthwhile but
there may have been an ulterior motive. The presence of other
women would have taken pressure off Freda, for Muriel was
increasingly unwell, which meant, at this point, mood changes. Dr
Deane's bills were expensive and aggravated the tension between
them. Freda must have been aware, from her own experiences, that
Muriel was going through a kind of breakdown; but Muriel had
been the strong one of the two, Freda had always relied emotional-

ly on her. She could not believe that Muriel didn't have the strength to snap out of it.

Any chance of that happening was negated by the news that Nell Cadogan, two years younger than Muriel, had died of peritonitis. Nell had always been dominated by her outgoing older sister but the pair had been very close. Muriel was devastated and felt sure she could somehow have prevented Nell's death if she had been back in Sydney. As well as her own distress, Muriel worried about her mother, whom Nell had been living with and caring for full-time.

Muriel's reasoning began to be affected as she sought to identify the cause of her problems. She began to believe that the Cadogans had been cursed from the moment that her grandmother, Marianne Cadogan, had forsaken the Cadogans for the Shaws. Muriel now saw the lectures that Alfred Shaw had given as taking control of her, in the same way he had ruined her father by wheedling his way in to get what he could of William Cadogan's savings. She was sure Alfred Shaw had used his knowledge of hypnotism to control her father. If he hadn't succeeded the Cadogans would have been rich (so Muriel's reasoning went). Nell would have survived, she (Muriel) would not have to be beholden to Freda and she would not be so angry with her. It was all so logical and, for a while, convinced Freda, who still had some way to go before she realised that Muriel was swinging from mania to depression, with fewer and fewer calm periods in between.

During this time Freda did hear some pleasing, though surprising news that Guy, at the age of 50, had married. His bride, Nina Suttor, was fifteen years younger, an independent woman who would work as a legal secretary most of her married life. Nina was acceptable socially as a daughter of the poor side of an establishment family.

Towards the end of that same year, 1927, Freda for better or worse decided to move out of Sea Road to Christchurch, a town Muriel particularly liked. Built on the confluence of the rivers Stour and Avon, and dominated by a medieval priory which separated the Solent from the main street, the town had a sense of community that Freda felt they had been missing. They would be closer to the Deanes on whom Muriel increasingly depended, and on whom Freda preferred her to depend, rather than the erratic and unsettling nature of her spiritualist friends. Because so much focused on money, an unspoken plus was that all of Sea Road could be let and they could get cheaper digs for a while and see how things worked out. A Miss Veal moved into their flat and Freda and Muriel moved to a house called Beaulieu at 3 Beaulieu Road, Christchurch. It was a nearly new home, with two storeys, built of orange-red brick with bay windows at the front. It stands in a small estate in an extremely neat suburban street, just off Barrack Road and about half a mile walk from the centre of Christchurch.On one side was a house called The Poplars, on the other The Outlook, so named because of its view down the bank to the River Stour. There was access from the street to the pleasant river walks down to Tuckton Bridge and the outlet of Hengistbury Head, with its views to the Solent and the Isle of Wight. They could swim at the beach which was free of tourists, buntings and traffic, then search for Iron Age relics, flints and old bits of pottery. There were also walks to the marshes. Pleasant hours were spent in the Stanpit Marshes Nature Reserve watching black and white oystercatchers dip their efficient bills into the mud, and slender white herons pose against the sky. For a while it felt like home.

The Deane family provided stability for Muriel although it was probably around this time that Dr Deane learned of Freda and Muriel's relationship. Muriel may even have confided in him. There is no reason why Dr Deane should have any other opinion on lesbianism than the current one: that lesbianism was a perversion.

And as things proved later, he probably believed that Freda was one of those types 'who found satisfaction in guiding and protecting weaker women'.[6]

Fearing Freda would be blamed, Muriel began to hide her perilous emotional state so that Freda's concern began to look like the real problem while the ideas Muriel exposed, only to Freda, moved into the realm of paranoia. It was the Shaws haunting her again. Muriel became convinced that Albert Shaw's lectures and hypnotic abilities had weakened her soul all those years ago, and had made her susceptible to the spiritualists, through whom evil spirits had entered her. She believed she was under their control, or rather Alfred Shaw was manipulating her, through them, from the afterlife. Muriel was sure Alfred's son, Cyril Shaw, was now out to ruin the next generation of Cadogans. Mrs Amanda Shaw and Cyril were in Vancouver, where they would live until moving to Pasadena in 1933, but there was no relief in that. If spirits could move between heaven and earth, or rather float somewhere in between and reach through the barriers to connect with susceptible people on earth, the Atlantic Ocean and the landmass of Canada wouldn't be a problem.

There were sleepless nights, then times when Muriel just stayed in bed, then got up and talked non-stop. There were moments, too, when Muriel would be perfectly well and Freda could believe, with the eternal hope of someone sharing a life with the chronically ill, that this time she would be all right. It was a terrible, uncertain year. Both Muriel and Freda were exhausted.

By Christmas 1928, Muriel was improving and Freda believed that if they could get through into the New Year it might be a turning point. They moved, again still in Christchurch, but to a boarding house in nearby Meon Road. They had definitely decided to return to Sea Road as most of their belongings were back there. The boarding house may have been an interim measure. Peace did not last. Dr Deane was soon calling. With him, during the Christmas holidays, came his young son, William, to mind the car when he made his calls. Muriel's instability continued into February 1929 when Freda again 'had no sleep as Miss Cadogan went insane and made a scene at the boarding house we were staying at'.[7] Later Freda would amend this to 'temporarily insane' but Muriel would have little life left ahead to prove its temporary nature. During that night, Freda managed to 'smooth her over' and at 8.00 a.m., the next day, completely exhausted and with a subdued Muriel, she arrived at Norman Deane's rooms, only a short walk away.

Muriel was calm until Freda began to explain what had occurred and the doctor began to question her. What was said was never recorded but it was enough, according to Freda, for Dr Deane, despite or perhaps because of the friendship, to shout at Muriel that, 'If she was not careful she would end up in a padded cell!'[8] Muriel, under such a threat, walked out. Freda ran after her and quietened her again but Muriel no longer wanted to be treated by Deane. She wanted Dr Morton, who had been the doctor treating their neighbour, Miss Canton. Dr Deane was, no doubt, relieved to refer Muriel. He had had enough; as a close friend it was too distressing and he was no expert on mental illness.

Freda and Muriel then walked to Southbourne, a few miles closer to Bournemouth. It is likely that Muriel refused to travel in Dr Deane's car, even if he had offered, and Freda may well have hoped that the walk would wear Muriel down.

They arrived at Dr Morton's surgery, The Lodge in Southbourne Road, Southbourne, later that morning. Morton was in his early fifties and carried with him all the superiority of a medical man who had trained in London, who had once been Senior Resident Officer at Hoxton House Asylum and was Medical Officer to the Outpatients of Royal Victoria and West Hants Hospital. Suitably cowed by such credentials Muriel, this time, did not interrupt as Freda explained their problem. Doctor Morton spoke only to Freda. He was reassuring; he could solve all their problems if she put Muriel in his hands. With gratitude, Freda did.

The relief was almost too much. The whole trauma, particularly the last year, the sleepless nights and the long walk without food, swept over Freda. According to her, she confessed that she was close to breaking point herself. To Dr Morton she was little different to Muriel. They were 'inverts' after all, therefore hysterics: 'a metaphor for everything unmanageable in the female sex'.[9] They had none of those things defining them as a woman: gentle natures, children, family connections, a husband.

Dr Morton recommended a stay at a nursing home of good reputation, Strathallan, at 3 Owls Road, Boscombe. Owls Road runs off Sea Road and the hospital can be seen from The Pines.

Freda and Muriel continued to walk on to Boscombe. Late afternoon put them outside the four-storeyed Strathallan. Designed to look out over the ocean and its classical garden of lily ponds, roses and weeping cherry, from the street it resembled a mausoleum with a hodgepodge of different sized windows, exposed plumbing, a variety of angled and flat roofs, and great square columns. It was not just a rest home but an extraordinarily well-set-up hospital, reportedly solely owned by the matron, Edith May Barton, although she may well have been a figurehead for a consortium of local doctors. It had vast operating theatres with terrazzo-type floors, the newest steel equipment and its own X-ray room. The hospital would later be described by Freda as sinister. Inside she was 'interviewed by a Dr whose name I do not know, in a dark corner of the hall'[10] before going to the office of Matron Barton. If she did feel any foreboding at the time, such was her relief at having Muriel in proper care that she ignored it and agreed they would both come in at six guineas a week. Leaving Muriel downstairs in the care of Matron Barton, she went up to check the rooms. The room she and Muriel were to share was charming and sunny, with wide windows, comfortable wooden beds and deep satin eiderdowns. On the same floor were sitting rooms with wing-back chairs, pretty lamps, writing desks and lace table cloths. Axminster squares softened the polished floors.

Optimistic now, she returned to the office only to discover Muriel was gone. Freda claimed the matron, in a blasé fashion, told her that Muriel had gone to collect clothes from Sea Road and 'there was no point going after her'. Freda, who had by then handed over her authority to those who professed to know, did as she was told and exhausted sat down to wait for Muriel's return. She may have been given tranquillisers as she fell asleep, waking later to find the matron and a nurse at the foot of the bed 'with folded arms like a soldier'. Freda was convinced she was hypnotised by a 'dark Indian looking doctor who looked me in the eyes and I felt myself falling'.[11]

A full day later she woke, very dazed and in a single room, not a double. Where was Muriel? Incessant questioning brought an answer. Miss Cadogan had returned with their clothes only to disappear again. Freda was dismayed. She had been asleep and Muriel had been allowed to run free. She asked for Doctor Morton. He arrived the next morning to report that Muriel had been 'found wandering' in Christchurch by the police. She had been 'penniless and disruptive'. The police could no more cope with Muriel than could Freda, so Dr Deane had eventually taken her back into his charge and admitted (or committed) her to a rest home, almost next door to his own rooms, on the corner of Barrack and Avenue Roads, Christchurch. This hospital, Broadlands, was run by Sisters W. McMillen and I.F. Mews. It was smaller than Strathallan, but the weekly cost was the same as Freda discovered when Dr Deane arrived to see her, accompanied by one of, what Freda called, the 'Jewish doctors'.

Norman Deane told Freda it was advisable for Muriel to stay in Broadlands so Freda agreed to be responsible for her friend's costs there. She wrote a note for Muriel which he took with him then. For the following week Freda, sure Muriel was now safe, took whatever medicine and food she was given and lay in a 'semi conscious state asleep all night and half the day'. She believed, particularly after leaving Strathallan when her head cleared, that she had been heavily drugged. She had bizarre experiences from hallucinations, although she believed they were caused by hypnotism and was sure she'd been awake. She had heard a voice, presumably that of the 'Jewish Doctor', saying 'You will have nothing of your own any more and never be as before. You have an inverted Hedonistic Persuasion at four points – will you become a Jewess and do as you are told or have eternal pain?'

She understood, however it was put, that the hospital and doctors felt that lesbianism, being an 'invert', was at the root of the problem. Freda rejected the strange offer. She was a lesbian but did not see herself as perverted. Hedonism had nothing to do with her sexual persuasion. She could not be influenced against her sense of right. As well she was Christian and nothing could persuade her from that.

Freda may have felt threatened by not only a man telling her how to live, but a Jewish one at that, as she appears to have believed, as many did in the area, that they were a danger to the English way of life. There was a reason in such a prejudice. The Jewish community in Bournemouth was centred on the East Cliffs, which verges on Sea Road. At one stage, there were 22 Jewish hotels and boarding houses supervised by Beth Din. These people, many who had gone to England to escape persecution in countries such as Russia and Poland, tended to isolate themselves; few spoke English and when they did their accents were considered to be barbaric. Their dress, particularly the Hasidic style, was regarded as ugly and primitive; their separateness was emphasised by intermarriage as a defence of their faith and against perceived and real hostility. The appearance of financial well-being did not endear them to a local population struggling against worsening economic conditions.

Sometime during the third week at Strathallan, perhaps because Freda was being taken off the sedation and there was concern about the effects of the treatment, a nurse, dressed in white apron and full veil over a pale blue uniform with stiffened cuffs and white shoes, sat in her room day and night. To Freda, this intrusion was imprisonment.

Finally, when she was fully awake and having used up what money she had with her, she decided to leave. Dr Morton attempted to discourage her and, as if to justify the treatment, informed her she had an unstable heart and should take care. But there was a more pressing need than her own health.

With only a few pennies and her suitcase, Freda left Strathallan, borrowed five shillings from a friend and arrived in Christchurch to visit Muriel, who had the keys for Sea Road, their bank book and some money. She took a room at a nearby hotel for the weekend so she could be close to Muriel, who 'was a little queer and confused but knew me and wanted me near her'.[12] The next morning, Dr Deane did not agree that Freda should stay near his patient. Only by removing Freda's influences and hence her lesbian power could Muriel recover and have a chance of adjusting to what the medical fraternity generally viewed as the more 'natural' relationship of heterosexuality.

Freda disobeyed and continued to visit Muriel for the next two days but, on the third, she was refused admittance on the grounds that Muriel had influenza. Freda forced her way in to find her 'flushed and feverish, she seemed drugged with her eyes half closed and did not know' her.[13] From then on, despite Freda's distress, she was not allowed to visit. She appealed to Dr Deane, who was formal and distant and firm. Muriel was now very ill. It would be better if she went back to Australia where she belonged, where it was healthy, with her family. On the strength of this he had sent for her sister, Beryl, who was taking leave from Crown Street Hospital in Sydney and would look after Muriel on the trip back.

Freda moved back into Sea Road, frustrated and confused by her own experiences. On the last day of May 1928, Muriel and Beryl came to see Freda to say goodbye and collect Muriel's belongings. Muriel was so changed Freda barely recognised her. Gone was that stalwart woman with the bright ideas. In front of her was a frightened, frail woman looking far older than her 45 years. In the so-familiar surroundings of the home they had set up together, amongst the paintings, the books, the furnishing they had chosen, Muriel clung to Freda weeping. She begged her to come with her. Freda couldn't immediately, as their finances were in a mess with all the moving about, and she had to sort out the house. In turn she pleaded with Muriel to stay but she was too far past the stage of changing any decisions, especially those made by people who professed to know what was good for her. After fifteen years of living together as adults, as lovers, Muriel was taken away from Freda and sent back to Sydney.

Early in June, Muriel and Beryl boarded the cargo boat, the *Port Heuon*, for Australia. For the next few days Freda tried not to worry and began, as quickly as possible, to organise the flats. Then a telegram arrived from the Red Sea. Muriel had died in the Bay of Biscay of 'Heat Prostration', so the report said. So devastated was Freda, that even six years later, she would say that Muriel had died in the Red Sea, an unusual mistake considering Grandpapa Woolley had died while sailing in the same piece of water.

It was all over. Freda would, as she had been threatened, 'never be as before',[14] but not directly through Muriel's death, nor her 'inverted persuasion', and not from an unstable heart, but from the inability to find out the real story about what had happened.

21 To The Ends Of The Earth

'... and these are the forces they had ranged against us,
and these are the forces they had ranged within us,
within us and against us, against us and within us.'

Adrienne Rich
In Search of a Common Language

Freda wanted answers as a way of dealing with the reality that Muriel was dead. To heal she had to understand what had happened but no one was willing to help her. Dr Deane professed to know as little as she did; he and Gertrude were also upset by Muriel's death and felt they'd done their best for someone they were very fond of. Freda brought trouble when they wanted to get their lives back on an even keel. After all, they had been under strain from Muriel too.

Communication with Dr Morton was useless. His answers were evasive; he described the treatment as a rest, nothing else happened. It was Freda's state of mind that was the problem. Freda, vulnerable in mourning and affected by her own stay in Strathallan, retreated. She was afraid and now confused. Was she crazy too, as Dr Morton implied? She doubted her memories yet she knew she had been drugged, as had Muriel. She suspected a conspiracy of the doctors to cover up their mistakes.

Hindsight can clarify the confusing events that led to Muriel's death and, as Freda would write, would 'ruin ... six years of my life'.[1] They had undergone what is one of the oldest treatments known to psychiatry, extended periods of sleep, commonly know as a 'rest cure'. It was a popular treatment, designed to alleviate symptoms of stress and mental disturbance, that found increasing favour in the hospitals and nursing homes during the nineteenth century and into the early twentieth century: 'The hapless patient was put to bed and injected at frequent intervals. After 48 hours he was roused for an assessment of his health (and his temper): any show of irritability and he was promptly knocked out again! This was then continued – almost indefinitely – until the patient was prepared to wake with a smile.'[2] Women, in particular, were felt to benefit from it, especially those who were intelligent and independent: 'Nervous susceptible women ... clearly the single more so than the married, are most frequently visited by hysteria; and such constitutions have always a greater aptitude to strong mental emotions, which on repetition will induce mental derangement.'[3] It was probably kinder than the fire or the ducking stool faced in earlier centuries, although in Muriel's case the result was comparable.

Bromides and perhaps chloral were used to sedate patients. It is entirely possible that Muriel underwent electro-shock therapy as well, as it was felt, by the medical fraternity, that a combination of techniques was 'valuable when the patients are too anxious and unco-operative ... In such a patient sleep treatment will reduce the excessive anxiety and permit a more rational attitude to treatment of choice.'[4]

It was firmly believed, by one of the strongest exponents of rest cures in Britain, Dr William Sargant, that the best subjects for such

treatment were persons 'of usually stable personality who have broken down as the result of a succession of severe stresses into a state
in which anxiety, depression and hysterical manifestations are all to
be seen'.[5] He could have been describing Muriel.

There was a genuine belief that in the short term the treatment was a success, although without follow-up treatment many
relapsed – but a patient confined to bed for weeks at a time was also
a good way for a hospital to make money. Muriel's later illness and
confusion appears to have been, if not caused by the treatment, at
least exacerbated by it. And the medical fraternity knew this could
happen.

The alarm had been raised about rest cures as early as 1926,
by Dawson and Barkas, the very people who had introduced the
treatment into Britain. In the *Lancet* they reported 'alarming com-
plications and fatalities'. Doctor Sargant terminated such radical
treatment after the deaths of two of his patients. Unfortunately
other doctors, some clearly in the rest homes in Bournemouth, felt
that modifications to dosage, different drugs and better daily care
would rectify any problem, although there was general acknowledgment that there was the risk of broncho-pneumonia, depression
of the respiratory centre, fever, toxic confusional states and cardio-
vascular collapse. Freda talked of Muriel's fever and confusion; she
officially died of a heart attack.

Freda's description of her experiences – the strange doctors,
the bizarre requests, the confusion, the poor health, the aggressive
attack on her to change her ways, her later confusion – was a pre-
cursor to other cases, many that ended just as tragically. Deep sleep
therapies, based on a bastardised version of Dr Sargant's work, but
without the special care by trained staff, were carried out by a
'Jekyll and Hyde' character, Dr Harry Bailey, at a Sydney hospital,
Chelmsford. During the 1960s at least 24 people died as a direct
result of the treatment. Many later committed suicide and more

would be unable to cope with the distressing after-effects. One patient reported, 'I would hallucinate, and instead of seeing nurses, I saw attacking goblins who were forcing liquid down my throat.'[6]

Freda may not have seen goblins but, for her, the Indian, the Jewish doctor and the soldier/nurse were just as strange. Without Muriel, there was no one to share and understand how disorientated she felt, so she used all her skills to hide her distress. Another recent patient of Bailey's described how she felt: 'The worst part about it ... I can't relate to real people.'[7]

In Sydney on 24 October 1929, probate was granted on Muriel's will in Australia, but the relief for Freda, that one more thing was organised, was overshadowed by another event: the 24th was also Black Thursday, the collapse of the stock market on Wall Street and the beginning of the Great Depression that would define Freda's last years as surely as Muriel's death would shadow them. It was another blow to what Freda felt were her fragile finances. She felt, too, that probate had taken an unnecessarily long time to be granted. Suspicious of the delay, unable to get information yet sure, as in the past, she could get through her depression and her uncertainty by attack, she decided to go to Australia and find out the truth from Beryl Cadogan. Then she could get on with her life.

Freda placed her English business with Mrs Ethel Cocker, a rare female lawyer and, even rarer, a partner in the reputable firm of Eaton and Cockers at 1 Yelverton Road, although she was married to one of the other partners. That done, she set sail on her mission before the new year.

Driven by such demons made it impossible for Freda to deal with events in Australia. She began by fighting with Hilton (Mick) Cadogan. Freda had expected all her money to be waiting for her plus a few bits and pieces of Muriel's. She was stunned to discover, when she visited Muriel's brother, that she was £700 short. His explanation was that Dr Deane had written to him, before Muriel's death, for £200, then after her death for another £500. Freda was given no explanation for these amounts; she consistently stated she had paid all Muriel's bills: £6 a week for approximately twenty-five weeks is still only £150 and she was always aware of where money went. The £500 could have included the boat fare organised by Dr Deane, plus his own personal expenses. Whatever the reason (and fraud cannot be entirely discounted) £700 was an enormous amount of money. It was about three times the annual basic wage for an Australian male at that time. Arguments raged between Freda and the mild-mannered, but firm, Hilton. Her sense of outrage was overwhelming, the stone-wall, to her, suspicious. She maintained Hilton had no right to send any money at all without her agreement as the money was hers but, as far as he was concerned, Muriel had given him the money and he was trustee. It was his obligation to pay off her debts before settling the estate.

Because of the arguments Freda did not get to see Beryl Cadogan to obtain her desperately needed explanation of Muriel's death. Nevertheless, Freda vowed never to give up. By attrition she would get through to the truth. She had to, it was the only way to recover. But there were no friends to calm her in Sydney, and the only peak she now was trying to conquer was misted with doubt and she couldn't even find a base from which to start to climb. Sydney was inhospitable as well, with the Great Depression hitting. There was no place with Guy, now focused on his new life with a wife. Staying with Bertie was brief and uncomfortable. Nephew John was growing, as Freda had feared, into a cold, unemotional young man. Her friendship with Wynifred was strained whenever Bertie was about. And what could she tell her sister-in-law? That she had been drugged and hypnotised in hospital? That Muriel had been killed? That her nest egg had been stolen? It was unbelievable.

Even worse Freda had begun to have bizarre thoughts and 'music in her head', as if a radio had been turned on, then turned off and she could not recall what she'd heard. She was frightened, as Muriel had often said, 'Listen to the words in the air!'[8]

Feeling that the only way not to expose her growing instability was to keep going, she escaped to the one person who would accept her, Enid. Enid denoted truth, even if it was of an acerbic kind. She could regain her sense of reality with her old friend, then go back into the fray. She also wanted advice from what she regarded as an untainted source, Von Haast, who had spent some time at the bar in Australia. Consequently, Freda left Australia for New Zealand.

What she did not take into account was that she was to go to Auckland for the first time and into the home of almost a stranger, Enid's new husband, John Ellis. Enid was busy with her concerns. The Ellis children, Barbara and Brian, twelve and fourteen years old respectively, were bearing the brunt and the benefit of Enid's enthusiasms. Many would sympathise with those who commented how 'tiring [it would be] to be brought up by Enid'. The children's new mater 'wore everyone to a frazzle'[9] with her demands and everything ended up like the Brownie uniform she was determined to make for Barbara which was without such finishing touches as sleeves and collars. Barbara wore it; who would argue?

Enid was as impossible with adults as she was with children, especially where finances were concerned. She loved to get involved, too quickly and unwisely, in business deals and unnecessary litigation which she would initiate, then leave the details to be picked up by her much more careful and kindly husband. Afterwards she loved to recount her schemes and how she wangled her way in and out of them, and generally enjoyed her lack of consideration.

Enid's stepchildren, filled with bedtime stories of Freda's exploits, both in the mountains and as a wicked young girl, were surprised to meet a small woman, with pale skin verging on sallow and dark hair brushed severely down. She appeared to them as a distant woman who hardly seemed aware of their existence.

When Freda arrived in Auckland in the middle of 1930 she looked terrible, according to Enid, who had always considered that whatever was going on with Freda was better than being normal and boring. A holiday would fix her up. Freda was bundled into the car with John Ellis, Barbara, baggage and food, leaving Enid and Brian to walk the cow, over two days, up to the holiday house in the Waitakere Ranges west of the city. It made good sense to Enid. She liked the cow, the cow had a right to go on holiday too, plus it would provide fresh milk. Freda might well have felt she wasn't so crazy after all.

The holiday house was small, built of heart kauri, a superb and by then rare native wood, by John Ellis and surrounded by beautiful native bush which cast a delicate green through the one big room downstairs. There were two bedrooms upstairs and a long dormitory, with a view back over the harbour to the east. Entry to the bathroom, which was in the basement, was through a trapdoor in the floor.

Enid continued to organise even on holiday. They all needed fresh air. Enid had done her part with the trek up into the hills so the children were ordered to take Freda out to climb to the trig station, the highest point on the ranges. It was pleasant, the children led at a pace Freda liked and the voices and anxieties in her head were stilled. They roamed upward, under the sweeping, bright needles of the rimu and past the remains of mammoth kauri, with tall trunks and thick canopies that created secret, mossy glades and winding, fern-edged tracks. The Waitakeres create a barrier between Auckland on the east coast and the isolated black sand of the western beaches, so at the top, they could perch on the base of the trig station and see in all directions. But the children had a problem. Should they take Freda back 'their own way'? Brian thought they shouldn't. As this Aunt Freda was a lady, they should return the way they'd come, but Barbara's answer was that she couldn't be a lady, she was a mountaineer.[10]

Truth won. They returned, heads down so no one would see them as they trespassed through the pastures and the backyards of other properties which were mostly covered in bracken that tore at their clothes and skin. Freda, according to Barbara, 'seemed to quite enjoy the experience'. When Freda spent the following two days in bed, the children, unaware of the interweaving dynamics of human behaviour and the causes of illness, believed Freda was just too old; 'their own way' had proved too much for her.[11]

If only the problem had just been physical, Freda might have been able to beat it. Instead she lay in bed to hide her precarious mental state. For the voices had come back, as they would now always come back, attacking her morals. She could deny their inferences about the unnatural ways of the invert, as she knew too many good homosexuals, especially Muriel, to consider them and their ways immoral. Nor would she take notice of narrow-minded religious zealots, heterosexual male doctors, old maid matrons, and Jewish psychiatrists. But her childhood was rooted in people who would have disapproved, and she may well have been susceptible to the suggestions in the hospital because of that upbringing. Her voices could well be regarded as an argument between the conscious and unconscious parts of her mind made more difficult because she could not confide in anyone, not in Enid, Ruth Abbott or her brothers or their wives, although her nephew John, as he grew older, recognised her sexual preference.

When the accusatory voices weakened and she felt secure once again, Freda left Enid's in early September to go south. The long train trip took her down through the centre of the country with clear views of the three active volcanoes of Mount Ruapehu, Tongariro and Ngauruhoe, partly smothered by a soft layer of steam that drifted and evaporated into the cool air. And west from there, if she strained her eyes she could see the perfect cone of Egmont. Just seeing the mountains was exhilarating. These were her forgotten peaks and they symbolised all that she valued in human beings. She was confident the New Zealand trip would heal her enough to continue her fight.

Freda stayed only briefly in Manakau. She had never been close to Sabrie and her Aunt Constance, although in her mid-eighties, still had an eye as sharp as her tongue. With memories of a depression thirty-five years earlier and as a way of maintaining control, Constance was well prepared for the current depression. She had cupboards stacked with everything from nutmeg to bottled fruits from the farm, drums full of eggs preserved in Vaseline and even piles of black, lisle stockings. There was enough to keep every member of the family for the next few years. Uncomfortable with her aunt, Freda pleaded that she had to catch the ferry and do business in Wellington, so departed in the middle of September 1930. Constance died the following year.

This time Heinrich Von Haast was hearty, as ever engrossed in his theatre and art, and planning to write a book on the life of his father. Freda was very impressed with all these activities, but would have been relieved that he was sharing chambers at 23 Waring Taylor Street with a younger lawyer, Mathew Oliver Barnett. A solicitor for nine years in Wellington, Barnett was extremely well organised, put all his working time into the business and looked after many of Von Haast's clients. Her finances were quickly re-organised: she deposited more money and another sum of £250 was lent out on mortgage. Von Haast was unable to advise her on Muriel's will. She should forget it.

Freda crossed by the night ferry to Lyttelton from where she felt confident enough to visit relatives of John Ellis, John and Margaret Coop, who farmed on the Banks Peninsula at Little River. While staying there she took a ramble up the local landmark, Mount Herbert, before returning to Christchurch and catching the train over the Southern Alps from where she took a service car, as buses were known then, to Franz Josef. She was beginning to enjoy herself. Australia and England were distant memories. New Zealand was working. She was even able to look forward to facing the Graham brothers. Compared to finally dealing with the Cadogans and the doctors, that would be nothing but pleasure.

Franz Josef did not disappoint. Despite the depression the Grahams were managing financially, helped by the fact they had many interests and worked as an extended family group with nineteen members of the family employed at one time. They owned the garage, had the guiding business and its associated tourist industry, and the hotel which, by then, had grown considerably. Add-ons and annexes had been built by Jack and Dave Graham, expert carpenters, whose farms also supplied food to the community.

But guiding, as Freda had experienced it, barely existed any more. During the Great Depression there were always wealthy tourists to take up the glaciers, but there were few clients wishing to make high climbs. Young climbers, the most likely to be tempted, did not have the money to hire guides, while those desiring a career in the mountains often 'were so poor that some had to write newspaper articles before they could buy their boots'.[12]

Alex and Peter and their families lived close to the hotel but in their own cottages. Peter had four children between three and thirteen years old: Garland, Hester, Keith and Stephen. Because of arthritis he rarely climbed but his wife Muriel still tackled the mountains. In 1935 she would take all her children, the youngest then seven, over the Copland Pass to stay at the Hermitage in the old hut that had been Peter's home as a young man.

Alex, his wife Louisa, commonly known as Louie, and their four children lived in a house behind the hotel. Louie found the isolation of the coast much harder to adapt to than Muriel Graham. She was not physically strong and at times was almost overwhelmed by her fears of the wild environment in which marriage had placed her.

To her relief Freda was not expected to stay with these busy families despite the fact that other old friends, like the regular visitor Dorothy Theomin, did. She felt they were strangers, watchful, busy men, with greying although still thick hair. Too much lay between them, too many years and changes, and she needed privacy. The bonus was that by staying in the hotel, she became friendly with Rose Graham. Although in partnership with her brothers-in-law, Rose, as licensee, lived in with her three teenage children. She was strong and attractive, with auburn hair and a cheerful way. As a widow, in effect a single woman, Rose made Freda feel comfortable as she had the knack of making a guest feel like a close friend. When one of the frequent power cuts hit the small settlement, she would boost up the fire, bring out the big old black kettles and cook in the living room, with as much casualness as Peter and Alex had cooked for their clients over a spirit stove.

Freda, according to some reports and all second-hand, did very little while staying there and 'sat like an old maid in the lounge',[13] but this was another of those negative attitudes about her that so many associated with the mountains seem to like to hold. She may not have been the great mountaineer she once was but she did long walks, some out along the tourist routes including up to the Franz Josef Glacier with its great hewn sides rising from the pearly grey moraine. She also visited the St James' Anglican Church and took photos from the altar window out to the glacial ice. Later she went down the river to Okarito on the coast.

The Graham families would carry on at the hotel but, by the

Second World War, their fortunate life was changing. Peter's son, Keith would be killed on a bombing raid. By the beginning of the 1950s Peter's arthritis had disabled him and Alex had heart trouble.

To respond to the new demands of tourists and to maintain mountaineering on the west coast, they needed to expand, but there was no private money available and they certainly had none to spare. The government felt it had made a success of the Hermitage, why not the Franz? In June 1947, the Grahams agreed to sell out to the government but, early in the morning, 5 July, the annexe caught fire. Four people died. Coupled with this disaster, the government refused to rebuild for the next eleven years. As men and women going into their seventies, without their old connections in Wellington, the Grahams could only sit back and listen to pathetic excuses and watch their work, mountaineering in the west coast, change into a successful centre for tourist coaches, full of daytrippers coming to admire the glaciers. Louie and Muriel died of cancer within six months of each other. Soon after, in 1957, Alex died from heart failure. In 1961, at the age of 82, Peter sat at his table writing his memoirs. He died as he finished writing about the ascent of the Minarets and how he had returned his clients, the Professor, Mr Earle and Freda Du Faur, safely back to Malte Brun Hut.

Despite feeling she had handled that leg of the journey well, Freda left Franz Josef as an outsider, with her place in mountaineering overtaken by young, confident women, dressed in knickerbockers and puttees, ties and tie-pins and wide scout hats, who had no regard for the past. Freda Du Faur meant nothing to them.

With renewed vigour, and believing she had stilled the voices, Freda began her quest again. With the help of the limited information she had from Australia and the better perspective distance and time had provided, she decided she could return to Bournemouth and this time, in full health, confront the doctors. To gain more ammunition, at the end of 1930 she booked on a sister ship of the *Port Heuon*, the *Port Brisbane*. As expected she found the 'Port' boats were 'not suitable for an invalid in Miss Cadogan's state of health'.[14] They were only cargo ships with berths for travellers and it was incomprehensible why Muriel had been booked on such a vessel. The only explanation was that the medical men had wanted her quickly off their hands and out of the country, a not unreasonable theory given the later history of the rest cure.

Once back in Bournemouth, the conspiracy theory was verified for her when Freda discovered that Hilton Cadogan had, on 19 November 1930, appointed Mr Ralph Neville Jones of Preston Redman Solicitors of Hinton House, Hinton Road, to handle probate of Muriel's will in England. For a simple will, with a small amount of capital, it had taken almost eighteen months to process – deliberately slow to thwart her, Freda was sure. A legal notice in *The Times*, 2 January 1931 gave notice of the pending grant of probate. It was granted on 4 February 1931. Freda finally received £1,150. The reality of the money made her even more determined to solve the loss, and then get back the £700 she was sure would have made all the difference between security and the destitution that was now apparent beyond the windows of The Pines. It had become a sad place: newspapers were calling Bournemouth 'an embattled dowager determined to maintain standards, while all else were dropping theirs'.[15] The town failed in this and never fully recovered as the orchestras and dancers disappeared, hotels emptied and the unemployed lined the streets.

For a brief period, there had been a chance Freda could recover from Muriel's death. During 1932 Freda met up with an old acquaintance, Hannah Dickson, who had trained with the Odbergs at the Swedish Institute before going out on her own as a masseuse.

Hannah had all the energy and confidence and openness that Freda had first loved in Muriel. Whether Freda had an affair with Hannah is conjecture but, during that year, Hannah lived in Sea Road with Freda, while a Mrs Frances Elizabeth Edwards occupied the Top Flat and the Little Flat was let to M.A. Hey. In the end, Freda could not let go her losses and recover. She could not admit that failure. Success was to be found in tenacious purpose, regardless of the pain.

Toward the end of that year, when she was 50, Freda realised returning to Bournemouth had been a mistake – more than that, a trap. The voices in the 'wireless' in her head had come back. She was not silly, she knew they didn't really exist, but she did know the cause was real: her Nemesis was still Dr Morton, whom she believed, had actually taken complete control of her mind through hypnotism and the drugs in Strathallan. She complained he 'knew all there is to know about my private affairs', and had begun to talk about them 'in the air' with none other than the dreaded Shaws. Freda said she could 'never stop hearing them and they never stop discussing my private business'.[16] She began to believe that Morton was in league with Dr Deane, Hilton Cadogan and the lawyer, Ralph Neville Jones – all men, all highly qualified, with standing in the community, who had swindled her.

Everything Freda believed did have a basis in reality – it was a matter of interpretation. The dictatorship of men was not only specific to her, but was actually occurring in Europe. By the end of January 1933, Adolf Hitler was Chancellor of the German Reich and Mussolini had been Dictator of Italy for eleven years. Freda was not among those who believed such power was a good thing. Everything she had read, every poet she had loved, every mountain she had climbed had denoted freedom of the individual. Now she equated the high-handed behaviour of Dr Deane, Dr Morton and Hilton Cadogan with the overbearing Fascist behaviour of the dictators. Common opinion was that they had 'a gang of criminals from Middle Europe',[17] as spies in England. Freda's thinking became more clouded by a common prejudice. Jews in Bournemouth were also Middle Europeans and thus part of the gang, those same Jews who had threatened her with eternal pain, if she did not join the world conspiracy against the free thinker.

'You will have nothing of your own any more and never be as before – will you become a Jewess and do as you are told or have eternal pain?' The words she believed the doctor had uttered in Strathallan went over and over in her brain during the long silent nights. It was convoluted thinking and put Freda in centre stage as one of the main targets of Fascists. To her, this bizarre thinking was entirely logical.

Freda had to escape her tormentors so, by the end of 1933, she was viewing the marvel of the century, the new Sydney Harbour Bridge. It had brought excitement and some work to the city but Sydney was only a warmer version of what she'd left in England. There too was the terrible despair, families living in tents, men scouring the country for jobs and children scavenging for food. It was even more incongruous in a rich country with enough food for everyone.

Once again Freda stayed with Bertie and Wynifred, who were living in one of the northern beach suburbs, Collaroy. Their house was on a battle-axe block, with steps up from the main coastal road, Pittwater Road. The house was small and bland, one of many of the houses being built in the new suburbs on poor soil, bereft of trees and with constant sea spray that discouraged real gardens. It suited Bertie, who now spent most of his free time down the coast looking for the elusive lode. When at home, he worked with John at the plant they had built in the backyard to extract minerals.

Despite Bertie's regular absences, tension soon began to develop between him and Freda. He was suspicious that Freda had been omitted from Aunt Frederica's will, only because she had already received gifts and probably money during her years in England. Even if Freda had bothered to explain, she couldn't have convinced him otherwise.

It may have been that two strong-willed women swamped the small wooden house and the men in it. As well, Freda was going through the menopause. Hair had grown on her face, which embarrassed her. Symptoms may well have added to her feeling of displacement and confusion. Just to function normally, Freda often had to concentrate to pierce the fog of the voices. Sometimes she talked to drown out the words. It made her wonder about Muriel and the way she had begun to talk so much. How long before her friend's illness became apparent had she too been trying to out-talk her voices? For the sake of sanity, Freda knew she would have to get a place of her own. The voices in the air were not going to go away of their own accord. She was determined to beat them. For that she needed privacy.

Freda rented a small, wooden cottage near Bertie's, called The Haven, in Cumberland Avenue, but at the lower end, near South Creek Road. Such a commitment put off her return to England indefinitely, but she hardly cared. Reports from Mrs Cocker were reassuring as the tenants at The Pines were paying regularly and Bournemouth was becoming a vague place, full of unhappy memories and threats. She would stay in Australia until she wrenched back her mind from the intruders and retrieved her lost inheritance from Hilton. Then she would go back fresh and ready to begin life again.

Unexpectedly Freda widened her social circle. There had always been Wynifred, but surprisingly she liked Guy's wife. With John, then sixteen, she visited Guy and Nina, or rather the Count and Countess, as they had begun to style themselves. Printed calling

cards, going out of fashion elsewhere, lay on the hall table beside
Nina's fresh white gloves. Favours were returned with the occasional garden party held amongst the daffodils and tennis racquets.
They drank sherry with the eyes of Cyprian and Sarah Du Faur
looking coolly down from either side of the mantelpiece. But this
life was a greater pretence than the fake titles,as it was maintained
by the gradual selling off of land. The original estate of 25 acres
would be whittled down to about an acre. With only Nina's wage to
support them, Guy had also begun selling his precious flowers to
the local florist.

Gradually a kind of friendship built up between Freda and her
sister-in-law whose affectations both amused and irritated her. She
did not mind Nina's sharpness. Outspoken people were far preferred, at least there were no secrets. As well, it was enough for
Freda that Nina adored her fragile husband and put a practical face
for him to the world. Someone had to. Nina, in her later years,
spoke well of Freda, although she was rather in awe of her and the
name Du Faur. Despite Nina's feelings that Eccleston was an overwhelming ogre, who had intimidated his wife and his elder son, she
would later write: 'The Du Faurs have been wonderful assets to
Australia and were men of vision ... I very much appreciate my
husband and his family.'[18] In 1959 this may have been a kinder
opinion than she had held earlier on, but by then Guy was dead as
were Bertie and Freda, and John was well away in Victoria.

Through Wynifred, Freda made friends in the straight world
and came to know two girls whose lives she would influence and
who would enable her to die with some kind of joy. Wynifred had
surrounded herself with an interesting group of women. Among
them were Maud Russell, a neighbour, an elderly woman of Irish
descent, who introduced her to the first girl.

Maud owned the Sydney Commercial Art School at 121
Bathurst Street, over the ES&A Bank and was a perfect Freda 'type'.

Her exuberance could be overbearing, but she had a generous sense of humour and the atmosphere at the art school was light-hearted and diligent. She had studied in Sydney, London and Paris to become an artist, but commercial art became Maud's compromise between the financial difficulties of the art world and independence. For a period of time, she created a haven for Freda by re-familiarising her with art in relation to the Australian landscape and lifestyle, and thus encouraged her to enjoy the area she was now living in. Dee Why became for Freda, as anything she appreciated did, the small detail: the flannel flowers growing in abundance along the hills behind the houses; the reeds on the tidal lagoons down on the flat; the shadows, light and winds. 'Out there' on long walks or artistic treks when she could paint landscapes or just roam as she had when a child, it was also easier to suppress the voices.

Maud had an ulterior motive for cultivating Freda. She had a protégé who needed a benefactor. The girl, Mary, a brilliant artist, was too unassuming, her family did not have high expectations for females (the one son was to receive most of the limited family finances) so Maud had been doing everything in her power to keep the girl's mother interested in all the school's activities. In October 1932 she wrote to her, in a tone full of appreciation, for the support Mary had already received: 'I think she [Mary] is very happy and relaxed at school and I think you are right to give her a good chance. She might go far.'[19] Maud worked on everyone this way. She invited Freda to her large airy studios and introduced her to the young artist. Her full name was Mary Abbott. Her mother was Freda's old friend, Ruth (Gerard) Abbott, who now lived at Gladstone Avenue, Woolwich.

When Freda had visited them at Quirindi in 1919, Stanley had been a stock and station agent and Mary scarcely three years old. Then the Abbotts were easy going and happy, with an open house full of guests and laughter, and an interest in art. They owned a small collection of high quality oils, watercolours and pastels which had aroused Mary's initial interest in painting. All the more reason, according to Maud Russell, why she 'should be finished properly'. Mary would attribute her love of art to two other influences as well: the art taught at school in Quirindi; and correspondence with a great-aunt, Louise Jopling-Rowe, an eccentric and exciting woman, a supporter of Oscar Wilde and a member of the Royal Academy in London. Unfortunately, her great-aunt's interest did not extend to leaving some of her fortune to her 'co-lover of art'.[20]

Stanley Abbott took up a grazing property but eventually the Great Depression and the fall in commodity prices forced them from the paddocks of New South Wales to Sydney. There he gained a position with the Rural Bank, as a land valuer, something he was immensely grateful for but also found particularly distressing. Despite the moratorium on foreclosures which was made law in 1930, there were many farmers unable to pay interest, even a year later. It was their farms Stanley had to value for sale, a dreadful irony as it was his and Ruth's families, the Gerards and the Abbotts who had helped develop the pastoral industry of New South Wales.

When Freda met Ruth and Stanley again, the bloom had gone. They were moral and kind people but conservative. Maud was right; Mary would be lucky to get the kind of break that would allow her to follow her artistic instincts unless she received help from else-where. All Freda's thwarted ambitions and the enjoyment she gained from young people merged in a desire for Mary to be a real artist.

Maud invited the sweet-faced, fair-haired Mary to stay the weekend at Collaroy. Freda and Maud also hoped they could save poor John Du Faur from his own dull personality and tried to set up a friendship between him and Mary. She thought he was completely unintersting, the ultimate nerd, and was not alone in her opinion. There were few young women who had any interest in John Du Faur. He was a 'hopeless proposition'.[21]

The second girl Freda became involved with was Jean Frances Lord, the grand-daughter of Wynifred's cousin, Ida Backhouse. The Backhouses were generally a well-off family. An uncle, Judge Backhouse, was prominent in Sydney society and had also been a serious supporter of many of Eccleston's activities. Another relative was Aunt Alice Todd Backhouse, after whom Alice Springs, the main town in the interior of Australia, was named. Frances, as the girl was commonly called, was to become Freda's favourite companion, 'a favoured niece'.[22] As Frances put it 'we just clicked'. Then thirteen years old, she was tall, with an open fresh face and long blonde plaits, with a simplicity that Freda knew she had once had, a quality that had encouraged her to believe she was capable of anything, before she had lost her way, before she had failed at the hospital and failed to take up mountaineering in Europe, before Muriel died and the voices started and still continued.

Every time the Lords visited Auntie Wyn, Frances went over to visit Freda, who demanded nothing more of her than her company, gave her plenty of attention and treated her like another adult with none of those 'aunty kisses and cuddles' which Frances hated.[23]

Through early spring and into summer of 1934 , they went for long walks along nearby Brookvale Creek, under vast stands of wattle that covered them in yellow pollen. Their walks extended up from the hills, into what was actually the eastern borders of Ku-ring-gai Chase where the sandstone cliffs and gnarled trees reached right down to the houses so there was little distinction between bush and backyard and even less distinction if a bushfire scorched through when the days grew hotter.

There was not only wattle growing but sweet smelling boronia, and native rose and banksia. Despite all she had been taught by her father, Freda could not resist picking tiny bunches of flannel flowers and Christmas bells. Careful not to disturb the roots, with 'only a bunch each', the pair brought them home, to decorate the house and make a change from the pelagoniums Freda grew in window boxes, which Frances thought were awful.

While they walked, Freda talked about the flowers, the bush-fires, about her life, what she believed in, about the Du Faur family, how she would change things. Frances listened and sometimes she didn't. Talk of mountaineering, talk of travel, none of that meant much to her even if Freda referred to it. Didn't all adult women do adventurous things? She was going to. All her mother's side went off travelling to Europe and to Britain and had interesting jobs and lives.

Lorna, her mother, had trained as a nurse at Prince Alfred Hospital. During the war she met her husband, Harry (Bill) Lord who according to Frances was 'a wonderful father tho' not the best of moneymakers'.[24] Bill Lord tried to do well. Before the war he had run his own 'paper and string business' (packaging) but had left it to enlist. When the Lords married in October 1918 they went into partnership with Bill's two brothers, on a sheep and wheat property of about fifteen hundred acres called Spring Grove, only thirty-five miles away from Ruth and Stanley Abbott in Quirindi. A year later, Frances was born, a year later a brother, John, then three years after that another brother, Peter.

Frances had a contented life as a child in the country, in a close-knit family with an easy-going father and a mother who could do everything from baking homemade bread to fixing broken bones and axe gashes. Frances was well aware that in that part of the country 'no person was more loved and respected than Mrs Bill Lord'.[25] Lorna taught her own children weekly correspondence lessons, then taught her neighbour so she could teach her own children. But despite all the determination and hard work the farm was not big enough to sustain three families so Bill leased a property on his own, called Wave Hill, sixteen miles from Narrabri, in the back-blocks of New South Wales.

Disasters followed. This was sheep country, but the Lords arrived at the beginning of the Great Depression. Sheep bought for thirty shillings dropped in value overnight to six shillings. It was lonely and hard, dry at the wrong times, wet at the worst. The youngest, Peter, developed malignant endocarditis. He died quickly, barely six. It was too much; the farm, the conditions and now the death of a little boy. The family moved again to Oaklands, six miles on the other side of Narrabri, to a fresh start where Frances had 'a nice home this time with a verandah right round it – great for chasings – a big orchard and of course Mother soon had all her vegetables growing. Our shoes were sometimes wanting but we ate like royalty.'[26] Her parents could ask for little else. There was a bonus for the isolated children too. They could now attend a real school by riding five miles to the Boral Subsidised School, on a local property.

By 1932 the Lords could not keep the farm going. Lorna and the children joined so many others on the exodus to the city, to rely on family and hope they had the skills needed to make a living. Lorna could survive, as Frances would, anywhere. Bill remained for a while in the bush before joining them in the city.

Believing there was now a chance for a contented life, Freda wrote that she was trying 'to get rid of the suggestion that was given to me … that a hypnotist can read my thoughts and will never leave me alone', but age had not necessarily made her wiser and, as usual, she believed she could get by on her own. She believed 'a trained hypnotic Doctor' could help her but the only assistance she sought was from a book, *Mind Control by Power*. For months she struggled, at least well into 1934, but she was 'unable to put the matter right' by herself.[27]

Still she did not get outside help. She had every reason not to trust the medical profession but even talking to a wiser head like

Maud Russell could have helped. But Freda was too proud to expose her weakness to people she admired. Her sexuality was an added difficulty. If she had any concerns about her 'inverted hedonistic persuasion', she would have considered it highly likely that the 'voices' in her head, her 'enemies' would use that against her. It would have been so easy for many to interpret Freda's interest, in both Mary Abbott and Frances Lord, as that of a lonely lesbian preying on young girls. If Freda had contemplated such a thing it certainly would have been easier for her to attribute such an intention to menacing outside forces that had taken over her mind. None of it was true. Not one of her young friends, women now in their seventies, were ever discomforted by being with Freda. They speak of her only with great affection. Frances was to say, 'I cannot remember a lot about Aunt Freda but always with a feeling of warmth.' Only much later would Frances think of Freda's 'great kindness': 'For a person of Aunt Freda's accomplishments, being kind enough to entertain and play with a young country girl, I now realise, must have shown her loneliness.'[28]

The Backhouse–Lord family did regard Freda as being 'strange', but as a perfect example of the dangers of spinsterhood rather than of sexual deviation. It is unlikely Freda's sexual preference was ever thought of. If it had been, neither of the girls, from such proper families, would have been allowed to associate with her, let alone go up and stay for weekends as Frances began to do.

Frances' relatives, the sophisticated city Backhouses, regarded the girl as naive, but there was only one occasion when there was a direct confrontation over her unusual friendship with 'the old witch', Freda. One of her aunts could not understand what she saw in 'the funny looking old thing'. Frances furiously defended Freda, then was made to apologise, which she did with little grace. 'I apologise because my mother made me but I don't want to', she said, stubborn to the end.[29] Frances was naive, although part of it was the intense politeness her mother, a very good disciplinarian, had instilled in her children. They had been taught to regard unusual characteristics unquestioningly, a particular requirement with Freda.

'Never mind, darling', Lorna Lord would say. 'Just because some people are a little eccentric, means sometimes they are not understood.'[30] Frances had no idea what eccentric or naive meant, but she was wily enough not to find out, because her naivety and her new Aunt Freda's eccentricity created an ideal friendship.

In September 1934, Freda was delighted when Barbara Bacchus came to stay on her honeymoon with her husband, Basil Duff Hewitt. As a wedding present, Freda gave her the Woolley silver. Barbara put it in her suitcase ready to take it back to New Zealand then left to do some sightseeing. Barbara, who had known Freda so well earlier on, did not think there was anything peculiar about her second cousin, but she would regret not locking that suitcase for the rest of her life because when she and her husband returned, the silver was gone. It appeared initially that Freda had decided that Duff was not trustworthy and retrieved it. Freda may have been right about Barbara's husband but the change of heart was not because of him; it was because she had chosen another to inherit and who wasn't a blood relative.

Freda was running out of time. She had failed to get rid of the voices that plagued her life. She knew as surely as they came to her, at the very moments that she believed they were gone, that they could only get worse. She knew she was behaving oddly and in fighting them off she would eventually become obvious. She was becoming desperate but refused to give up. There had to be a solution – some schrund that could be skirted then relief found, like a snow cave full of exquisite beauty. Then gradually it came to her. It was obvious. The solution was right there in front of her, in fact had been there during the last year of torment. She could resolve everything through the two people she most cherished: Mary Abbott and Frances Lord. As her brothers were the combination of her father, she came to believe that the girls were a combination of her; one artistic and sensitive; the other strong and physical, a free spirit, who carried the undamaged part of Freda's soul. No matter what, through them she would endure.

Freda decided to set up her own 'reincarnation', so that all she valued in her ruined self, might begin again. She ceased to be concerned with curing herself and instead focused on Mary and primarily Frances. She actively began to pass on her knowledge to them, in the hope that it would give the girls the courage to be whatever they wanted to be.

She recognised the madness, but there was also logic in it and most of all relief. The voices could no longer touch her and she was harming no one but herself. They certainly couldn't get to the new 'Freda' in the girls. She had won. She felt wonderful.

Early in February 1935, Freda caught a train to Eastwood, a suburb in the north-west of Sydney and walked the short distance to 2 Hillview Road, the office of the one person she believed could help her finalise her plans, the lawyer Marie Byles.

22 COCOON

'It slayeth and it saveth, nowise moved
Except unto working out of doom;
Its threads are Love and Life; and Death and Pain
The shuttles of its loom.'

Sir Edwin Arnold
THE LIGHT OF ASIA

The meeting between Marie Beuzeville Byles and Freda was both tense and exhilarating. Both were tiny although Marie at five foot two inches and seven stone was the smaller. Marie was also eighteen years younger than Freda, but both women had been the same age when they climbed Mount Cook. Marie felt she already knew Freda, in a sense had already met her. Before Marie's own climb, on 27 January 1929, she and a close friend, the respected New Zealand climber Marjorie Edgar Jones, were staying at Malte Brun Hut, in that small room for women with 'not very clean kapok mattresses', during a storm that made going to the latrines like 'soldiers going over the top'.[1] Marie had been waiting with her own supportive guide, Alf Brustad, just as Freda had waited with Peter Graham, eighteen years earlier for storms to abate. When Marie's companions gave up and returned to the Hermitage, Brustad suggested they 'take a look at that old fellow straight away'.[2] Beyond the Haast Hut they stood, for a reverential moment, at the place where Freda and Peter Graham had bivouacked before setting off to succeed in their climb. When Freda first met Marie, the lawyer had only just returned from the Southern Alps where she had made a number of first ascents in the nearly inaccessible Hooker Range. By 26 February, the two women had worked out the will Freda wanted and she signed it. Freda left everything under trust with Marie Byles, 'for or towards the maintenance education or benefit of my niece Jean (Frances) Lord'. But Freda had no intention of passing over easy money. The intention was that when Frances reached the age of 21, the remaining estate was to be divided. The first half she would receive outright but, if she died before that, Mary Abbott would inherit the money. Frances was to have an income from the second half of the estate until she was able to earn her own living and had been in receipt of an income from a profession or occupation of not less than £2 10s per week, for the space of at least six months or until she reached 28 years of old. At that point if she had not earned that amount of income or had died before that age, the half estate would go to Mary Abbott absolutely. It was complex but clear. Marie approved of it; the demand that a certain amount of independence be achieved may well have come from the lawyer.

Freda respected and admired Marie; she was everything Freda would have desired to be. The gap in their ages had made all the difference to their lives. Marie loved climbing as much as Freda and was still climbing, but importantly she had control of every aspect of her life. She worked hard to do so. The family nickname for her was 'Mrs Mahabili Pushbar: the lady what gets things done'. She spent her life clarifying her thoughts and releasing herself from the wayward confusion of desires and fears. Marie believed in 'imaginative dreaming, active exploration and finally practical action',[3] whilst Freda's dreams and her experiences became mixed together in such a way that she found it difficult to plan any action.

Born in 1900, at Ashton-on-Mersey, England, Marie came to Australia at the age of eleven when her father, Cyril, obtained a job as a signalman on the railways. He encouraged his children to love the outdoors and not be afraid of what the world presented. Marie's mother was a Suffragette who refused to wear corsets or long dresses that so stupidly trailed in the mud. She and Marie were always vegetarians.

Marie may have spent her early life as an agnostic and preferred to save her emotions for nature, but she would eventually investigate the Unitarians, Congregationalists, Theosophists and attempt to join the Quakers; however, on finding she was too opinionated, the intense young woman took up the philosophy of Mahatma Gandhi and learned to discard all that was not in accord with the law of love and truth. Surprisingly, there was always room for more. She added Aldous Huxley's opinion that 'to judge not' was the greatest saying of Christ and to this mix added the teachings of Tenkho San of Japan who 'searched for all the evil of the world and found that it lay in his own heart'.[4] Ultimately she would wrap such truths in Buddhist meditation and its five precepts,[5] but discarded the religious observances. 'I am not a Buddhist', she would say, 'but a student of Buddha'.[6]

Marie described herself as having a 'good but not brilliant brain' along with a flimsy body and enormous discipline that would provide her with a first class honours degree in history and enabled her to withstand three years of being the only girl studying for a Bachelor of Laws. In 1924 she became the first woman lawyer in New South Wales and an articled clerk, although only after her father paid the firm a bond of £200 (men paid £100) and agreed to provide her with 'all manner of necessary and becoming apparel'. Having to succumb to that was the most difficult aspect of becoming a lawyer. Five years later, she had her own office in the partitioned foyer of the

Duke of York Cinema, funded by a bank loan, £40 from her mother and a brass plate donated by her father. To the disgust of many, she hired married women 'who should have been at home'.

That brain, discipline and philosophical interests also provided Marie with the guts to head off on a cargo boat to England, Scotland, Norway, North America and New Zealand.[7] And to climb mountains. She was a conservationist when few had heard of the word, let alone comprehended the need. She also formed bushwalking clubs. With her experiences in law and, after a battle to save the Blue Gum Forest in the Blue Mountains, she helped persuade the government to set up what was to become Bouddi National Park, north of Ku-ring-gai across the Hawkesbury River. Her house, Ahimsa, in Beecroft, Sydney, was built in bushland and was designed to interfere as little as possible with the environment. At home, surrounded by pieces from her travels – Chinese and Tibetan rugs, porcelain and her books – she wore a long blue tunic, blue trousers and black slippers, the uniform of a Chinese woman of the scholar class.

None of Marie's ideas were new to Freda but she had never met anyone who had combined so many ideals and was managing to live up to them. In that last year, 1935, Freda had found another best friend. It was actually the perfect friendship for Freda. There was no sexual involvement. Marie described herself as a 'natural celibate', although kinder friends saw her as 'pure mind'.[8] She was not anti-sex and although not anti-homosexual, she had some difficulties with the latter concept. She commented cryptically 'men's and women's bodies are not made for this, I have no suggestions.' If she suspected Freda's sexuality, she would never have brought the subject up anyway. Marie had found 'a middle way'. What she believed in was not a relationship between two individuals but 'spiritual growth through the increasing consciousness of oneness with all things'.[9]

Marie had 'chummed up' with two little girls, Rosemary and Betty, the children of her parents' tenants and was in the habit of taking them out on Sundays for bushwalks. They began to call past Freda's and often she went with them, down to the beach, or around favourite tracks into the hills. With the little girls running on ahead, the two women talked. There was so much they agreed on: mountaineering; the horrors of 'the sacrifice of beauty for the mad scramble for material wealth';[10] and the opinion that civilisation was a disease that gradually destroyed the land and the people. Both were interested in photography; Freda gave Marie some of her original photos of Mount Cook which Marie intended to use in one of her books. Marie kept printing equipment and an enlarger in her kitchen. Both loved poetry and Marie was as keen as Freda on Tennyson and Browning. They both believed in the power of nature to heal both itself and human beings.

Marie was stronger than the 'voices' in Freda's head but unfortunately she was not curious about people she met. If she liked them she showed it, if she didn't there was no pretence.[11] She expected her companions to be as open as she was and when they weren't she did not question them. On those walks the women talked about ideas, rarely about personal things, next to nothing about life in Bournemouth and nothing of Muriel. Frances was never included in the walks and yet she would have been about the same age as Rosemary and Betty. Marie was only aware of Freda's friendship with Mary Abbott and Frances Lord because of her will. Marie heard about safe subjects like Possie, the dog, but never even knew Freda had relatives in Sydney, although they would have walked right past Bertie and Wynifred's house.

Marie went off regularly on bushwalks up the coast with a groups of close friends including the novelist Dymphna Cusack. She also went skiing to Kosciuszko in the Snowy Mountains, south of Sydney, but she could not persuade Freda to go with her. Yet, when Freda locked herself out of her house and climbed up through a high window to get the key still inside, Marie was amazed at the ease with which she did it. Obviously, while still fit and loving being active, Freda could not face trips such as Marie suggested. She could not face the loss of giving up climbing so long ago and the acknowledgment that her body was fading, but more importantly, Freda had become obsessed with another subject and could not bear to go away and lose track of what was going on. Just as meeting the girls, and then Marie, had great significance for her which she then incorporated 'logically' into her interior life, in those last months she had become fascinated by a case that had been running in the papers, which confirmed that the 'spies' she had escaped from in Britain had reached Australia

The case concerned an anti-war, anti-Fascist European, Egon Erwin Kisch, who had been invited to Australia by the Australian Anti-War Council to lecture. Two months before he was due to arrive in November 1934, he had been forbidden because of 'information received from British authorities in London which apparently verified he was a communist agitator'. Nevertheless, he arrived in Australia by ship, *The Strathaird*, on 6 November and was refused landing as a prohibited immigrant. During this voyage round the coast to Sydney he reported 'police interference with conversations with friends and visitors on *The Strathaird* and of interruptions by officials'.[12] Freda identified immediately with his plight.

On 17 November, a Kings Counsel hired to defend Kisch gave evidence that his client was not a communist nor had he been banned from entering the United Kingdom, but that, 'a gang of criminals from Middle Europe were operating in Sydney and England and before the case was over he [the KC] would show who they all were'.[13] Freda was sure that these names would include Dr Morton, Cyril Shaw, Hilton Cadogan and perhaps even a Jewish/Indian doctor.

The fact that the names were never published was further proof of the conspiracy.

The counsel for the prosecution, Mr Manning, KC, said, 'Kisch's future movements might be subject to scrutiny where ever he went.' In a letter to Frances, Freda quoted his statement as an example of what was happening to her. She was not a criminal, she complained, she wasn't even political and yet her movements were subject to similar scrutiny all the time. Even a poem by Browning, one she had known and loved for years, became highly significant. The lines she quoted were:

Only be sure thy daily life
In its peace or in its strife
never shall be unobserved.

Freda did not find such observation 'a pleasant process as Browning's heroine thought she might'. Freda pointed out to Frances that the Fascist spies were a 'well known group' and that 'Browning's poem, ... was staged in Middle Europe'. It was obvious to her, from all these clues, that the spies were closing in on her. Browning's heroine did not see them as a danger and Kisch could escape his enemies when eventually the court found in his favour, but there was no legal system capable of redressing the daily wrongs being inflicted on Freda. She felt she had escaped the voices only to be confronted with the real people, and there was only one way to get away from them.[14] Whether she intended to kill herself before she made her will has not been established but, through Marie Byles, her new companion, she found a philosophical approach that she could twist into justifying suicide.

Marie was opposed to suicide. She was afraid of only one thing – her mind would die before her body – but she sincerely believed, and stated often, that 'You learn from everything. Everything is fated, nothing happens by chance. Everything is alright once you accept it.' Also on those pleasant walks together, Marie, when she discussed her life (and Freda did not), mentioned her mother's view of life and death. Mrs Byles had regarded death as 'a butterfly out of the cocoon'.[15] Marie would also, half jokingly, quote Peter Pan: 'To die would be an awfully big adventure.' Freda did believe there was an afterlife but she had not been convinced it would be any better than the one she was living. The idea of her life being a rather dull, constricting cocoon and death as a winging into the sunlight began to appeal to her. The grey pressing down, the crushing of the voices, her inability to change and the weariness were perfectly explained by a cocoon. So why not break it with one violent blow …

It was all so logical.

The freedom of the climber, the heart beating against the warmth or chill of a mountain. She could feel that again on gauzy wings that would take her to the heavenly view.

But her death would be like a climber coming down, having almost made it to the summit; distressed, exhausted and careless.

On the night of 10 September 1935, Freda placed a number of her favourite books in a large box. They included *The Light of Asia*, the Browning she had been reading, Tennyson and her own book, *The Conquest of Mount Cook. An Account of Four Seasons Mountaineering on the Southern Alps of New Zealand*.

On top of that, wrapped in cloth, went the silver, all those knives, forks, spoons, and napkin rings adorned with the flourish of the Woolley W. Beside them Freda placed her favourite paintings, nothing valuable, nothing she had painted: watercolours by Amalfe, by Battista, a landscape by Worsley and some unsigned works. She folded in her best dresses, her favourite shimmery stole from Bournemouth days, then placed her brooches, the waratah, turquoise rings, bracelets, a gold ice axe tie-pin, her Mount Cook badge then, finally, a hand mirror with intricate leaves and gumnuts entwining the initials F.D.F., all carved over long winter evenings. On top of that Freda finally placed a card on which was written: To Frances from Aunt Freda.

Inside this card was a letter Freda had written which she believed explained why she no longer wished to continue living. She closed the box. On the top she wrote: For Jean Frances Lord, Mosman, Sydney. Freda had done all she could to ensure the futures of Frances and Mary Abbott and to ensure eternal life for herself.

She was entirely in control of her life at that moment. Everything was exactly as she wished. She turned on the gas and placed her head in the oven.

While Freda lay dead on the floor of her small plain kitchen, an article in the 'Women's Supplement' of the *Sydney Morning Herald* asserted:

> A decided swing towards wholesome romance. Women on the most part have given up pretending they like exploring. They like to read of other women who have lived and loved, suffered and even died in an atmosphere of romance, an atmosphere charged with sentiment, tinged with passion, suffused with illusions even if crowned by disillusionment.

Freda died on 11 September 1935, three days before her father's birthday and five days before she turned fifty-three. Two days later, her nephew John arrived to see where she was. Perhaps it was uncollected mail that made Wynifred wonder, or the Bertie Du

Faurs may have watched out for Freda more than she realised. Not yet twenty, John would never forget that moment when, on getting no answer, he broke in to find his aunt's body. He would mourn, not his aunt, but the lost chance of ever getting to know her and would say years later that she was 'the most fascinating woman I ever met'.[16]

Bertie dealt with the difficult matter as quickly as he could under the circumstances. Guy and Nina remained quietly and sadly at home.

There was no post-mortem. The official report attributed Freda's death to 'Carbon Monoxide poisoning wilfully caused by inhaling a quantity of coal gas while of unsound mind'.

Marie Byles was returning from a pleasant week in the Snowy Mountains, skiing at Mt Kosciuzko with a friend, Jean Trimble, when she read Freda's death notice.

Du Faur – Sept.13th,1935 at her residence, the Haven, Cumberland Ave, Dee Why. Freda Du Faur aged 53 years. Privately Interred.

It stated that Freda had died on the day John found her. Her age was slightly inaccurate. Anyone interested in attending her funeral was discouraged as there was no service and no mention of the cemetery but it was the final statement 'privately interred' that upset Marie the most because 'Freda had expressed in writing her desire to be cremated.'[17] Putting the best on the situation, Marie reasoned the family may not have have known that Freda had a lawyer or known of her preference but she would later view the burial in an entirely different light.

On 20 September, Freda was buried in the Manly Cemetery, in the Church of England section, in haste and shame by her brother Bertie, who loved the earth more than he loved and comprehended

Freda. She lies between strangers, Henry Stephenson and Francis Wyndham, without a gravestone.

In death, Freda finally found a place in the Alpine Club of England, with an obituary written by a mountaineer, H.E.L. Porter, who climbed in New Zealand during the 1920s, who never met her, but admired her. He summarised her record as a climber and commented: 'The Mount Cook district in her time had some resemblance to the Swiss Alps of sixty years ago. Virgin peaks were still numerous, bivouacs frequent, ladies not yet emancipated.'

In June 1936, Freda's obituary appeared in the *New Zealand Alpine Journal*. The editor, J.A. Sim, was familiar with *The Conquest of Mount Cook* and quoted freely from it in order to establish her place in climbing in that country. He wrote in particular about her enthusiasm, her relationship with Peter Graham, her effect on climbing for women and her achievements. The article finished on a note of great credit: 'Perhaps one other climber only has bettered her in the matter of major ascents, but as a woman climber she stands supreme.'

Marie Byles appointed Ethel Cocker in Bournemouth to re-seal probate in England, and Heinrich Von Haast to do the same in New Zealand. When Bertie Du Faur heard Freda's will left nothing to him or even to John, he was outraged. That Freda had left her money to Wynifred's relative, Frances, was even more outrageous. Once again Bertie felt he had been dealt a blow by domineering women. He was suspicious of Marie Byles, and of Frances, and angry with her parents for allowing Frances to ingratiate herself with his sister. Marie Byles, for whom material goods were completely irrelevant, was appalled by the behaviour of the Du Faurs. Bertie and John Du Faur 'now stepped in claiming Freda was incapable of making a will on account of insanity'. Marie was astounded by their claim that Freda was mad and she saw no reason why a relative should automatically inherit. The Bertie Du Faurs invaded her rooms and made no pretence of their feelings, those 'angry relatives on the other side of the desk with their greed and failure'. This was the first time Marie 'had come up against the rapacity of relatives and was genuinely shocked'.[18]

The Guy Du Faurs kept entirely out of the matter but they would later feel the direct effects of this 'rapacity'. Nina, after Guy died in 1957, was to warn her nieces and executors, Marjorie and Rosalind, to be wary of John for 'he had come round after Guy died putting pressure on me as last of the family'.[19] Nina, who outlived John, left everything, including the Du Faur heirlooms, to her own nieces.

Before Freda's death Marie had already been in contact with Von Haast over accounts in arrears. In 1930, Von Haast had lent £550 of Freda's money on mortgage to an Olive Annie Haybittle, who had quickly got behind in payments. Freda was still owed £46 at her death. Another account with Von Haast was better and £670 mortgaged out a year earlier, was repaid. There was also nearly £200 at the main Wellington Post Office.

Sorting out English finances was more difficult because of the time involved in communications. The remaining contents of Sea Road had to be assessed and the house itself sold. Dealings with death duties dragged on. Most of the death duty on the New Zealand assets had to be paid in New South Wales, yet there was less money there than anywhere else. Marie had to request a refund of the death duties from New South Wales so she could then pay the death duties in New Zealand before assets were released.

These difficulties were useful to Bertie Du Faur. Determined to fight his sister's will, he had time to work out tactics. He had a caveat placed on it, hired a barrister and 'brought forward a certain amount of evidence which might have indicated that she [Freda] was not in her right mind when she made the will'.[20]

Miss Byles instructed the barrister, Mr G. B. Thomas, to defend Freda's decision and therefore her state of mind. Marie stated that 'To me Freda seemed to know very well what she was doing … she seemed sane enough to me.'[21] But somewhat tongue in cheek, and in private, she said, 'Of course they said she was insane. They said I was insane too. All mountaineers are insane especially women mountaineers.'[22]

On 10 December 1935, the *Sydney Morning Herald* recorded a contested will.: 'An order nisi has been made in the matter of the will of Miss Freda Du Faur, deceased, calling on John Bertram Du Faur, one of the next of kin and caveator, to show cause why probate of the will signed by the deceased on February 26th should not be granted to the executrix, named therein, Miss Marie Byles.'

The judge felt there was enough doubt of Freda's sanity to discharge the order nisi and ordered that the matter should proceed in the way of a contested suit. It would require barristers and solicitors for days. The Du Faurs' evidence seems to be based primarily on her suicide but Marie did not believe the court system was an efficient and logical way to deal with disputes. All that was certain was, that if they went to court, a good part of the estate would be eaten up in legal costs.

Meanwhile, the situation was slightly simplified by the Abbotts. Always honourable, it was clear to Ruth Abbott how they should behave. Any money left by Freda by right belonged to the Du Faurs as most of it had originated from the Du Faur and Woolley family anyway. It should remain there. The decision was made by the Abbotts to remove Mary from consideration. The judge queried the decision carefully. He took Mary aside to check that she 'fully understand what was occurring, what she could be giving up'.[23] Reaching 28 years old was a lifetime away for a teenager and Mary was not one to question parental decisions. If her parents felt it was the right thing to do, she would do it.

Ruth Abbott later told her daughter that Freda had killed herself because she was suffering from cancer. Freda's old childhood friend was the only person, on record, to have suggested such a thing. It may be true but was unlikely, as it would have been brought forward in evidence that Freda had a sound reason for killing herself and would surely have been mentioned by Marie Byles. It is more probable that cancer was the only reason the high-minded Ruth could find for someone to commit suicide.

The Lord family was different. Despite, or because of, the enmity of Bertie, they decided that Freda had meant the estate to go to their daughter. Moreover, they saw the careful thought that had been put into the process so Frances would not be spoiled by such a windfall. Consequently they would not back down.

Marie Byles found her 'middle way' and negotiated an agreement with the Du Faurs and the Lords, in which approximately half the estate went to Frances. She would eventually receive almost £3,000 plus, untouched, the box of favourite things Freda packed for her. Probate was finally granted to Marie Byles on 1 April 1936 but her work was not finished. She immediately applied to have Freda's body exhumed so it could be cremated. She was informed that she was too late and was told that exhumation was allowed only after seven or eight years.

Marie's last act for Freda was to persuade Allen and Unwin to bring out a second impression of *The Conquest of Mount Cook* in 1936.

23 PILGRIMS

Oh may I join the choir invisible
Of those immortal dead who live again
In minds made better by their presence

George Eliot

Marie Byles continued to climb; in that year of Freda's death she returned to New Zealand with her friend, Marjorie Edgar Jones, and another New Zealand climber, Dora De Beer. In 1938 the three women went on an expedition organised and led by Marie to Western China with the intention of climbing Mount Sansato, the White Dragon, which was approximately 19,000 feet high. Accompanying them were two New Zealand guides, Kurt Suter and Mick Bowie, and another climber, Fraser Radcliffe. They climbed many smaller peaks but the White Dragon eluded them as they were kept from the summit, so often the case in the mountains, by 'the Black Dragon', bad weather. For the next forty years, Marie continued to free herself from attachment to everything including, when her feet were damaged in 1941, her beloved climbing and bushwalking. She believed it was for the best as she had become too attached to climbing and her damaged feet stopped her stagnating on life's 'pilgrimage'. She wrote in her unpublished autobiography:

339

'My mountaineering adventures, the grand passions of my life, ended with my foot operation. But they have been transcended by a far greater adventure, the quest for Nirvana … You learn from everything. Everything is fated, nothing happens by chance. Everything is alright once you accept it.'

Such a philosophy was to be tested when, at the age of 67, an intruder attacked her and smashed her skull and jaw. She was to suffer from the effects of these injuries for the rest of her life. For three more years Marie continued her work until 1970, when she disassociated herself from all her clubs, societies and legal work, then handed over her house and extensive grounds to the National Trust of Australia. Freda's 'short-time' walking companion to the last 'spurned medication and refused to be hospitalised. She departed her life with the dignity [with which] she lived it'[1] in her eightieth year.

It may have been easier for the Abbotts to turn down a possible legacy than a probable one. As Frances survived, Mary would never have actually inherited it all, but the process of turning down that opportunity for their daughter may have made it difficult for the Abbotts to turn down others. Maudie employed Mary as an art teacher but kept pushing for her to go overseas, to increase her confidence and develop her abilities. England was the preferred choice. It was the tradition of 'going Home' and there were still relatives to visit. Mary's brother was making his second trip to Germany in 1936 and as Maudie and her sister planned a trip over a few months later, so it seemed an ideal time for Mary to go away to art school. Ruth was determined to give her daughter a chance as an artist. She, not her husband, borrowed money to send Mary to England.

Despite this support, the trip turned out to be a compromise. Mary, on arriving in London, didn't just study but had to use her commercial art abilities and immediately got a job as a designer with Ciro Pearls in Regent Street, at £2 a week. The plan, in theory, was that she would leave after three months to study but her mother 'advised Commercial Art and Miss Russelll, Fine Art'.[2] As Mary was never to learn to be less retiring, she tried to please both women by attending the Chiswick Polytechnic four evenings a week but continued working. This became a strain, but it wasn't work but art that was cut back, although on holidays she managed to visit the galleries of London, Paris and The Hague and attended summer sketching school in Suffolk.

While she was still in London, a letter arrived for Mary in the elderly woman's handwriting, but with the address by another. The letter had not been finished. Maud had taken a break from writing it, had gone out into the garden and dropped dead. She left her oil painting case to Mary, of great symbolic encouragement but little else. To risk taking on the life of the full-time artist she was capable of being, Mary needed private finance which she was never to get.

On her return to Australia in 1937, Mary continued to keep herself as a commercial artist by setting up a studio with another artist. On spare evenings and Saturdays, she followed her heart and attended the leading Sydney Art School, later Julian Ashton's, at the Mining Museum Building almost under the Harbour Bridge.

Mary never had a lucky break and was probably too unassuming to grab it. The closest she came was as one of the three finalists in the NSW Travelling Scholarship, an award that would have given her the opportunity to paint full-time. Such was her ability that, in 1943, she became assistant teacher at Ashton's. In 1947 she married and in 1949 had a daughter, Christine. She also held solo exhibitions and exhibited in such diverse shows as the Archibald Prize every year between 1954 and 1958 and in 'Project 21: Women's Image of Woman' at the Art Gallery of New South Wales. In 1958, after her husband was injured in a car accident, they moved to

Bathurst in the Central West of NSW, and she began teaching again at the Orange Technical College from 1965 to 1974.

Although Mary would later acknowledge that if it had not been for her mother's sacrifices 'during the difficult depression years, I may never have had the opportunity to study art at all',[3] there is still an unanswerable question. How far would this 'serious, disciplined and gifted student and teacher'[4] have gone if Maudie Russell had won her fine arts versus commercial debate and there had been money, as there was for Frances Lord? Such was Freda's nature, that despite Mary's need and her initial intentions, she in the end concentrated everything on Frances, on that young girl, her alter ego.

Frances Lord, now in her mid-seventies, has never forgotten 'Aunty Freda'. She lives with her husband Ray near Kingaroy, Queensland, an area renowned for conservative, can-do politics and narrow religious fervour. Beyond the town, the countryside on the way to their farm is equally dry, as gradually plantations of peanuts and the pale harsh foliage of sugar cane give way to scrubby farms. The gravel road becomes a rutted dirt road that pushes through tall rattling eucalypts and tussock until reaching the vividly lush half acre of green lawn containing the farmhouse. White hens scatter to hide under old sheds as a car approaches. The house is really a barn with corrugated iron walls and roof; the money allocated to a proper one had to go into fencing.

Frances comes through the glass doors. She is lean and muscular, wearing faded pants and a loose shirt. According to some who wish to rewrite history in the light of their own prejudices, romantic natures or who cannot think of any other reason why Freda would have left the girl her property, she is Freda and Peter Graham's love child. Unfortunately for these theorists, Frances' birth certificate makes no mention of adoption and her maternal aunt, present at her birth, has graphically described to Frances the moment when she was born to her mother: Lorna Lord.

Another version of Frances, according to Freda's blood relatives, is that she was a sly child who ingratiated herself with Freda for her money and who had parents too greedy to give it back. This elderly Frances looks innocent enough, now that all those people who fought and criticised are dead. If anything she looks kind of intellectually dotty as she squints intently through her most dominant feature, her spectacles, narrow lensed with a thick and very black upper rim. She takes them off, then brushes back grey-brown hair. Suddenly her eyes are a clear blue, with lids that slant down, giving her a wise and curious look. She has a strong, slightly curved nose and a straight mouth and chin. She speaks quickly checking to see if what she is saying is being accurately followed and proves to be as determined and smart, simple and enthusiastic as when Freda first met her sixty years earlier. But she is no longer that girl with long blonde hair, plaited and wound around her ears, who worked in a bank to earn the essential £2 10s a week, who joined the air force and rode on the back of a motorbike, her face pressed to the uniformed back of her future husband.

Freda, of course, had not imagined Frances' dynamism. Apart from the farm and the work Frances did before they married, she set up a number of successful businesses and at one stage she and her husband were the dominant producers and marketers of the ubiquitous meat pie throughout New South Wales. Frances and her husband believe that with five children to bring up, their life would have been a struggle without Freda's money. What Freda also did was to give them the freedom to choose their lifestyle, to bring their children up on a farm, and to move them into the city for schooling when necessary.

In the last decade, when others their age retired, they bought land that had been overstocked, overfertilised and poisoned, and turned it into a successful Murray Grey cattle stud. Much of the work has been physically done by Frances as, despite Ray's appearance in the flat cap and tweed jacket of a robust English gentleman farmer, he has been unwell for a long time. Always a hard worker he was temporarily then permanently disabled during the war and years of farming with sheep dips, tick and prickly pear sprays and suspect chemicals have given him arsenic poisoning. As well, his energy has been sapped by the Ross River virus, a disease transmitted by the mosquitoes which are common in the swampy areas and rivers of northern Australia.

Inside the house, on that day, it is calm and comfortable. Sleeping quarters are divided off from the main room by a large cupboard, a yellow cotton curtain is pulled back revealing a sun room. A velvet couch, with carved legs, sits immaculately in front of a log-burning stove on which pots simmer. A long bench beneath the windows that overlook the sheds is covered in jars and utensils, bowls of home-grown vegetables, fruit and eggs. A table is set for lunch, the cutlery is solid silver engraved with a curling old English W. The napkin rings bear the same; W for the Woolley family, for Emmeline, Blanche and for Freda. On the walls are paintings that belonged to Freda, including the Battista and another watercolour of an Italian scene. Others have been painted by Frances' daughter, Nadine, who also runs four-wheel-drive expeditions into the Kimberley Ranges in Western Australia.

Frances writes poems that are not classical or romantic, but are narratives, based on her daughter's letters, full of humorous ideas and easy language. She reads aloud, proud and excited. Everything is interesting; other people's experiences are more interesting than her own.

Frances takes out a shawl in which she swaddled all five of her babies and drapes it over the velvet couch. Soft colours are blended by soft fabric. Freda's shawl, still pale-grey, is tinged with turquoise. Frances becomes eager to share that time and that person. There is Freda's mirror, the glazing slightly mottled and, on the back, her initials *F.D.F.* entwined in gumnuts. It hangs by a leather thong near the door and is used every day. And there is Freda also, the person the young girl Frances knew, in clear precise memories.

There are no more Du Faurs in Australia. There are names on mountains and gates and plaques, there are rocks and islands, chateaux and buildings and an entire national park. There is a box of Du Faur history stolen from Nina Du Faur by nephew John and retrieved from his house when his wife, the last to call herself a Du Faur in Australia, lay in madness, dying. There are words on paper, copperplate and typed, books and paintings, there are houses that still stand – Flowton and Pibrac. There is one unmarked grave in the cemetery above the beaches of Manly, on the edge of the Tasman Sea. And there are people living. Peta, the grand-daughter of Freda's 'favoured niece', wears Aunt Freda's wishbone brooch with the waratahs on it. Other grandchildren, themselves have had children.

Frances says, and her eyes are as intent as that girl-child in 1935, 'While my family is still alive, so is our Freda.'

ACKNOWLEDGMENTS

For someone writing about a woman, it came as a surprise to realise it was three men whose patience and assistance I couldn't have done without. The first is my father, Ces Irwin, who always worried for me, but chased up all the details and photos in New Zealand. To Roger Simpson who believed this book would one day be finished, and that one day I'd be grateful for ever having begun it, and Dr Graham Langton, whose obsessive attention to historical and mountaineering detail has made this book what it is.

Throughout my research I was constantly humbled by the generosity of others. At the very beginning I discovered I was not the only writer on the trail of Freda, and I would particularly like to thank Pip Lynch and Colin Monteath both from Christchurch, New Zealand. Pip without hesitation handed me a considerable amount of earlier research, an act as brave (I consider) as her mountaineering. Colin, explorer, publisher, photographer, allowed me complete access to what must be the greatest library of 'The Ice' – mountains, Antarctic and Arctic literature – in the Southern Hemisphere.

In Australia I would like to thank my true believers, my children, Blake and Darcie; the latter in particular, has lived with this book her entire life. I was also privileged to meet and to be given access to the memories of Freda's two 'girls', Mary Abbott-Roberts and Frances Lovell. As well I was helped by George Bendell, Kate Blackett, Clare Brown, Dorothy Butler, Max Cadogan, Judith Colville Smith, Keirin Cook, Gillian Coote, Max Dupain, Roslyn Hayman, Marjorie Hercus, Jean Hudson, Ray Lovell, Nadine Lovell, Billy McManis, Velma (Nagle) McMullen, Secretary' Norma', Mrs Maltby, SCEGGS Archives, Helen Malcher, Dr D.J.Mulvaney, E.J.(Jake) O'Donnell, M. Palmer, Gail Percy, Andrew Roberts, Dr Kingsley Rowan, Fenella Souter, Phil Taylor, Mr. Williams, Margaret Wyatt.

I received invaluable assistance from the Genealogical Society, Ku-ring-gai Chase Archives, Ku-ring-gai Historical Society, Lady Davidson Hospital, Mount Morgan Historical Museum, *Mosman Daily*, The Mitchell Library, The State Library of NSW, the staff of the Stanton Library, North Sydney, Mount Wilson Progress Association, Geelong Grammar, Sydney Homeopathic Archives (Balmain Hospital), Sydney University Archives, the Victorian State Library.

In New Zealand I would like to thank Andy Anderson, Logan Brewer, Barbara Ellis, Angela England, Dorothy Fletcher, Sir Edmund Hillary, Anna Hobbs, Sue Irwin, Guy Mannering, Elinor McEwan, Elayne Nilson-Reid, Rae-Ann Sinclair, Barbara Swabey, Margaret Westmacott, Mount Cook Archives, Canterbury Museum, The Hocken Library, the Turnbull Library, Otaki Historical Society.

In the United Kingdom: Anne Adams, the Bryans family – Max Bryans, Sheila Bryans – Doctor William Deane and his wife, Ruth Deane, John Edginton, Roger Guttridge, J.G.R. Harding, Frank Heywood, Kaye Hitchcox, D.J.E. Neville-Jones, R.W. Thomson, Erica Westmacott, Ursula Westmacott-Crocker, Patrick Young, Bournemouth Council, Bournemouth Evening Echo, the British Museum Library, Dorset Health Authority, Dorset Police, East India Office,the Fawcett Library, General

Medical Council, the Guild hall, the Imperial War Museum, the Women's Service Bureau Archives, Harrow Civic Library, English Alpine Club, Ladies' Alpine Club Archives, Nat.Assoc.of Mental Health, *Mind*, Otmore Productions, the Pinner Public Library, the Pinner Historical Society, Strathallen Nuffield Hospital, *The Times* Archives.

In Canada: the Whyte Museun, Banff, the Canadian Alpine Club.

I would also like to make special acknowledgement of the exquisite writing in the quotes used: Adrienne Rich, *The Dream of a Common Language Poems 1974-1977* W. Norton and Company, New York 1978; Earl Denman, *Alone to Everest*; Thomas F. Hornbein, *Everest: The West Ridge*, The Sierra Club, San Francisco 1993: Walt Unsworth, *Everest* Grafton Books London 1991.

Endnotes

1 Dream weavers

1 Freda Du Faur, *The Conquest of Mount Cook and other climbs. An Account of Four Seasons' Climbing in the Southern Alps of New Zealand*, George Allen and Unwin, London, 1915, p.27.

2 F.D.F. *The Conquest*, p.103.

3 F.D.F. *The Conquest*, p.104.

4 So rotten is the top of Mount Cook that in December 1991 approximately 70 million cubic metres of rock and ice came off and tumbled into the Tasman Valley. The mountain is now 3,754 metres (12,316 feet).

5 F.D.F. *The Conquest*, p.106.

6 F.D.F. *The Conquest*, p.108.

7 Rosalind Miles, *The Women's History of the World*, Paladin, London, 1989, p.256. Miles also comments on a meeting between the reformer and writer Beatrice Webb, who was given the following advice by a Professor Marshall of London University in 1889, who said 'that woman was a subordinate being, and that if she ceased to be subordinate, there would be no object for a man to marry...Hence the woman must not develop her faculties in any way unpleasant to the man: that strength, courage, independence were not attractive', p. 224.

8 Letter from Professor Baldwin Spencer written from Malte Brun Hut, 8 January 1910 to his daughter Chappie (Alline) concerning his stay at Mount Cook. Held by Alline's son, Kingsley Rowan.

9 This edict which ended the French wars of religion in 1598 gave the Huguenots religious and civil rights in most areas, although in practice

this was not necessarily so. Eventually this edict was eroded and from 1679 on direct action was taken against the Huguenots.

10 Eccleston Du Faur, Freda's father, gathered together oral reminiscences (in possession of author) and this comment comes from these files.

11 Outside work hours Eccleston Du Faur spent ten years compiling a complete map of New South Wales. It was destroyed just as the finishing touches were being put to the maps when the Garden Palace, a beautiful glass and stone building in the Botanic Gardens, burned down, six days after Freda's birth.

12 Professor John Woolley from *Sermons*, Rossall School, 1847.

13 Professor John Woolley to Edward Hawkins, Secretary of the Society of the Propagation of the Gospel, 30 April 1849.

14 Lord Bishop of Manchester, Testimonials for Rev. John Woolley. 14 July 1849.

15 Joseph Romilly, Diary 21 April 1851 vol. XIII, p. 110, Cambridge University Library.

16 John Woolley, Inaugural Lecture of Wollongong School of Arts, 28 May 1861. In Emmeline Woolley Papers, Fisher Library, University of Sydney.

17 Letter from John Woolley to his wife Mary. In the possession of the Hewitt family.

18 John Woolley, Lecture on *The Idylls of the King* by Tennyson. Darling Point Mutual Improvement Society, 18 Dec 1860.

19 John Woolley, *Idylls* Lecture.

20 From a speech by Sir Alfred Stephens, Chief Justice, concerning the death of John Woolley quoting from *The Times* report of the wreck of *The London*, 26 March 1866.

21 Sir Charles Nicholson, one of Woolley's closest friends, arranged a public meeting to testify to the 'Public Sympathy' with Dr Woolley's family, 26 March 1866.

2 God's Work

1 Freda's Aunt Emmeline Woolley, with her partner, Ethel Pedley, were frequently written about in the papers of the time. The public, particularly 'Society', adored their performances and their musical compositions, *Sydney Morning Herald*, 27 June 1882, 29 June1895.

2 Funeral of Captain Bacchus, *SMH*, 31 July 1878.
3 John Woolley, Lecture on the *Idylls of the King* by Tennyson, Darling Point Mutual Improvement Society, (18 Dec 1860).
4 John Woolley, *Idylls* Lecture.
5 E.D.F. *The Conquest*, p.58.
6 Conrad Kain, *The Millionaire Guide*, Whyte Museum, Banff, Canada.
7 Ethel Turner, *Seven Little Australians*, Ward and Lock, 1894, p.5.
8 Mary Abbott-Roberts, Notes from memories and tape from a conversation with my mother, Frances Ruth Abbott.
9 E.D.F. *The Conquest*, p.26.

3 NATURA ARS DEI

1 Du Faur did think things were going too far when there was a proposal to copy Mount Rushmore and instead of presidents, huge faces of local explorers were to be carved into the face of the rocks around Govett's Leap, a beautiful waterfall and picnic spot favoured by the Du Faur family. It brought immediate action as he lobbied furiously and wrote letters to the papers until the proposal was dropped.
2 Eccleston Du Faur, from a Speech to the N.S.W. Academy of Art, Personal files, E.Du Faur.
3 Eccleston Du Faur, 'To the Bottom of Govett's Leap', *Sydney Morning Herald*, 5 Oct 1875.
4 'A trip to the Valley of the Grose' by 'A Correspondent', *SMH*
5 Inglis, S *Our Australian Cousins*, MacMillan & Co., London, 1880
6 Letter from Comte de Pibrac to E. Du Faur, E. Du Faur files, 28 Sept 1888.
7 'Eccentric on a Bicycle', review of *Architect Extraordinary, The life and work of John Horbury Hunt 1838-1904*, Cassel, Australia,1971.
8 Interview with Margaret Wyatt, Ku-ring-gai Historical Society, Gordon.
9 H.E.L. Porter, *Farewell to Dampier*. Porter and his climbing partner, Marcel Kurz, began the next major wave of mountaineering in the Southern Alps in 1927 when with extensive use of crampons made some major climbs including the first traverse of Tasman, the second ascent of Haidinger, the fourth traverse of Mount Cook and the traverse of Haast and Lendenfeld.
10 Dr E.D.Hopen, 'Ku-ring-gai', *SMH*, 4 April1900.

11 Letter from F.D.F to Otto Frind, 6 Jan 1914.
12 F.D.F. *The Conquest*, p.26.

4 SCHEME OF CREATION.

1 A Great Pioneer of Secondary Education, Sydney Church of England Girls Grammar School, Archives, p.44.
2 SCEGGS Old Girls Letters, 1895-1920, p.45. What prize Freda was reputed to have won has not been established. It may have been little more than rumour and no one who knew Freda has mentioned it.
3 SCEGGS Old Girls Letters, 1895-1920, p.43.
4 Old Girls Notes, 1912.
5 SCEGGS magazine, *LUX*, July 1912.
6 Ethel Anderson, *Letters from Old Girls,* pp.138-41.
7 Edith Badham, Presentation Speech, 1895, SCEGGS
8 Sheila Jeffreys, *The Spinster and her Enemies: Feminism and Sexuality 1880-1930*, Pandora Press, 1983, p.88.
9 F.D.F letter to Otto Frind. 6 Jan 1914, Personal Papers, New Zealand Alpine Club Archives, Hocken Library, Dunedin, New Zealand.
10 Letter from Louisa MacDonald to Eleanor Groves (Pixie), July 1895. Letters between Groves, her great friend and mentor, Principal of Bying College, England, and MacDonald, 1892-1897, are in the Mitchell Library, Sydney.
11 Letter from Louisa MacDonald to Eleanor Groves (Pixie), July 1895.
12 Lillian Faderman, *Surpassing the Love of Men: Romantic Friendship and Love between Women from the Renaissance to the Present*, Women's Press, London, 1981.
13 E. Du Faur, Letter to trustees of Ku-ring-gai Chase, 7 March 1900.
14 F.D.F. *The Conquest*, p.26.
15 F.D.F. *The Conquest*, p.26.
16 F.D.F. *The Conquest*, p.26.
17 F.D.F. *The Conquest*, p.26.

5 HEAVENLY BODIES

1 Louisa MacDonald, a comment in Eleanor Groves letters, 1892-97 Mitchell Library, Sydney.

2 F.D.F. *The Conquest*, p.37.

3 F.D.F. *The Conquest*, p.26.

4 *Lux*, SCEGGS magazine, April 1902.

5 Homeopathic Hospital minutes and records, 2 July 1902, which are maintained at Balmain Hospital, Sydney.

6 Hospital minutes, F.D.F. engagement as probationer, Dec 1903.

7 Hospital minutes, March 1904.

8 F.D.F. *The Conquest*, p.78.

9 E. Du Faur, Letter to *SMH*, 22 Jan 1907.

10 J. Cowan, *Official Record of the New Zealand International Exhibition of Arts and Industries*, 1905-6 p.75. During Parliamentary Financial Statement preparation, 1903, the New Zealand Prime Minister, Richard Seddon, conceived the possibility of such an exhibition.

11 J. Cowan, *Official Record of the New Zealand International Exhibition of Arts and Industries*, 1905-06 p.373.

12 F.D.F. *The Conquest*, p.84.

13 J. Cowan, *Official Record of the New Zealand International Exhibition of Arts and Industries*, p. 211.

14 F.D.F. *The Conquest*, p.33.

15 The mountain is named, so the legend goes, after a young Maori boy named Aoraki who, travelling by canoe with other members of his tribe down the east coast of the South Island, was wrecked in a storm. The survivors moved inland to explore but would remain forever as mountains when the early morning sun turned them to stone. Aoraki, who was riding on the shoulders of his grandfather, became the highest peak in the country. The mountain is also called Aorangi.

16 F.D.F. *The Conquest*, p.33

17 F.D.F. *The Conquest*, p.28.

18 F.D.F. *The Conquest*, p.28.

19 Peter Graham, *Peter Graham: Mountain Guide*, A. H & A.W. Reed, 1965. The guide died just before his 83rd birthday, 7 April 1961, unfortunately only getting to the beginning of his climbing years with F.D.F. on the Malte Brun climb,1910. The autobiography was edited, with the use of

Graham's notes and Freda's book, by the New Zealand mountaineering writer John Pascoe.

20 F.D.F. *The Conquest*, p.28.
21 F.D.F. *The Conquest*, p.28.
22 Peter Graham, *Peter Graham: Mountain Guide*, p.141.
23 F.D.F. *The Conquest*, p.29.
24 Peter Graham, *Peter Graham: Mountain Guide*, p.159.
25 The first guide, Tom Fyfe, had been appointed in 1896, the year after he, George Graham and Jack Clark(later Clarke) were the first to climb the high peak of Mount Cook. The first hut, Ball Hut was established in 1891 and Malte Brun Hut in 1898. In 1901 Clarke became chief guide and in 1903 hired Peter Graham.

6 NON OMNI MORIAR

1 Letter from Eccleston Du Faur to *SMH*, 22 Jan 1907.
2 *Peter Graham: Mountain Guide*, p.164.
3 *Peter Graham: Mountain Guide*, p.152.
4 The explorer Shackleton sailed on the sealing ship *Nimrod* to Antarctica in August 1907 with the intention of reaching both the South Pole and the magnetic South Pole. Because of difficulties in finding a wintering-over location, his polar journey couldn't begin until the end of October 1908. The four men ended up eating frozenhorse meat, came within a hundred miles of being the first to reach the pole and only just made it back to catch the ship home.
5 *Peter Graham: Mountain Guide*, p.158. P.G. was as fond of the eccentric Professor as Freda and the two had an informal friendship as equals rather than guide and client.
6 A poem collected by Eccleston Du Faur, contained in his collection of family reminiscences.
7 E.Du Faur, from a letter to his sister, Frederica Du Faur. Held by the Bryans family, London.
8 Prof. D. J. Mulvaney, *So Much that is New: Professor Baldwin Spencer 1860-1929*. From a letter from Spencer to his daughter, Alline (Chappie), p.26.
9 F.D.F. *The Conquest*, p.29.

10 F.D.F. *The Conquest*, p.29.

7 A PLACE

1 *Peter Graham: Mountain Guide*, p.164.
2 Cicely Williams, *Women on the Rope*, Allen and Unwin, London, 1973, p.26.
3 *Women on the Rope*, p.43.
4 *Women on the Rope*, p.94.
5 *Peter Graham: Mountain Guide*, pp.174, 175.
6 *New Zealand Freelance Magazine*.
7 F.D.F. *The Conquest*, p.32.
8 F.D.F. *The Conquest*, p.35.
9 F.D.F. *The Conquest*, p.36.
10 Letter from Professor Baldwin Spencer to his daughter, Alline, from Malte Brun Hut (8 Jan)1910. In possession of her son, Kingsley Rowan, Melbourne.
11 F.D.F. *The Conquest*, p.36.
12 F.D.F. *The Conquest*, p.36.
13 F.D.F. *The Conquest*, p.36.
14 F.D.F. *The Conquest*, p.37.
15 *Peter Graham: Mountain Guide*, p.189.
16 F.D.F. *The Conquest*, p.39.
17 F.D.F. *The Conquest*, p.40.
18 F.D.F. *The Conquest*, p.40.
19 F.D.F. *The Conquest*, p.42.
20 F.D.F. *The Conquest*, p.44.
21 F.D.F. *The Conquest*, p.45.
22 D. J. Mulvaney, *So Much that is New: Professor Baldwin Spencer 1860 – 1929*. Letter to Professor Baldwin Spencer from Julian Ashton, p.342.
23 Professor Baldwin Spencer and F.J. Gilbert. Preface to *The Arunta: A Study of Stone Age People*, Macmillan and Co.England,1927.
24 F.D.F. *The Conquest*, p.49.
25 F.D.F. *The Conquest*, p.50.
26 F.D.F. *The Conquest*, p.50.
27 F.D.F. *The Conquest*, p.51.

28 F.D.F. *The Conquest*, p.52.
29 F.D.F. *The Conquest*, p.52.
30 F.D.F. *The Conquest*, p.55.
31 F.D.F. *The Conquest*, p.56.
32 F.D.F. *The Conquest*, p.58.
33 F.D.F. *The Conquest*, p.59.
34 Professor Baldwin Spencer, letter to Chappie from the Hermitage, 11 Jan 1910. Held by Kingsley Rowan.
35 F.D.F. *The Conquest*, p.62.
36 Professor Baldwin Spencer. Letter to Chappie from the Hermitage, 11 Jan 1910.

8 PIERCING THE CLOUDS

1 F.D.F. *The Conquest*, p.64.
2 F.D.F. *The Conquest*, p.65.
3 F.D.F. *The Conquest*, p.69.
4 F.D.F. *The Conquest*, p.71.
5 F.D.F. *The Conquest*, p.72.
6 F.D.F. *The Conquest*, p.74.
7 F.D.F. *The Conquest*, p.77.
8 F.D.F. *The Conquest*, p.80.
9 *Peter Graham: Mountain Guide*, p.39.
10 F.D.F. *The Conquest*, p.81.
11 F.D.F. *The Conquest*, p.85.
12 An interview with Conrad Kain, *Christchurch Press*, 28 Feb 1914.
13 F.D.F. *The Conquest*, p.85.

9 VENUS

1 The Dupain Institute was still active in the 1960s and trained such sports people as the tennis player Evonne Cawley, the Australian cricket team and the members of the yachting challenge for the America's Cup.
2 George Zepherin Dupain, *Are you satisfied with your physical condition? Exercise and the Woman*, Atkins McQuitty, Sydney, 1909.

3 Muriel Cadogan, *Dupain Quarterly,* Jan-March 1913.

4 Muriel Cadogan, *Dupain Quarterly,* Jan-March 1913.

5 Muriel Cadogan, *Dupain Quarterly*, Jan-March 1913.

6 Interviews with Max Cadogan, youngest brother of Muriel, 1992, 1994.

7 F.D.F. *The Conquest*, p.163.

8 F.D.F. *The Conquest*, p.90.

9 F.D.F. *The Conquest*, p.90.

10 F.D.F. *The Conquest*, p.91.

11 F.D.F. *The Conquest*, pp. 93,94.

12 *Peter Graham: Mountain Guide*, p.195.

13 F.D.F. *The Conquest*, p.100.

14 F.D.F. *The Conquest*, p.101.

15 F.D.F. *The Conquest*, p.100.

16 F.D.F. *The Conquest*, p.110

17 Douglas Cresswell, *Canterbury Tales: Mount Cook Bows to a Woman* Kathleen Cresswell, 1951, p.147.

18 F.D.F. The Conquest, p.111.

19 Douglas Cresswell, *Canterbury Tales.*

20 F.D.F. *The Conquest*, p.163.

21 F.D.F. *The Conquest*, p.37.

10 STEPPING STONES

1 F.D.F. *The Conquest*, p.117.

2 It was the first and last time Alex Graham would become ill climbing. Freda always regarded De La Beche as an unlucky mountain. Theirs was the third ascent ever but two other previous attempts by others had also been called off near the summit and both times through the rare event of illness.

3 F.D.F. *The Conquest*, p.122.

4 Fitzgerald, Zurbriggen and Clarke bivouacked there in 1895 for a number of cold, wet nights before successfully striking for Tasman.

5 F.D.F. *The Conquest*, p.124.

6 F.D.F. *The Conquest*, p.125.

7 F.D.F. *The Conquest*, p.127.

8 A Climber of Mountains – *An Australian Lady's Alpine Exploits. First Ascent*

of Mt Dampier, Weekly Press, 1912.
9 F.D.F. *The Conquest*, p.130.
10 F.D.F. *The Conquest*, p.130.
11 F.D.F. *The Conquest*, p.140.
12 F.D.F. *The Conquest*, p.141.
13 F.D.F. *The Conquest*, p.144.
14 F.D.F. *The Conquest*, p.146.
15 F.D.F. *The Conquest*, a dedication to Muriel Cadogan.

11 A DELICATE BALANCE

1 Interview with Jean Hudson concerning Wynifred Du Faur and John Du Faur, and the Dee Why years, Feb 1993. Also interview with Andrew Roberts, brother-in-law of Mary Abbott-Roberts.
2 F.D.F. *The Conquest*, p.163.
3 F.D.F. *The Conquest*, p.148.
4 F.D.F. *The Conquest*, p.149.
5 F.D.F. *The Conquest*, p.150.
6 F.D.F. *The Conquest*, p.150.
7 F.D.F. *The Conquest*, p.151.
8 F.D.F. *The Conquest*, p.152.
9 F.D.F. *The Conquest*, p.153.
10 F.D.F. *The Conquest*, p.156.
11 Review of *The Conquest of Mount Cook, New Zealand Alpine Journal*, Vol. 111, No 10 March, 1921.
12 F.D.F. *The Conquest*, p.172.
13 F.D.F. *The Conquest*, p.175.
14 F.D.F. *The Conquest*, p.104.
15 F.D.F. *The Conquest*, p.179.
16 *Peter Graham: Mountain Guide*, Epilogue by John Pascoe from Graham's notes p. 202.
17 *Peter Graham*, p.201.

12 VAST SILENT PLACES

1 F.D.F. *The Conquest*, p.192.
2 F.D.F. *The Conquest*, p.192.
3 Letter from Erica Westmacott to Margaret Westmacott, 27 November 1984.
4 Letter from F.D.F. to Otto Frind, 12 Dec 1913, Personal Files NZAC. Hocken Library, Dunedin, New Zealand.
5 Letter from Erica Westmacott to Margaret Westmacott, 27 November 1984.
6 F.D.F. *The Conquest*, p.198.
7 *Peter Graham*, Appendix p. 240.
8 *Peter Graham*, Appendix p. 241.
9 F.D.F. *The Conquest*, p.199.
10 F.D.F. *The Conquest*, p.200.
11 F.D.F. *The Conquest*, p.202.
12 F.D.F. *The Conquest*, p.203.
13 F.D.F. *The Conquest*, p.205.
14 F.D.F. *The Conquest*, p.207.
15 F.D.F. *The Conquest*, p.208.

13 THE LAST

1 From notes in Ladies' Alpine Club minutes, 2 Jan 1912, by the Bishop of Bathurst.
2 F.D.F. *The Conquest of Mount Cook*, p.208.
3 *Peter Graham: Mountain Guide*. In the Epilogue provided by John Pascoe, Graham mentions how he was advised against the climb.
4 F.D.F. *The Conquest*, p.210.
5 F.D.F. *The Conquest*, p.211.
6 F.D.F. *The Conquest*, pp. 214-15.
7 F.D.F. *The Conquest*, p. 220.
8 Notes on Samuel Turner from the Epilogue, *Peter Graham: Mountain Guide*, pp. 214-17.
9 Notes on Samuel Turner from the Epilogue, *Peter Graham: Mountain Guide*.
10 Notes on Samuel Turner from the Epilogue, *Peter Graham: Mountain Guide*.

11 F.D.F. *The Conquest*, p.223.
12 F.D.F. *The Conquest*, p.229.
13 F.D.F. *The Conquest*, p.230.
14 F.D.F. *The Conquest*, p.231.
15 F.D.F. *The Conquest*, p.235.
16 F.D.F. *The Conquest*, p.237.
17 F.D.F. *The Conquest*, p.238.
18 F.D.F. *The Conquest*, p.238.
19 F.D.F. *The Conquest*, p.239.
20 Letter from Erica Westmacott to Margaret Westmacott, 27 November 1984.
21 F.D.F. *The Conquest*, p.242.
22 F.D.F. *The Conquest*, p.245.
23 F.D.F. *The Conquest*, p.246.

14 Ground work

1 Letter from A. O. Wheeler to Otto Frind, 3 Jan 1913, Canadian Alpine Club, Whyte Museum, Banff.
2 Letter from F.D.F. to Otto Frind, 30 Sept 1913, NZAC files, Hocken Library, Dunedin.
3 F.D.F. *The Conquest*, p.208.
4 Comment by Otto Frind, Personal Papers, NZAC. Hocken Library, Dunedin.
5 Conrad Kain and J. Monroe Thorington, *Where The Clouds Can Go*, The American Alpine Club, New York, p.349.
6 F.D.F. *The Conquest*, p.244.
7 Letter from F.D.F. to Otto Frind from Flowton, 4 Dec 1913, Personal Papers, NZAC Hocken Library, Dunedin.
8 An article about Otto Frind, 'An Alpine Enthusiast', *Christchurch Press*, 15 May 1914.
9 Letter from F.D.F. to Otto Frind from Flowton, 4 Dec1913, Personal Papers NZAC. Hocken Library Dunedin.
10 Letter from F.D.F. to Otto Frind from Flowton, 6 Jan1914, Personal Papers, NZAC.
11 Letter from F.D.F. to Otto Frind from Flowton, 6 Jan 1914, Personal

Papers, NZAC.

12 Letter from F.D.F. to Otto Frind from Flowton, 6 Jan 1914, Personal Papers, NZAC.

13 Letter from F.D.F. to Otto Frind from Flowton, 6 Jan 1914, Personal Papers, NZAC.

14 Letter from F.D.F. to Otto Frind from Flowton, 4 Dec 1913, Personal Papers, NZAC.

15 ELYSIAN FIELDS

1 F.D.F. *The Conquest*, p.184.

2 Interview with Conrad Kain, *Christchurch Press*, 28 February, 1914.

3 Letter to F.D.F. from Otto Frind, 4 April 1914, Personal Papers NZAC Hocken Library, Dunedin.

4 Presidential Report by Lucy Walker, Ladies Alpine Club, 1913.

5 Interview with Captain McCarthy, Canada, 19 Nov 1927, NZ Alpine Club Papers.

6 Cicely Williams, *Women on the Rope*, Allen and Unwin, London, 1973, p.45.

7 Cicely Williams *Women on the Rope*, p. 100.

8 Cicely Williams *Women on the Rope*, p. 95.

9 Andrew Rosen, *Rise Up, Women*, Routledge and Kegan, 1974, p.233.

10 Ray Strachey, *Women's Suffrage and Women's Service, The Cause: A Short History of the Women's Movement in Great Britain*, Bell and Sons, London, 1928.

11 Letter to F.D.F. from Otto Frind, 24 April 1914, Personal Papers NZAC Hocken Library, Dunedin.

12 Comment by Otto Frind on bottom of above letter. Dated 2 Jan 1928.

13 Virginia Wolf had intended writing a sapphist novel called *The Jessamy Brides* but as the main character came close to that of her bisexual friend, Vita Sackville West, and lesbians 'had fallen into such disrepute by 1928' (Faderman) she changed it to *Orlando* and wrote instead of androgyny and sex change.

14 Letter from F.D.F. to Frances Lord, September 1935.

15 Lillian Faderman, *Surpassing the Love of Men: Romantic Friendship and Love between Women from the Renaissance to the Present*, London, 1981.

Introduction p. 6.

16 LANDLOCKED

1 Eccleston Du Faur wrote to Harrow concerning Mrs Crummer, his mother-in-law from his first marriage. In Greece, as a young woman she had known Lord Byron well. At the time of his letter in 1902, Eccleston felt she was one of the few persons still alive with personal knowledge of the famous poet.

2 *Pinner through the Ages: The Changing Years*, King & Hutchings Ltd, 1937.

3 Joan Baringer of Harrow, spinster, was found to have practised the detestable arts of witchcraft on and against Rose Edlyn, daughter of Richard Edlyn of Pynnore, with the intention of murdering the same Rose, who languished from the effects of the said diabolical practice 'til she died thereof on 17 March then next followin'. Baringer persisted in her pleas of innocence.

4 *When I was a Child: Memories of a Childhood in Pinner*, Pinner Local Historical Society, p. 23.

5 *When I was a Child: Memories of a Childhood in Pinner*, p.51.

6 *Pinner through the Ages: The Changing Years*, p.127.

7 Imperial War Museum, Women's Bureau Records, *Account of work since outbreak of war NUWSS, Report of NUWSS, Women's War Services, Work of Women's Volunteer Reserve, Millicent Fawcett. Hospital Units. Notes from our Work NUWSS*.

8 Ladies' Alpine Club (London) *Year Book*, 1916. The first year book was published in 1913.

9 *Lux*, SCEGGS magazine1915.

10 Notes in Personal Files, Otto Frind, NZAC Hocken Library, Dunedin, New Zealand.

11 Letter from Otto Frind to Johannes Anderson, 8 June 1915. Notes in Personal Files, Otto Frind, NZAC Hocken Library, Dunedin.

17 DARKENED LANES

1 The loss of almost an entire raiding party due to cold weather on

19 October 1917 put an end to most Zeppelin raids.

2 Letter from the Head of the Department of Health and Resources, New Zealand, Mr Wilson to Otto Frind, May 1915, Personal Papers NZAC, Hocken Library, Dunedin.

3 Interview with Erica Westmacott by her niece Ursula Westmacott-Crocker, 2 March 1994.

4 *The Times*, 5 Sept 1916.

5 Clio, 'Australian Brigade', *Punch Magazine*, March 1918.

18 THE BEACON SOUTH

1 F.W.G. Miller, Cradle to Grave, *Memoirs - New Zealand Yesterday*, Readers Digest, 1984.

2 Interview by phone with the secretary, 'Norma', of John Du Faur while in the Department of Productivity, NSW government.

3 Bernard Smith, *Art in Australia*, Oxford University Press, Melbourne.

4 Interview with Barbara Ellis, concerning her stepmother, Enid Bacchus, Auckland, January1993.

19 SEA ROAD

1 Eleanor Winthrop Young. From the *Journal of the Pinnacle Club*. p.6.

2 After Shelley drowned in Via Reggio, Italy, at the last minute his heart was snatched from the funeral pyre on the beach and, so the story goes, was returned to Mary Shelley in a silken scarf. She kept the heart preserved between the pages of the Pisa edition of *Adonis* and eventually it was interred in the family vault at St Peter's Church, Bournemouth.

3 A comment by Osbert Sitwell, grandson of Edith Sitwell, *The Book of Bournemouth*, p.22.

4 Interview with Bournemouth journalist/historian, Roger Guttridge, July 1994.

5 Foreword by Lady Arthur Conan Doyle in *The Spirit of Irene* written by William Tyler, Boscombe 1923.

6 From the *Bournemouth Magpie and Society Pictorial*, Feb 1923, placed by the Bournemouth Spiritual Church.

7 From the *Bournemouth Magpie and Society Pictorial*, Feb 1923, from an interview with Daisy Groves, local spiritualist.
8 Inscription on postcards from Freda Du Faur to Enid Bacchus.

20 CRACKS

1 Radclyffe Hall, *The Well of Loneliness*, London, 1928.
2 Marie Stopes, *Married Love*, Putmans London, 1918; *Enduring Passions*, Hogarth Press, 1928.
3 Ray Strachey, *Women's Suffrage and Women's Service, The Cause: A Short History of the Women's Movement in Great Britain*, Bell and Sons, London, 1928, pp.114-15.
4 Interview with Max Cadogan by author, March 1992.
5 At the annual meeting of the Royal Society of Tasmania, a new form of *Milligana densifloria* (the Tasmania native lily) gathered in Cradle Mountain and Mount Humbolt was introduced. It was named after the indefatigable collector, Mrs Lindon.
6 Lillian Faderman, *Love Between Women in 1928: Why Progressivism is not always Progress*, California State University, p.30. The quotes come from Dr Phyllis Blanchard in 1929.
7 Letter from F.D.F. to Frances Lord, Sept 1935.
8 Micale, untitled research paper, 1990
9 Letter from F.D.F. to Frances, Lord.
10 Letter from F.D.F. to Frances Lord.
11 Letter from F.D.F. to Frances Lord.
12 Letter from F.D.F. to Frances Lord.
13 Letter from F.D.F. to Frances Lord.

21 TO THE ENDS OF THE EARTH

1 Letter to Frances Lord from F.D.F. Sept 1935.
2 Ian C.A. Martin, 'Some Therapeutic Concepts of Sleep', *Nursing Times*, 9 Oct, 1975, p.1611.
3 Jane Ussher, *Women's Madness: Misogyny or Mental Illness*, Harvester Wheatsheaf, 1991. The rest cure would be used on such notable women

as the writers Edith Wharton and Charlotte Perkins Gilman, who wrote about the cure in her book *The Yellow Wallpaper*, reprinted by Virago, London, 1988.

4 Sargent and Slater, *An Introduction to Physical Methods of Treatment in Psychiatry*, E.& S. Livingston, 1963, p.139.

5 Sargent and Slater, *An Introduction to Physical Methods of Treatment in Psychiatry*, E.& S. Livingston, 1963.

6 Interview with Bob Stokes in the film of Chelmsford *Deep Sleep*, a film by John Edginton.

7 Melanie McFadgeon, 'The Endless Sleep', *The Independent on Sunday*, 28 June1992.

8 Letter from F.D.F. to Frances Lord, 1935.

9 Interview with Barbara Ellis, stepdaughter of Enid Bacchus on the Ellis family. Auckland 1993.

10 Letter from Barbara Ellis to author,14 June 1992.

11 Letter from Barbara Ellis to author.

12 G.Mannering, *Memories of Mountains and Men: A general survey of New Zealand Mountaineering*.

13 Interview with Andy Anderson, journalist and mountaineer, and close friend of the Graham family, during his time as a teacher on the west coast. Christchurch, New Zealand, December, 1991.

14 Letter from F.D.F. to Frances Lord, 1935.

15 David Sievewright Young, *The Story of Bournemouth*, Bournemouth Public Library.

16 Letter from F.D.F. to Frances, Lord 1935.

17 Letter from F.D.F. to Frances, Lord 1935.

18 Letter from Nina Du Faur to Max Bryans, 7 Oct 1959. In possession of Bryans family, London.

19 Letter from Maude Russell to Frances Ruth Abbott (nee Gerard) 8 Oct 1932.

20 Mary Abbott-Roberts, 'Notes from memories and tape from a conversation with my mother, Frances Ruth Abbott', held by author.

21 Interview with Mary Abbott-Roberts by author, 12 Mar 1992.

22 Letter to the author from Frances Lovell (nee Lord) concerning her friendship with F.D.F. and her own life, 1993.

23 Letter to the author from Frances Lovell.

24 Letter from Frances Lovell.

25 Letter from Frances Lovell.

26 Letter to the author from Frances Lovell.

27 Letter from F.D.F to Frances Lord, Sept 1935.

28 Interview with Frances Lovell, 8 June 1992.

29 Interview with Frances Lovell, 8 June 1992.

30 Interview with Frances Lovell, 8 June 1992.

22 COCOON

1 Marie Beuzeville Byles, *By Cargo Boat and Mountain*, Seeley, Service and Co, Sydney,1931.

2 Marie Beuzeville Byles, *By Cargo Boat and Mountain*.

3 Dorothy Butler, Salute and Farewell to Marie Byles, unpublished ms in Marie Byle collection, Mitchell Library.

4 Marie Byles, Scrapbook, held in Mitchell Library.

5 The Five Buddhist Precepts are: to refrain from taking life (human and animal); to refrain from taking what is not given (stealing); to refrain from taking alcohol or drugs; to refrain from inappropriate sexual behaviour; to refrain from telling lies. There is no punishment; the individual undertakes to observe the precepts and pass their own judgement.

6 Marie Byles, Autobiography, unpublished ms, held in Mitchell Library, Sydney, Box12–13.

7 Marie Byles wrote a book on the experience, *By Cargo Boat and Mountains*, in 1931. Later there were other books about her interests: *Footprints of Gautama the Buddha* (1956); *Journey into Burmese Silence* (1962); *The Lotus and the Spinning Wheel* (1963); *Paths to Inner Calm* (1965).

8 Interview with Dorothy Butler, climber-bushwalker, close friend and supporter of Marie Byles, by author, 10 January 1994.

9 Marie Byles, Scrapbook. From an article 'Sex and Spiritual Growth'.

10 Marie Byles, Scrapbook. From an article 'Sex and Spiritual Growth'.

11 When Marie finally retired from the Bushwalking Club in 1947, she finished her resignation by saying, 'Finally, Mr Secretary, please don't let your wife waste her valuable time writing a reply in flowery style to this letter. I detest such stuff'.

12 A.H. Charteris, *Notes on Egon Kisch Case*, Aust.and N.Z. Society of

International Law, Vol. 1, 1935, pp.174. Kisch was a trade unionist, author and lecturer. He was banished from Germany because of his anti-Nazi/anti-Fascist stand. Because of pressure from that country he was later refused entry to England, but Australia was the only other country to try and prevent him speaking on the basis that he held 'subversive views and communistic association'.

13 Letter from F.D.F. to Frances Lord, Sept 1935. Egon Kisch's case against deportation was a cause celèbre in the papers of the day from November 1932 through to late January 1933.

14 F.D.F. letter to Frances Lord, Sept 1935.

15 Marie Byles, Autobiography, unpublished ms. Held in Mitchell Library.

16 Jake O'Donnell, Letter to the author, 11 September 1990; Letter and interview with John Du Faur, in the process of writing *The Australian Dictionary of Biography* entry for Freda Du Faur.

17 Marie Byles, Autobiography.

18 Marie Byles, Autobiography.

19 From interviews with Marjorie Hercus and Roslyn Hayman, nieces of Nina Du Faur, April 1992–93.

21 Marie Byles, Autobiography.

22 Letter from Dorothy Butler to Alison Rutherford, Capper Press, 3 March, 1978.

23 Mary Abbott-Roberts, Letter and Interview with author.

23 PILGRIMS

1 Dorothy Butler, Salute and Farewell to Marie Byles, unpublished ms.

2 Interview with Mary Abbott-Roberts by author.

3 Interview with Mary Abbott-Roberts by author.

4 David E. Wilson, Chairman Bathurst Regional Gallery, catalogue entry, 'Concerning Mary Abbott-Roberts'.

PHOTO REFERENCES

1 Making New Zealand Collection, Turnbull Library, Wellington, N.Z

2 a, Portrait file – Mitchell Library, b, Photo from original painting –
Roslyn Hayman, Sydney

3 a, b, Author's photos c, Sydney University d, Angela England, Wellington, N.Z

4 a, Du Faur file, held by author, b, Ku-ring-gai Historical Society

5 a, b, 6, 7, Du Faur files

8 a, SCEGGS archives b, from the watercolour held by author c, author's

9 a, Max Dupain, Sydney b, Portrait file – Mitchell Library

10 Ex Archives N.Z Alpine Club, ms-1164-2/34/9. Hocken Library, Dunedin, N.Z

11, 12, Freda Du Faur – *The Conquest of Mount Cook*

13 a, Dennistoun Collection b, Freda Du Faur – *The Conquest of Mount Cook*

14 a, b, Ex. Archives N.Z Alpine Club. ms-1164-2/77/13 Hocken Library

15 a, author's b, Pinner Historical Society, c, postcard, Angela England

16 a, b, Dr W. Deane, Christchurch, England c, Dot Butler, Sydney

BIBLIOGRAPHY

ABBREVIATIONS
SMH Sydney Morning Herald

ARCHIVAL AND MANUSCRIPT SOURCES

New Zealand
Hocken Library, Dunedin
New Zealand Alpine Club, including personal papers of H.O. Frind,
  MS 1164/41.
Theomin, D.M., letters to family, 1914-32.

Turnbull Library, Wellington
Annual Reports of the Department of Tourist and Health Resorts, 1902-09,
  1913-22.
Bacchus, E., MS 1372.
Du Faur, F., MS 1006 4 P165.
Otaki Historical Society Journals. 1900-07.
Tapuhi-NZ Shipping Company Passenger Lists. 1902-05.
Von Haast, H., MS 37, MS 466, MS 1372 1.9, 1.12, 1.17.

Australia
General
Homeopathic Hospital Minutes (Balmain Hospital Archives, Sydney) 1902-05
Ku-ring-gai Chase Archives, Ku-ring-gai Headquarters. Minutes,
  Management Meetings.
SCEGGS Archives (Darlinghurst, Sydney) School Reports 1898-1912

Mitchell Library, Sydney
Arnold, M., papers A821.
Butler, D., 'Salute and Farewell to Marie Byles', unpublished article, ML MSS 3833/4.
Byles, M., papers, ML MSS 38 33/1; ML 719/71
Charteris, A.H., notes on the Egon Kisch Case, *Aust. and N.Z. Society of International Law*, 335.4 K.
Du Faur, E., notebook, on Mt Wilson, A1629 NC.
Dupain, G. Z., Papers, *Dupain Quarterlies*, ed. M. Cadogan, 1912-13.
MacDonald, L., correspondence, 1892-1897.
Russell, M., Freehand Drawing, 1926, pamphlet, 740/R
Scott, R., correspondence with Louisa MacDonald, 20XCY 1222.
Shaw, A., 1871-91, papers, ML MSS 923 N/C
Woolley, E., Australian Women, article Q.A. 90.7.

University of Sydney Archives
Scott, R. Papers Collected, 1852-1922, vols ML MSS 38, 58, 59.

United Kingdom
Bournemouth Library
Bournemouth Magpie, 1923.
Edwards, Elisabeth, 'Is there a curse on Boscombe?' article, Oversize LPC, U7697;
Read, E., *Bournemouth Memories*, U769.091;

English Alpine Club
Alpine Club Journals, 1908-14.
Canadian Alpine Journals. 1914-19, 1935-38.
Ladies Alpine Club Archives. Year Book 1913-35

Harrow Civic Centre Library
Harrow Monthly Gazette, 1914-15.

ARTICLES
'Australian Deep Sleep Report', *British Medical Journal*, January 1991 (no author cited).
Bacchus, Captain G., *SMH*, 31 July 1878.

Bailey, Dr H., '"Dr Jekyll" Patients', *Daily Telegraph*, 21 December 1990.

Clio, 'Australian Brigade', *Punch Magazine*, March 1918, p. 12.

'The Conquest of Mount Cook' (book review), *Times Book Review*, 8 April 1915.

'The Conquest of Mount Cook' (book review), *Times Literary Supplement*, 18 March 1915.

Cowan, J., *Official Record of the New Zealand International Exhibition of Arts and Industries*, 1905-6.

Du Faur, E., articles in:

North Shore Times, 24 November 1971;

SMH, 5 October 1875, 14 April 1900, 23 April 1900, 12 October 1901, 26 January 1901, 5 September 1902, 10 April 1906, 9 February 1907, 29 March 1910, 15 March 1904, 1 January 1907, 22 January 1907.

Du Faur, F., articles in:

N.Z. Freelance, 4 May 1912;

Otago Witness, 1 May 1912;

The Press, 4 January 1910, 31 May 1913;

SMH, 6 December 1910, 20 September 1935, 28 July 1936;

The Weekly Press, 9 October 1912, 25 June 1913.

Du Faur, F., 'High Climbs in New Zealand', *Lone Hand*, 1 April 1914, pp. 341-4.

Du Faur, F., 'Alpine Climbing in New Zealand', *Lone Hand*, 2 March 1914, pp. 265-8.

'Handfighting at Flers', *The Times*, 25 September 1916.

Harnett, R.H., 'The Mosman Daily Centenary Supplement', *The Mosman Daily*, 25 March, 1993.

Jenkins, J.B., 'Electro Sleep Therapy', *Nursing Times*, 21 October 1971, pp. 1310-12.

Kisch Case, *SMH*, 17 January 1935, 19 January 1935.

Lynch, P.A., 'A History of Women Mountaineers in Victorian New Zealand Society', Research Essay (B. Phys. Ed.), University of Otago, 1985.

McFadgeon, M., 'The Endless Sleep', *Independent on Sunday*, 28 June 1992, pp. 8-9.

Marc Wallace, C., 'Modified Narcosis and the Nurse', *Nursing Mirror*, 14 February 1969, pp. 46-7.

Martin, I.C.A., 'Some Theurapetic Concepts of Sleep', *Nursing Times*, 9 October 1975, pp. 1612-14.

Porter, H.E.L., 'Farewell to Dampier', *New Zealand Alpine Journal*, no. 253, 1936.

Ross, F., 'A Lady Mountaineer in the New Zealand Alps', *Wide World Magazine*, December 1900, pp. 275-82.

Shaw, C.D., obituary of, *Brisbane Sun*, 7 January 1969.

Sim, J.A., 'In Memorian', *New Zealand Alpine Club Journal*, vol. VI, no 23, 1936.

'Women's Supplement', SMH, 12 September 1935.

Woolley, E., articles in SMH: 29 June 1895, 30 June 1895, 19 March 1908. With Ethel Pedley, *Sydney Mail*, 29 June 1895.

Woolley, Prof. J., SMH, 16 March 1866, 26 March 1866; letter from Sir Charles Nicholson to *The Times*.

BOOKS

Anderson, J.C., *Jubilee History of South Canterbury*. Whitcombe & Tombs, Christchurch, 1914.

Anon., *Pinner through the Ages: The Changing Years*. King & Hutchings Ltd, London, 1937.

Arnold, Sir E., *The Light of Asia*. Privately published, 1926.

Byles, M., *By Cargo Boat and Mountain*. Seeley Service, London, 1931.

Cresswell, D., *Canterbury Tales: 'Mount Cook Bows to a Woman.'* Kathleen Creswell, Christchurch, 1951.

Department of Lands and Survey (NZ), *The Story of Mount Cook National Park*, Wellington, 1986.

Du Faur, F., *The Conquest of Mount Cook: an Account of Four Seasons' Mountaineering on the Southern Alps of New Zealand*. George Allen & Unwin, London, 1915.

Dupain, G.Z., *Are you satisfied with your physical condition?: Exercise and The Woman*. Atkins McQuitty, Sydney, 1909.

Faderman,L., *Surpassing the Love of Men: Romantic Friendship and Love between Women from the Renaissance to the Present*. Women's Press, London, 1981.

Flecker, J.E., *Hassan*. Heinemann, London, 1922.

Freeland, J.M., *Architect Extraordinary: the life and work of John Horbury Hunt, 1838-1904*. Cassel, Australia, 1971.

Graham, A., and Wilson, J., *Uncle Alec and the Grahams of Franz Josef*. John McIndoe, Dunedin, 1983.

Graham, P., *Peter Graham: Mountain Guide*. Reed, Wellington, 1965.

Hall, R., *The Well of Loneliness*. Jonathan Cape, London, 1928.

Halstead, G., *The Story of St Ives* (N.S.W.). Nungurner Press, Sydney, 1975.

Hardy, T., *Tess of the D'Urbervilles*. Osgood M'Ilvaine and Co, London, 1891.

Hughes, G., *The Story of Mount Wilson*. Mount Wilson Progress Association, 1960.

Inglis, S., *Our Australian Cousins*. MacMillan and Co., London, 1880.

Jeffrey, S., *The Spinster and Her Enemies: Feminism and Sexuality*, 1880-1930. Pandora Press, London, 1983.

Kain, C., *The Millionaire Guide*. Whyte Museum, Banff, Canada (n.d.).

Kain, C., and Thorington, J.M., *Where The Clouds Can Go*. American Alpine Club, New York, 1935.

Mannering, G.E., *Eighty Years in New Zealand*. Simpson & Williams, Christchurch, 1931.

Miles, R., *The Women's History of the World*. Paladin, London, 1989.

Mulvaney, D.J., *So Much that is New: Professor Baldwin Spencer, 1860-1929*. OUP, Melbourne, 1985.

Pascoe, J.D., *Great Days in New Zealand Mountaineering*. Reed, Wellington, 1958.

Rosen, Andrew, *Rise Up, Women*. Routledge and Kegan, London, 1974.

Ross, M.A., *A Climber In New Zealand*. Edward Arnold, London, 1914.

Sargent, W., and Slater, E., *An Introduction to Physical Methods of Treatment in Psychiatry*. E. & S. Livingston, London, 1963.

Scott, G., *Sydney Highways of History*. Georgian House, Melbourne, 1958.

Sievewright Young, D., *The Story of Bournemouth*. Bournemouth Archives (n.d.).

Spencer, B., and Gilbert, F., *The Arunta: A Study of Stone Age People*. McMillan and Co., London, 1927.

Stopes, M., *Married Love*. Putmans, London, 1918.

Stopes, M., *Enduring Passions*. Hogarth Press, London, 1928.

Strachey, R., *Women's Suffrage and Women's Service, The Cause: A Short History of The Women's Movement in Great Britain*. Bell and Sons, London, 1928.

Turner, E., *Seven Little Australians*. Ward, Lock and Co., London, 1894.

Turner, S., *The Conquest of the New Zealand Alps*. T. Fisher Unwin, London, 1922.

Tyler, W., *The Spirit of Irene Speaks*. Privately published, Boscombe, 1923.

Ussher, J., *Women's Madness: Misogany or Mental Illness*. Harvester Wheatsheaf, London, 1991.

Williams, C., *Women on the Rope*. Allen and Unwin, London, 1973.
Wilson, J.G. Aorangi, *The Story of Mount Cook*. Whitcombe and Tombs, Christchurch, 1968.

LETTERS
All copies held by the author, unless stated otherwise.

Bryans, M., to Pip Lynch, Christchurch, 29 June 1988.
Butler, D., to A. Rutherford (of Capper Press, NZ), 3 March 1978.
Byles,M., to C. Monteath, 14 March 1978; Ashima, 23 April 1978;
Deane, Dr N. (of Christchurch, UK), to author, 6 November 1993.
Du Faur, E., to F. Du Faur, (n.d.), held by S. Bryans, London.
Du Faur, E., to Harrow , 18 April 1905.
Du Faur, F., to E. Du Faur, 1 September 1908, held by S. Bryans, London.
Du Faur, F., to Frances Lord, Kingaroy, September 1935.
Du Faur, J., to E.J. O'Donnell, of Crossmaglen, NSW, 11 September 1990
Du Faur, J. G. Sydney, to A. Rutherford (of Capper Press, NZ), 9 March 1978.
Du Faur, J., to M. Bryans, London, 14 June 1963.
Du Faur, N., to M. Bryans, London, 7 October 1959.
Edginton, J., to author, 10 December 1993.
Ellis, B. (of Auckland), to author, 14 June 1992-94.
England, A., Bacchus family letters, 3 August 1992.
Guttridge, R. (of Bournemouth), to author, 12 December 1992.
Lovell, F. (of Kingaroy), to author, April 1992
O'Donnell, J., to author, 11 September 1990.
Rowe, M., to C. Monteath, (n.d)
Russell, M., to Ruth Abbott, Sydney, 8 October 1932.
Spencer, Sir Baldwin, to Alline Spence, from Hermitage, January-February 1910
Swabey, B. (of Manukua Historical Society), to author, 22 November 1992.
Taylor, T., to C. Monteath, 14 March 1978.
Thomson, A., to author, Harrow Civic Library, Pinner, 4 March 1993.
Westmacott, E., to Margaret Westmacott, Waimate, N.Z., 27 November 1984.
Woolley, Dr J., to his family, held by David Hewitt, Sydney.

INTERVIEWS
All interviews were conducted by the author, unless stated otherwise. In most cases

the subject of the interview is stated.

Anderson, A., at Christchurch, 18 January 1992: the Graham family.

Abbott-Roberts, M., in Sydney, 2 April 1992: the Abbott family and Freda's last years.

Bendell, G., at Vine Cottage, Pinner, 25 August 1994.

Brown, C., at the Dupain Institute, Sydney, 27 May 1992.

Butler, D., in Sydney, 18 January 1994: Marie Byles and mountaineering.

Cadogan, Max., in Sydney, 15 January 1991 -97: Muriel Cadogan and family.

Colville Smith, J., in Sydney, 18 February 1992: Jean Lord.

Coote, G., in Sydney, 1995: about her film A Singular Woman (Marie Byles).

Dupain, M., in Sydney, 27 March 1992: George Dupain, of the Dupain Institute

Deane, Dr W., at Christchurch, UK, July 1993: the Deane family.

Ellis, B., in Auckland, 7 January 1993: the Bacchus family.

Fletcher, D., at Westport, 15 January 1992: the Graham family.

Guttridge, R., in Bournemouth, UK, July 1993: Boscombe history.

Hayman, R., in Sydney, May 1992: Nina and Guy Du Faur, and family paintings.

Hercus, M., in Sydney, May 1992: Nina and Guy Du Faur, and the Du Faur family.

Hudson, J., in Sydney, May 1992: the Dee Why years of the Du Faur family.

Lovell, F., at Kingaroy, 10 June 1992: her childhood and friendship with Freda.

McManis,B., in Sydney, 10 May 1992: Guy and Nina Du Faur.

McMullen,V., in Sydney, 30 May 1992: Guy and Freda Du Faur.

Palmer, M., in Sydney, 8 May 1992: Nina and Guy Du Faur.

Roberts, A., in Sydney, April 1992: John Du Faur, Du Faur family, and Dee Why.

Secretary, 'Norma', in Sydney, 19 May 1992: John Du Faur

Westmacott, E., interviewed in UK by Ursula Westmacott-Crocker, 2 March 1992, 8 February 1992, and 27 November 1994.

INDEX